PIANO
WORKBOOK

Carl Humphries

To my loving wife, Agnieszka, without whose endless support and patience it would not have been posssible to write this book.

Piano Workbook
A complete course in technique and performance

Carl Humphries

A Jawbone Book
First Edition 2007
Published in the UK and the USA by Jawbone Press
2a Union Court,
20–22 Union Road,
London SW4 6JP,
England
www.jawbonepress.com

ISBN 978-1-906002-03-9

EDITOR John Morrish
DESIGN Lisa Tai

Printed by Colorprint Offset Ltd (Hong Kong)

1 2 3 4 5 11 10 09 08 07

CONTENTS

INTRODUCTION

I'd like to welcome you to *Piano Workbook*, the sequel and companion volume to *The Piano Handbook* – the best-selling guide to learning the piano that I wrote several years ago. The continuing popularity of the *Handbook* went way beyond anything I expected. It not only integrated classical and popular approaches to piano playing but linked the learning of repertoire classics to a wide range of creative techniques and skills, such as composing and improvising. The idea was to allow the piano to become a real tool for personal self-expression.

Yet the techniques and repertoire associated with piano playing and creative music making at the piano are so vast that a second book was called for, not just to give readers access to a wider range of possibilities but also to offer a fresh, alternative perspective on the whole process of learning the essentials. That's why I've now written *Piano Workbook*. Like the *Handbook*, it takes you through the central points connected with posture, technique, styles of playing, and ways of using harmony and melody; but it illustrates these with quite different repertoire, a fresh choice of styles and new topics.

This means that if you're looking for a fast-paced tutor you can simply choose between *Piano Workbook* and the original *Handbook*, knowing that both reflect the same approach but with a different emphasis. But you also have the option of using both books simultaneously to create a more leisurely and richly illustrated course – something that'll be especially good if you don't have previous experience with this instrument. (Take a look at both books together if you can: you'll see they follow the same structure, so each unit in one book deals with material linked to that in the equivalent unit in the other book, at a corresponding level of difficulty. This makes cross-referencing between the two volumes completely straightforward.)

The Piano Handbook included more background information on the history of the instrument, as well as a comprehensive repertoire guide and discography. By contrast, *Piano Workbook* focuses on the practicalities of technique and interpretation, and on the essential theory you need to know if you want to be successful as a composer or improviser. It contains practical tips on songwriting, and features some really up-to-date topics that other books on piano playing seem to miss, such as the implications of world music for modern styles of piano playing and improvising.

Maybe you've already started using *The Piano Handbook*, liked the approach you found there, and would just like to add more material to your piano course? If so, you can do so easily with the help of this book. Equally, if you just want a more practical, 'nuts'n'bolts' guide to the whole experience of learning the piano, but using the same distinctive approach as in that book, then this volume should definitely work for you.

Either way, I wish you the best of luck. To quote myself in the other book, do keep in mind that "the really important things in your experience of piano playing aren't going to come from this or any book. They will come directly from you."

CARL HUMPHRIES   2007

UNIT 1

TIPS FOR BEGINNERS

Before you get started on this book, it's worth taking time to clarify some really basic and important points connected with how you approach learning and playing. This will make your progress through the book a lot smoother and more enjoyable.

ACOUSTIC OR NOT?

Sophisticated modern technology means that some modern electronic keyboards are designed to function as alternatives to the traditional acoustic piano: these are normally known as "electronic pianos". (They're quite different from the older "electric pianos" used in jazz, which were never intended to produce a realistic likeness to the piano.) If your main interest is jazz or popular music, or you don't expect to reach an advanced level in classical playing, then a modern electronic piano certainly has some appealing features. For example, it's usually more economical on space, and there's an option to hear yourself just through headphones – something that can make for better relations with neighbors, especially in modern flats with thin walls. Modern computer mapping also means that the best instruments combine touch sensitivity with a pretty realistic sound, and some offer recording/playback facilities. Even so, if you have the resources there is still no substitute for a reasonably sized, good quality acoustic piano. In fact starting out with one of these from the beginning is certainly better if you plan to take your classical playing up to a serious level, at which point it will be essential anyway.

YOUR INSTRUMENT: The first question to ask is whether you have a suitable instrument. It's no good trying to work through this book on a piano that is so old that the keys keep sticking, or which has notes that carry on sounding even after you have released the keys. That should only happen when you have the right-foot pedal held down, and then the notes should stop sounding the moment you release the pedal. (Also, the left pedal should soften the sound noticeably. If your instrument has a third, middle pedal, you don't need to worry about that right now.) Make sure your piano has been tuned and regulated recently, and remember that it needs to be tuned regularly – two or three times a year.

SITTING COMFORTABLY: To get the best from your instrument and from yourself, you really need an adjustable piano stool. If you have to make do with an ordinary chair, make sure you have a good pile of newspapers you can use to bring it up to exactly the right height. If it's already too high, find a different one! It's best not to use cushions – they're too soft to support you properly.

PRACTICING: Before you get involved in playing, take some time to think about how you will organize your practice time. Be realistic but disciplined. How much time would you like to spend at the piano each week? How will this fit in with the rest of your life? Try to spread your practice evenly throughout the week. Remember the old motto of piano teachers everywhere: A little but often is better than all at once!

TECHNIQUE: Every time you sit at the piano, start by checking your **posture**. Are you sitting at the right **height**, **distance**, and **angle**? These points are connected, so first you need to check that your back is straight (but not stiff). Then place your hands on the keyboard: there should be a very slight downward slope from the elbow to the wrists. When you've adjusted your height to get this right, check you can play comfortably across the whole keyboard without having to lean backwards, and that you don't have to lean forwards just to play at all.

It's also important to think about **hand shape**: when you're about to play something the normal shape of the hands is with the fingers cupped or rounded – as when holding a tennis ball – and the thumb curved in slightly towards the hand. Try to keep the knuckles reasonably level, so that the side of the hand with the weaker, smaller fingers is supported and doesn't collapse down onto the keys.

The most important thing of all is physical **relaxation**: make sure your shoulders are as relaxed as possible, so that your arms literally hang down – at least as far as the elbows. Especially when practicing a lot, or trying something difficult, take regular breaks, and give your wrists a shake to make sure that they're loose. If you feel pain or tension in your arms, wrist or hand, don't force yourself to carry on; you might injure yourself, and your playing certainly won't benefit. Better to take a break; maybe it's time to make yourself that nice cup of coffee you were thinking about…

LEARNING THE KEYBOARD

Notice how black keys alternate with white keys, except where two white keys sit next to each other with no black key between them. This creates larger gaps between some of the black keys, which fall into a nice alternating pattern of groups of two and three. We use this pattern to locate the different notes or pitches. Note that we use the first seven letters of the alphabet to refer just to the white notes. (We'll learn the black notes later.) You can see that when we come back to the same place in the pattern we reach the same letter-name again; we call this distance between two notes with the same place in the pattern and the same letter-name an **octave**.

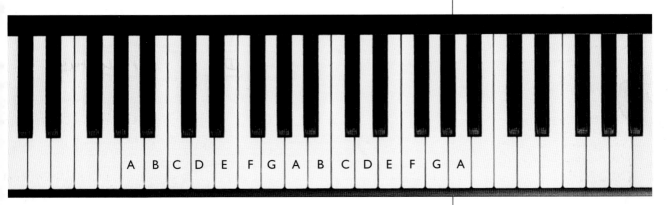

Practice finding every A on the piano, then every B, every C, and so on. Make a special note of the C right in the middle of the keyboard on your piano. (Usually parallel with the keyhole for locking the lid.) This is **Middle C**.

The piano keyboard with the names of the white notes marked. Notice the pattern formed by the white and black keys.

PRACTICING READING

You'll have noticed that notes to the right are progressively higher in pitch, while notes to the left get progressively lower. This is reflected in music notation. Notes are indicated by their vertical position on a set of five horizontal lines known as the **stave** or **staff** (always pronounced 'stave'). They can appear on the lines or in the spaces between them. In piano music we normally have two staves running parallel – one for the right hand and one for the left. Each has a different sign at the start of the line of music, called a **clef**. This is important, as the letter-names come in different places on the staff depending on whether they are for right hand (with treble clef) or left hand (bass clef).

Note that reading just the notes on spaces, or just the notes on lines, in ascending order, gives a pattern of letter names that we can memorize; we can either read the pattern as a word, or make each letter the beginning of a word in a phrase. Here they are for treble and bass clefs (over page):

TREBLE CLEF (RIGHT HAND)

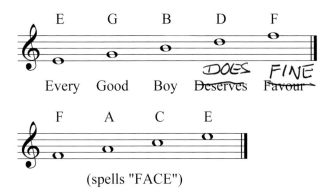

Every   Good   Boy   ~~Deserves~~ *DOES*   ~~Favour~~ *FINE*

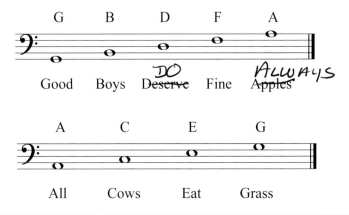

(spells "FACE")

BASS CLEF (LEFT HAND)

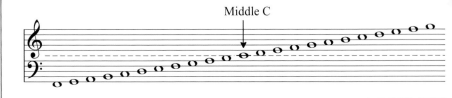

Good   Boys   ~~Deserve~~ *DO*   Fine   ~~Apples~~ *ALWAYS*

All   Cows   Eat   Grass

The diagram below shows how the two clefs fit together. Middle C comes above the bass clef and below the treble clef, with a small line through it. This line is called a **leger line**, and represents an extra horizontal line that runs between the right and left-hand staves but which is only shown when it is needed for particular notes.

Middle C

Sometimes the notes need to continue beyond the staves, and so extra leger lines are added to accommodate them. This can simply be because the notes are too high or low to be shown on the clefs.

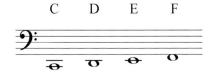

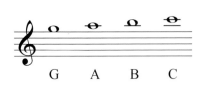

But leger lines are also used when the left hand plays above Middle C or the right plays below.

EXERCISE 1.1

First try reading the names of these notes aloud. Then find them on the piano as quickly as you can.

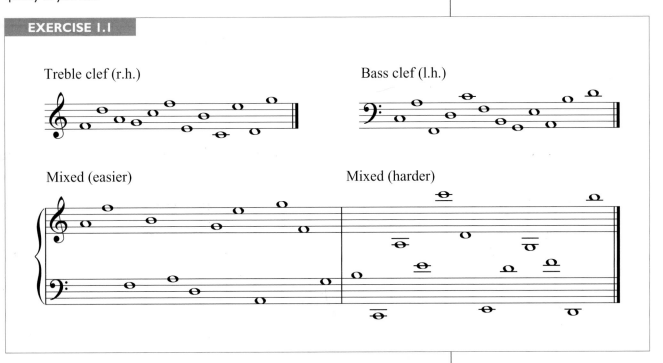

EXERCISE 1.1

Treble clef (r.h.)

Bass clef (l.h.)

Mixed (easier)

Mixed (harder)

PRACTICING COUNTING

We normally control **rhythm** in music by relating notes of varying durations to a regular underlying **pulse**. This pulse falls into regular cycles of beats, which we call the **meter** of the music. When learning music, it often helps to count out these beats silently, in our head (or even aloud), while we are playing, to make sure that our timing is accurate. Later we learn to feel how the rhythm relates to the meter.

This is reflected in the way the music is written: it has regular divisions, called **measures** or **bars**, separated by vertical lines called **barlines**. Each bar corresponds to a metrical cycle. A **double barline** indicates the end of a piece. Two dots before a double barline, whether at the end of the piece or before the end, indicate that you should return to the start and repeat either that section or the whole piece. A double bar with two dots after it indicates that you should start your repeat from there rather than from the start of the piece.

Rhythms are expressed as different time-values, corresponding to successive halvings of the longest commonly used time-value, which is known as the whole-note in America and northern Europe and the semibreve in Britain and some other countries. In the American system, the names for the smaller time-values simply reflect those successive halvings: whole-note, half-note, quarter-note, etc. In the British system, different names are used for each time-value, derived from French and Latin.

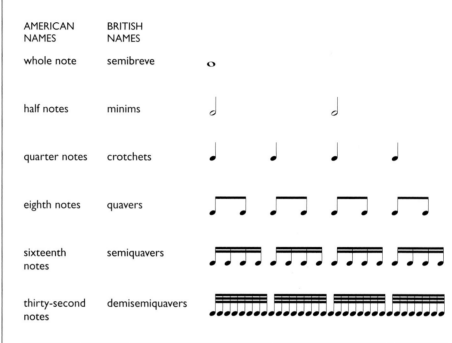

AMERICAN NAMES	BRITISH NAMES	
whole note	semibreve	
half notes	minims	
quarter notes	crotchets	
eighth notes	quavers	
sixteenth notes	semiquavers	
thirty-second notes	demisemiquavers	

For every note, there is an equivalent **rest**, indicating a period of silence of exactly the same duration. (NB: A rest lasting for a whole bar is always shown with the sign for a whole-note rest, even when the bar itself is longer or shorter.)

NOTE:	REST:	NOTE:	REST:

In practice, it's often easier to think of time-values as divisions or multiples of whatever time-value represents the actual pulse of the music. This time-value, along with the number of beats per bar, is indicated at the start by the **time signature** – two numbers which look and work rather like a fraction. The lower number states the time-value corresponding to one unit of the pulse, as a division of the longest time-value – as in the diagram above. The upper number shows how many of these fit into one bar.

SIMPLE DUPLE TIME:

2 eighth-note beats per bar

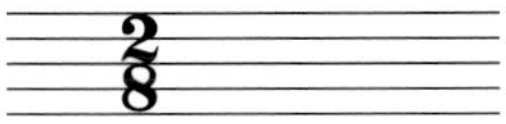

2 quarter-note beats per bar

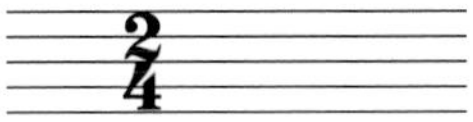

2 half-note beats per bar *alla breve*

or

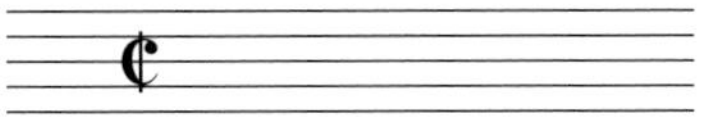

SIMPLE TRIPLE TIME:

3 eighth-note beats per bar

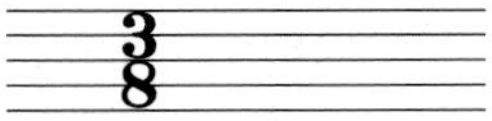

3 quarter-note beats per bar

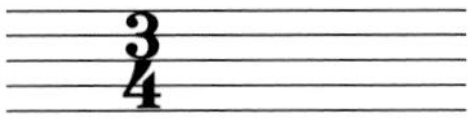

SIMPLE QUADRUPLE TIME:

4 quarter-note beats per bar

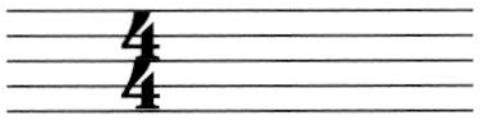

'common time'

or

Here are the most common time signatures. (Note the alternative names and signs for some of them.)

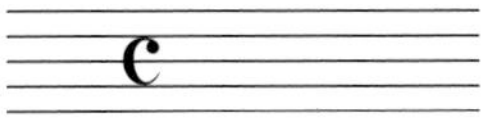

To indicate note durations that are not available using the basic time-values, you have to join notes together, using a curved line called a **tie**. For instance, to indicate a duration of three quarter-notes, you can tie a half-note to a quarter-note. This rhythmic pattern, in which a note is extended by half its length, is very common. Another way of indicating it is to use a dot: placing a dot after any time-value adds half as much again to the value of the note. Placing a dot after a rest also adds half as much again to its length.

EXERCISE 1.2

Let's practice clapping different rhythms, counting the beats of the bar aloud at the same time, so we can hear how the rhythms relate to the beats. With each new bar we start over again, counting from 'one'. We can also count divisions within a beat if necessary: the halfway point as 'and', a quarter of the way through as 'er', and three-quarters of the way through as 'a'. The first beat of each bar is always the strongest, and with four beats per bar the third beat is also slightly emphasized. Notice the curved line in the fourth line, connecting the last note of the second bar to the first note of the next: this is a tie. It means that instead of playing or clapping the second note you hold the first note on for the combined value of both.

EXERCISE 1.2

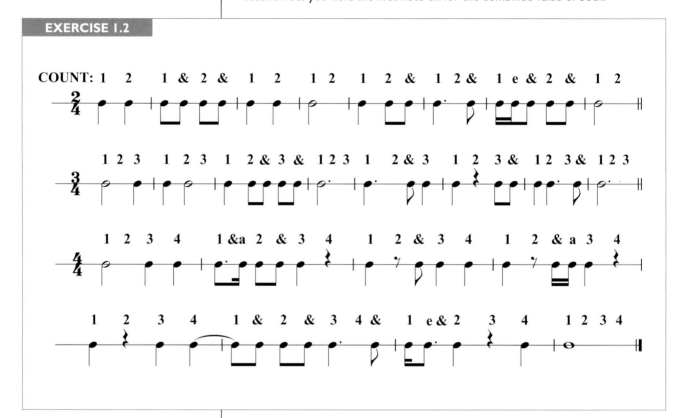

HANDS SEPARATELY

Now it's time to start playing some music. The simplest place to begin is by positioning both hands on the piano with the thumbs on Middle C, and with each of the other fingers positioned directly over an adjacent white note. (Remember to curl your thumb inwards slightly so it doesn't cover more than one note.) This is the 'basic five-finger position'. In a moment we'll learn to extend it to cover more notes, and to move it around to different parts of the keyboard.

Look at the piece below. Note the small numerals written above or below the notes. These tell you the **fingering**. Each hand is numbered outwards from the thumb (=1), through the index (=2), middle (=3), and ring (=4) fingers to the little finger (=5). This means that fingering is symmetrical between the hands.

With all of the pieces in this unit, try to connect each note to the next without a gap – what we call 'joining notes smoothly'. You can do this by releasing each note just fractionally after you play the next one.

Be careful, though: if the same note is repeated immediately, as in the next piece, we can't do this. In fact, we must even shorten the first note slightly to allow extra time for the finger and key to return to their original position, so that they are ready in time for the second note to be played.

EXERCISE 1.3

CD TRACK 1

First note the time signature, and try to clap the rhythm, counting four beats per bar as in Exercise 1.2. Then look at the notes. Where does each hand start? Find the first note in each hand using the finger indicated. Then position the other fingers of the hand on adjacent notes. In this piece the hands never play at the same time, but you might still find it easier to start by playing just one hand at a time, all the way through. When you combine the hands in sequence, it's important to achieve a smooth transition from one to another, so resist the temptation to take either of them away from the keyboard while the other one plays. Don't forget posture and hand shape – and keep as relaxed as possible. Try to make all the quarter-notes the same length, and all the eighth-notes even as well. If you find it hard to play in time, or to keep the fingers over the right keys, it probably means you're playing too quickly. Remember the golden rule, which is 'Don't rush!'

EXERCISE 1.3   DANCE OF THE SQUIRRELS

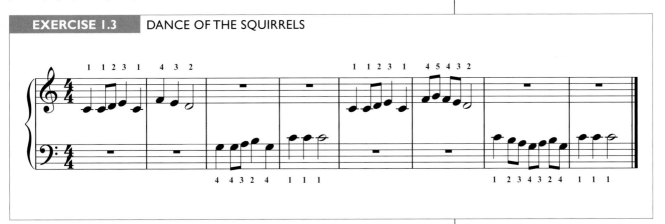

In this next piece each hand keeps the 'basic five-finger position', but the left hand has been moved to a lower place on the keyboard, so that it is exactly one octave below the right hand.

CD TRACK 2

EXERCISE 1.4

Start by looking carefully at the music for each hand. Notice the places where the notes move directly from one line to the next, or one space to the next. In both cases this means a leap of two steps – missing out the white note (and the finger) in between. Also, try to work out the letter-names of the notes in the left hand by using the rhymes mentioned earlier, rather than by counting down from Middle C. Now look at the time signature. It's in 2/2 time, which means that each beat of the pulse corresponds to a half-note. This doesn't mean you have to play the quarter-notes faster than in the previous piece. It just means you feel them as divisions of a slower beat rather than as corresponding to single beats themselves. Singing the tune while clapping on the half-note beats as you go along will help you to get the feel of this.

EXERCISE 1.4   CLAPPING SONG

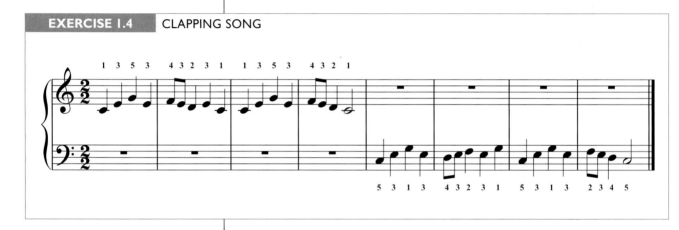

SHIFTING POSITION

Now that we're familiar with the basic hand positions we can try extending them to cover more notes.

EXERCISE 1.5

CD TRACK 3

Look at the rhythm in bars 1, 5, 9, and 13. It's a dotted rhythm, so you have to feel the division of the beat into three-quarters and one-quarter. You'll also need to move each hand a little to make room for the other to play. You can see that in bar 4 and 12 we extend the left-hand thumb upwards by one extra note, while in bar 7 we bring the right-hand second finger over the thumb, while the latter is still playing. In bar 15 note how we first contract the right hand, bringing the third finger next to the thumb, and then open it out again so that the thumb reaches down to B – a bit like a crab walking sideways. Where no fingering is marked, we use the fingers that lie naturally over the notes in the basic five-finger position.

| EXERCISE 1.5 | MARCH |

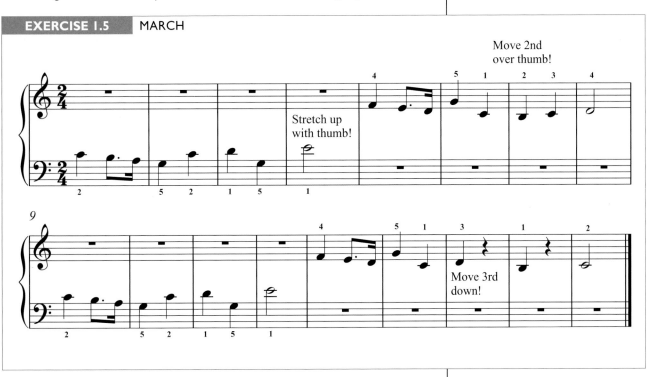

CD TRACK 4

EXERCISE 1.6

Here the hands start off one octave apart, as in Exercise 1.4. Notice the crab-like movement in the right hand in bar 14 – just like in the last piece. Now think about the left hand in bar 29. Here you can first let go of the previous note and then quickly jump down with the whole hand, so that the thumb is ready to play on E. Watch out for dotted half-notes tied together – they last for a total of six counts.

EXERCISE 1.6   LITTLE BOY

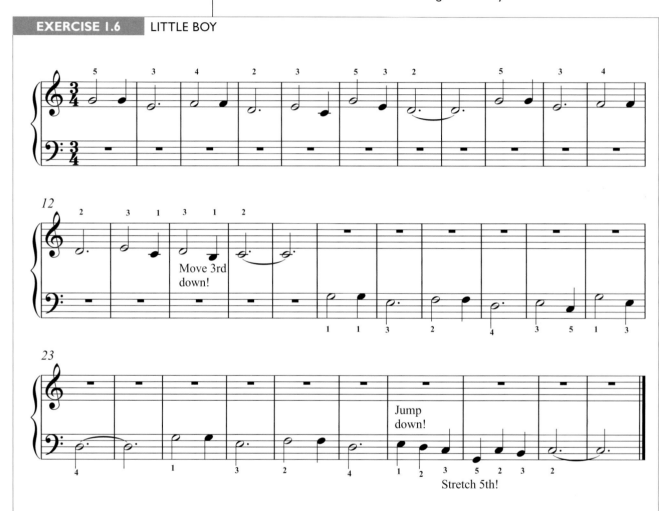

LINKING THE HANDS

Let's take a look at how the two hands can be interlinked in more complex ways.

EXERCISE 1.7

Here the hands are back in the middle of the piano again, with both thumbs on Middle C. Notice how often the melody passes between the hands. Sometimes this happens as it moves between different notes, so you can try joining these smoothly: they should sound as if played by the same hand. Sometimes it's the same note played first by one hand, then the other, so you'll need to release the first one a little earlier, as well as quickly making room for the other hand to come in.

CD TRACK 5

EXERCISE 1.7 HOP AND SKIP

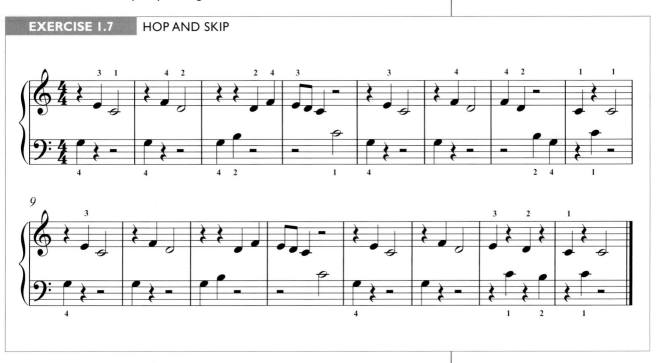

HANDS TOGETHER

One of the simplest ways for the hands to play together is to play notes with the same letter name at the same time – usually one or two octaves apart. This allows both hands to play the same tune simultaneously. The piece below uses this technique a lot of the time.

CD TRACK 6

EXERCISE 1.8

This is one of Beethoven's most famous tunes. Try to observe carefully how the fingers fit together when the two hands play the same notes an octave apart: opposite fingers (eg, thumb and fifth, fourth and second, etc) come together, except for the third fingers, which coincide. Watch out for bars 7-8 and the final two bars: here the hands play different material at the same time, so they must work independently. Practice each hand separately for these passages before combining them very slowly. Then bring them gradually up to speed.

EXERCISE 1.8 ODE TO JOY

Beethoven

DEVELOPING THE THUMB

The thumb is the source of a lot of physical problems for pianists. This is because, unlike the fingers, it has to move at an unnatural angle. It's tempting to let the hand tilt in the opposite direction, away from the thumb, because this makes the angle of movement of the thumb more natural. However, it unbalances the rest of the hand and prevents the weaker fourth and fifth fingers from working independently. The challenge, then, is to maintain the correct angle for the hand and the thumb – with all of the knuckles roughly level – while keeping everything loose and relaxed, in spite of the resulting unnaturalness. This requires very slow practice and takes time, so don't expect overnight results.

At the same time, you need to develop control of the movement of the thumb across the keys, and of its speed of attack. The thumb is more cumbersome than the fingers, so it tends to play too loudly anyway, and this is made worse if the muscles supporting it have been forced to work and have become stiff. What then usually happens is that the whole hand moves instead of just the thumb, and this is even harder to control.

EXERCISE 1.9

CD TRACK 7

This exercise takes you through all three aspects of the problems connected with thumb control. First concentrate on slow, relaxed movements of the thumb up and down, keeping other fingers in contact with the keys, knuckles level, and the wrist relaxed. Then focus on developing the agility of the thumb as it moves sideways from one note to another. Use the long notes to relax, and try to keep the short notes light and even. Play all the notes using just the thumbs, without combining the hands

EXERCISE 1.9	THUMB STUDY

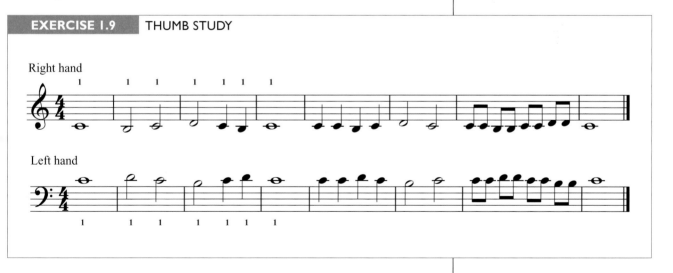

SCALE RHYTHMS

Playing up and down the white notes by step for one or more octaves, starting on C, produces the **Scale of C major**. When we get to the third finger in the right hand we must pass the thumb under to give enough fingers to get to the top. The left hand does the same on the way down. This is reversed when going in the opposite direction: we stretch third over the thumb to play the next note. It's important to aim for evenness of both tone and time in scales, and a good way to develop this is by practicing the same scale in different rhythms, as shown below.

EXERCISE 1.10

This exercise shows you the different rhythms in which you can practice your scale of C major. Stressing the notes that fall on the beat will help to give a stronger sense of rhythmic pattern. When you are confident playing hands separately, try playing both hands at the same time, moving in opposite directions, in the same rhythm (so both hands start and finish on Middle C.) Dotted eighth-notes are worth three quarters of a beat, sixteenth-notes one quarter. This exercise shows you how the overall rhythm can be varied by lengthening and shortening alternate notes.

TRIADS AND INVERSIONS

Western music consists of both melody and harmony. Harmony is made up of chords
– particular groups of notes that the ear learns to recognize as a single unit, because
they have a distinctive sound when played together. The most basic types of chord in
Western classical and non-classical music consist of three notes, each spaced two steps
apart. We call these **triads**. However, we can also change the sound of a triad by varying
which of the three notes is placed at the bottom. This creates **inversions**, which are also
useful for creating smoother progressions between chords.

EXERCISE 1.11

The first part of this exercise shows you the basic triads and inversions for a
C major chord, in both hands. In each hand the fingering changes for one of the
inversions, using second finger instead of third for the middle note, and it's a
different one depending on the hand. The second part shows how moving
between different triads sometimes requires us to use a different fingering from
the one used just to play the chord itself. (See the chords marked with the
asterisk.) Note also how the thumb is sometimes required to slide between
adjacent notes.

Right hand

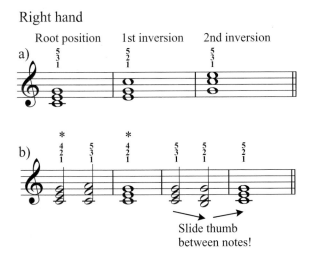

Left hand

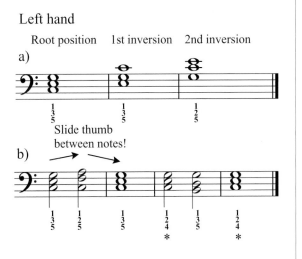

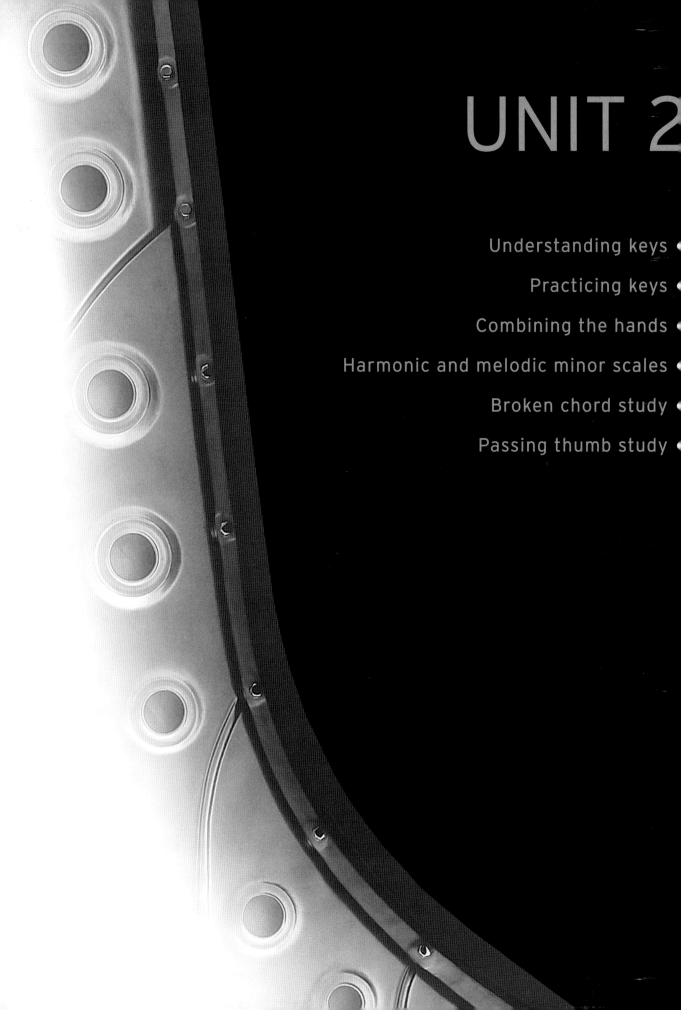

UNIT 2

UNDERSTANDING KEYS

So far all the music we've been playing has been based on the scale of C major. This means that the note C functions as the principal point of arrival and departure for melodies, and the chord (or triad) based on C is the principal reference point for harmony. We express this by saying that the music is in the **key** of C major.

The word **major** here refers to the type of scale used: major scales use a particular pattern of larger and smaller steps that generally make for happier sounding music. If an alternative pattern is used, it's usually the **minor** scale, which tends to make for a sadder feel. It just happens that when we play the pattern for major scales starting on C, we only get white notes: if we start anywhere else, we have to use one or more black notes to maintain the pattern. This means that if we want to play in keys other than C major, we need to know how to read and play black notes.

Take a look at the diagram (right), which shows how each of the five different black notes can have two possible names. This is because we think of black notes as alterations of neighboring white notes, so we can treat each one as an alteration of the white note either to the left (ie, just below) or to the right (ie, just above). In the former case it is as if we were slightly raising the pitch of the white note, so we call it a **sharp**. In the latter case it is as if we were slightly lowering it, so we call it a **flat**.

Here's how we write these:

In written music we place these signs just in front of the notehead, on the same line or space. A **natural** sign cancels a sharp or flat, meaning that you just play the normal white note.

We can write the signs for sharps, flats and naturals in front of individual notes, in which case they are known as **accidentals**, and affect that particular note (in that particular octave only) for the remainder of the bar, unless cancelled by another sign. However because most music uses the same scale, or stays in the same key, for a lot of the time, this is inefficient. It's simpler just to show the sharps or flats for that key at the beginning of each line of music, using what we call a **key signature**. This means you must remember to apply these alterations automatically to any note in the music with the corresponding letter-name (in any octave). It's important to remember, however, that these signs can still be overridden by accidentals in the music, which will affect a particular note right up to the end of the bar in which the accidental appears.

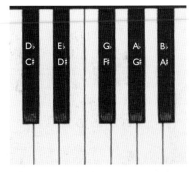

Each black note has two possible names. It is called either the sharp of the white note to its left or the flat of the white note to its right. Which one is used depends on the musical context.

Here are the key signatures for the most common major keys. It's worth memorizing the flats or sharps for each of them.

Sharp keys

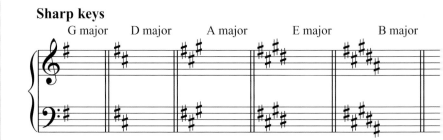

Flat keys

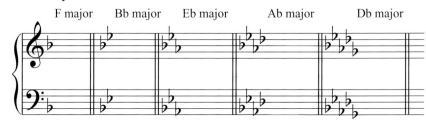

PRACTICING KEYS

When music changes from one key to another, we say that it **modulates**. A **modulation** can be shown through a change in the key signature, but if the music only remains in the new key for a short time it is more likely to be indicated using just accidentals. Try reading through the music for Exercise 2.1 (below) and see if you can spot the modulations. You should be able to identify the keys that the music passes through by matching the accidentals with the key signatures given on the previous page.

CD TRACK 8

EXERCISE 2.1

'Morning' is a famous tune by the Norwegian composer Edvard Grieg. Read the key signature at the beginning carefully. Keep a look out for changes in hand position in the right hand, and try to prepare all the fingers at once, so they're all ready to play in the new position. Notice how the left hand keeps mostly the same chord shape throughout. However, it uses a different fingering in bars 17-24, to avoid putting the thumb on a black note in bar 22, which would be awkward. In the last four bars, read the right-hand notes carefully, and be ready to pass the second finger over the thumb at the end of each phrase, as in bars 8 and 40. Also, the lower stave changes to treble clef here – but this needn't confuse you. These notes are still played by the left hand, but go quite far above Middle C, so it's simpler to write them as if for the right-hand. Leaning over a little to the right here will give your left hand room to cross over, but you must make sure your legs are resting firmly on the floor in front of you, and that you are not too close to the keyboard.

EXERCISE 2.1 MORNING

continued over page

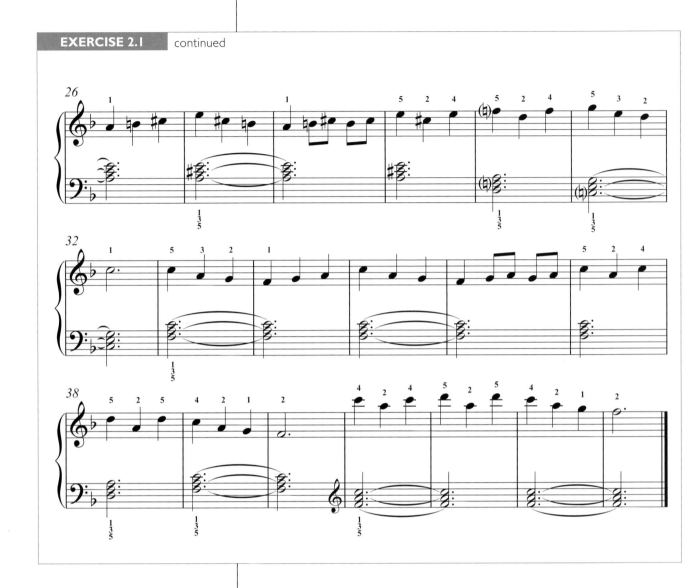

COMBINING THE HANDS

In the last piece the hands were playing together, but the left hand only had to play slow chords, so not much independence was required. Often in piano music both hands are equally active, though, even when one hand has the melody and the other is providing an accompaniment. This means it is necessary to first master each hand separately, before fitting them together carefully at a greatly reduced speed. Only when you've done this should you try playing hands together all the way through, approaching the proper speed a little more closely each time.

You've probably noticed how the end of each piece is indicated with a thick and a thin line – called a **double barline** (or just 'double bar' for short). However, if there are two dots in front of a double barline, it just means you should repeat the music up to that point, starting from the beginning again without a pause. However, if there is a double barline earlier in the piece that is followed by two dots, then you should repeat from there. (You can see both kinds of **repeat sign** in Ex.2.2. opposite.)

EXERCISE 2.2

This gavotte is by George Frideric Handel, in his time the most famous composer and improviser in the whole of Europe. Notice the key signature of D major – which sharps must you remember to play? It should feel like a cheerful dance. Stressing the first beat of each bar will help to achieve this, but be careful, as each section starts and finishes halfway through the bar – a special effect known as 'anacrusis.' Look out for the unusual right-hand fingering at the end of each section: this is required so that we can change fingers on the repeated D, which gives clearer repetition and saves the heavier thumb for the strong beat. Note the repeat marks. You play to the first set of repeat marks, midway through bar 5, then return to the beginning, then play through to the end of the piece. At that point you return to the double barline followed by two dots in the middle of bar 5 and play on from there to the end.

EXERCISE 2.2	GAVOTTE

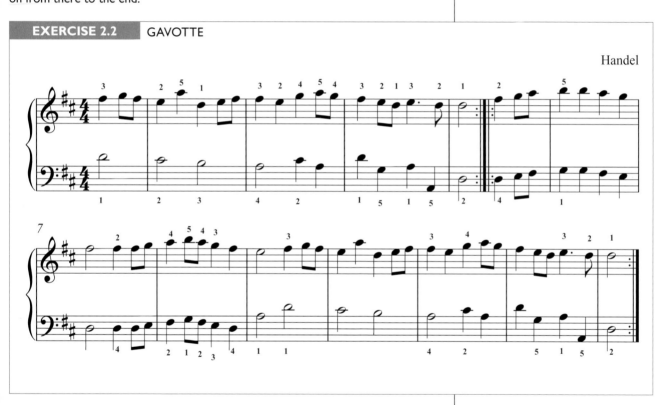

Handel

HARMONIC AND MELODIC MINOR SCALES

There are two main forms of the minor scale in regular use throughout classical and non-classical music. These are the **harmonic minor** and the **melodic minor**. (Other variations, such as the natural minor and jazz minor scales, are used less widely: we'll learn those later.) The harmonic minor scale lowers the 3rd and 6th degrees of the major scale by the smallest step possible on the piano, which is known as a **half-step** or **semitone**, and it does this whether you're ascending or descending. On the other hand, the melodic minor scale flattens only the third in its ascending form, but flattens the 3rd, 6th, and 7th on the way down. This makes for a smoother melodic effect.

HALF-STEPS

If you include both white and black notes then any two adjacent keys on the piano are a **half-step** or **semitone** apart. And as you would expect, two half-steps make a **whole step** or **whole tone**. We call the different distances between notes or scale degrees **intervals**.

For each major scale there is an equivalent minor scale that shares the same key signature. (These are then known as the **relative major** and **relative minor**). However, some notes are different in the actual minor scales, and these have to be written as accidentals.

With the exception of scales on F and B, all other scales starting on white notes follow the standard C major fingering for two-octave scales, as shown below. Note how we pass the thumb under the third finger, then under the fourth to move into the second octave, and then under the third again – reversing the sequence when going in the opposite direction. (You can remember this as 'three-four-three,' and it works equally well for both hands.)

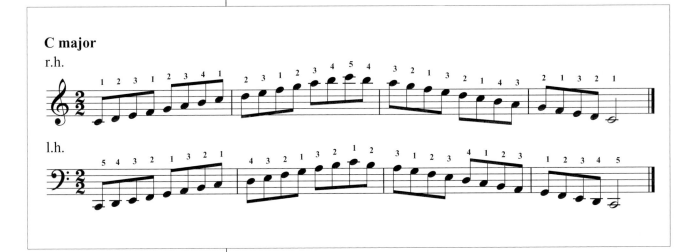

Try reproducing this pattern, starting on G, D A and E, adding the appropriate sharps from the key signatures given earlier in this unit. This will give you the scales of G, D, A and E majors with the correct fingering. (When you've done this, if you want to you can check the notes and fingering against the versions of these scales given in Unit Four.)

Here are both the harmonic and melodic versions of the minor scale with the same key signature as C major: A minor. Note that the fingering pattern is the same:

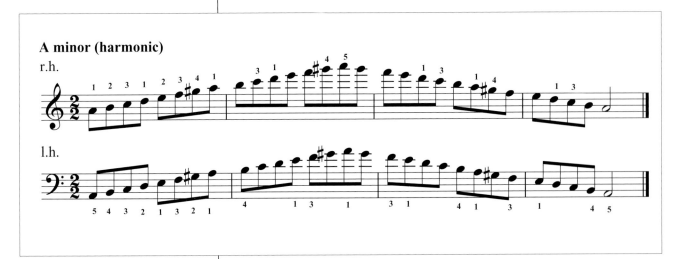

A minor (melodic)

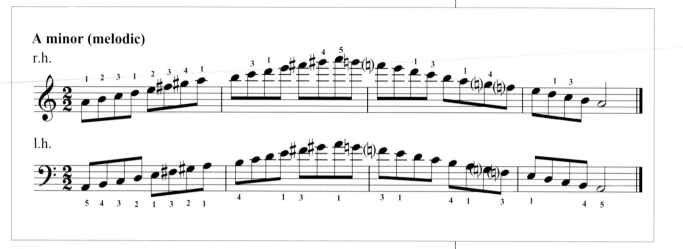

Here are some other melodic minor scales you should also know, also with the C major fingering pattern. See if you can work out what the equivalent harmonic minor forms are. Can you tell what their relative majors would be, just from the key signatures? If so, try practicing them as well.

D minor (melodic)

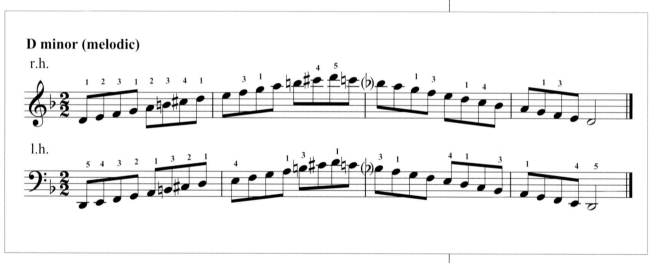

E minor (melodic)

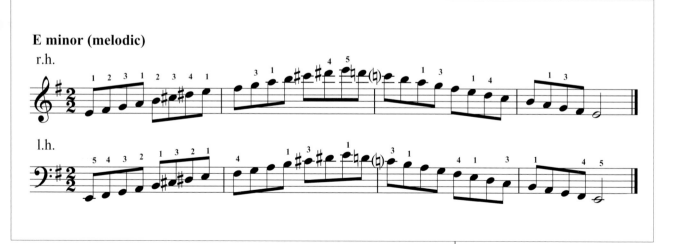

Finally, here are the two major scales on white notes that have different fingerings. Note how the 'three-four-three' pattern is changed to 'four-three-four' for F major in the right hand, and for B major in the left hand, while the other hand in each case uses the C major pattern. Also note how the top note in the right hand in F major is played with fourth, while in B major the left hand begins on fourth instead of fifth at the bottom.

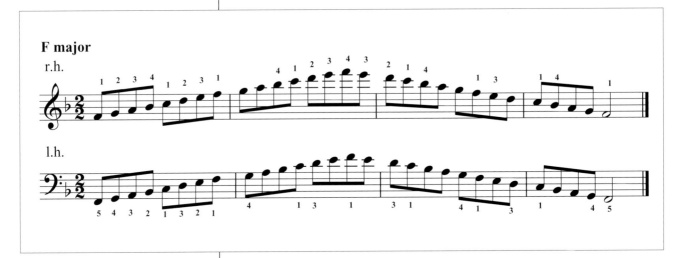

F major

B major

EXERCISE 2.3

This is the first part of a well-known piece by Christian Petzold. The great composer J.S. Bach thought it so fine he included it in a special collection of pieces he presented, luxuriously bound, to his wife as a gift. It's a minuet, a European courtly dance with a relaxed character, so even though the tune is rather melancholy there should be a strong sense of rhythmic pattern. The key signature has two flats, but look out for accidentals in the music as well. It starts in G minor (the relative minor of B flat major), with the descending form of the melodic minor scale in the left hand, but modulates to the relative major at the end.

EXERCISE 2.3   MENUET

Petzold

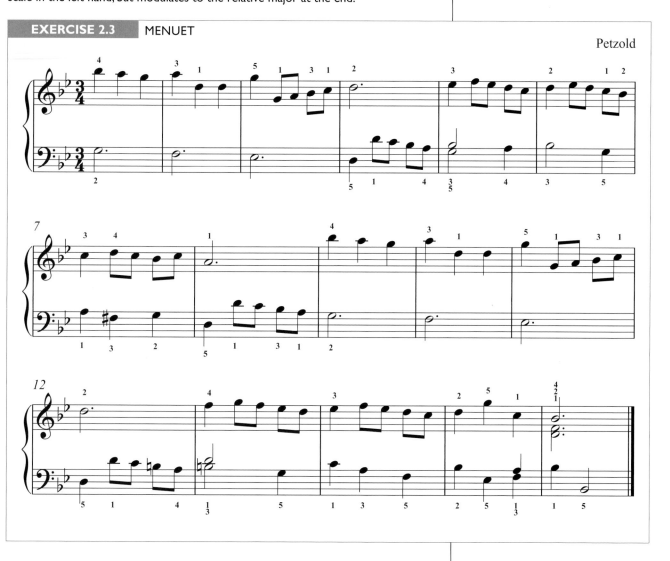

CD TRACK 11

EXERCISE 2.4

'Autumn Song' also uses elements of the melodic minor scale – this time in the key of E minor. The piece should be played softly and smoothly throughout. Be careful with the time signature: 3/8 means three eighth-note beats in a bar, so sixteenth-notes only divide the beat into halves, not quarters. Note the marking 'D.C. al fine' at the final double bar. 'D.C.' stands for Da Capo,' Italian for 'from the beginning,' while 'Fine' means 'end.' So when you arrive at the final barline you should repeat from the beginning, but only as far as the marking 'Fine' in bar 16, which is the actual end.

EXERCISE 2.4   AUTUMN SONG

BROKEN CHORD STUDY

A broken chord is a pattern that takes us through all of the different positions of a triad, in a single melodic sequence. It's useful for practicing chord fingerings. Here's an example, based on C major. When you've learned it, try to reproduce the same pattern, starting on G and on F, and then on A, D and E, using just white notes. (Notice that these last three have a different feel, because keeping to the white notes here gives rise to minor chords.) Don't try to combine the hands: unlike scales we only practice broken chords hands separately.

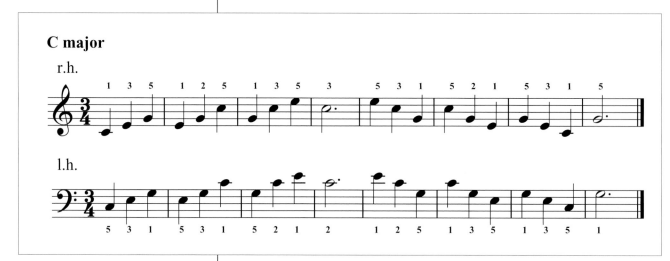

CD TRACK 12

EXERCISE 2.5

This study will help you to develop rhythmic control in broken chords and familiarity with the typical fingerings. Try and maintain a consistent rhythm by using your fingers to slightly stress the notes on the beat. As is usually the case, though, the first beat of every bar needs an even stronger emphasis. The way to achieve this is to let the whole hand push or sink into the keys just for a moment, with the help of the wrist and forearm. However, the sixteenth-notes that come just after the beat must remain light.

EXERCISE 2.5   BROKEN CHORD STUDY

PASSING THUMB STUDY

When you practice scales, you should pay special attention to the process of moving the thumb underneath the third or fourth finger in order to continue into a new position. Try to pass the thumb under the fingers as they are playing, rather than waiting to the last moment and making a sudden jolt. Resist the temptation to let the elbows swing out away from the sides of your body: this makes it easier on the hand and wrist but harder to control in the long run. Make the thumb, hand, and wrist do the work.

EXERCISE 2.6

Here's a preliminary exercise for practicing the passing thumb. Keep the second and third fingers held down throughout while you jump between the other two notes with just the thumb, aiming for a light and bouncy feel. You can repeat the exercise several times in each hand, leaving the second and third fingers down all the time. However, make sure you stop if you feel pain or tension in the wrist.

EXERCISE 2.6

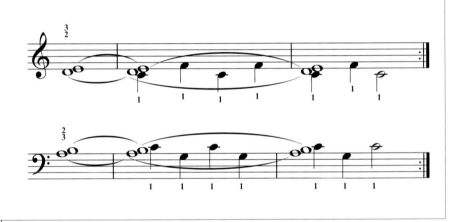

XERCISE 2.7

his study will help you to develop this technique. Be careful in bar 28: the thumb
nust jump straight to the new position to start the descending scale. Practicing this
iece will also be useful for developing the reverse technique, where we pass the
hird or fourth finger over the thumb to continue a scale.

EXERCISE 2.7

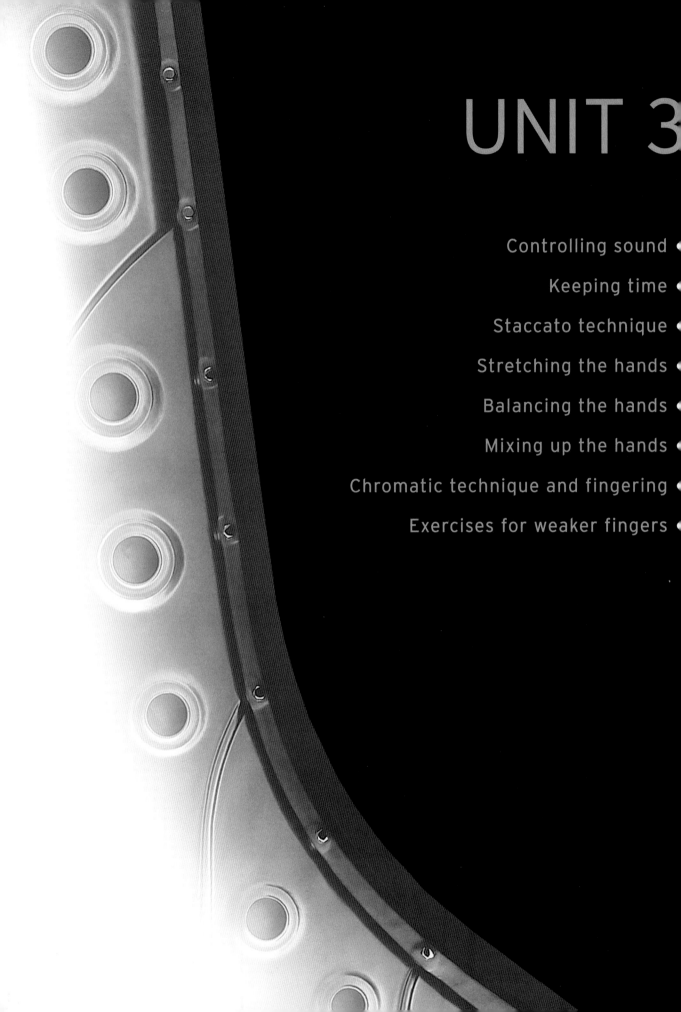

UNIT 3

CONTROLLING SOUND

When playing music it's important to be aware of how loudly or softly you are playing: this is what musicians call **dynamics**. Composers usually indicate the dynamic level of the music using dynamic markings, which take the form of Italian terms, or abbreviations for these, or certain other symbols.

It's also important to be aware of how the composer wants particular notes or groups of notes to be played. Should they be joined smoothly, or played and released quickly, leaving a gap before the next note? Should they be accented (ie, stressed) or not? We call this aspect of playing **articulation**.

You will find that nearly all piano music, apart from early music written for the harpsichord, has both dynamic markings and articulation markings. They are an important part of the music that cannot be ignored. However it doesn't stop there: as the performer you are also expected to add more subtle shadings of dynamics and articulation yourself. This is part of your role as an interpreter of the music.

THE MAIN DYNAMIC LEVELS

Italian	Abbreviation	Explanation
pianissimo	*pp*	very soft
piano	*p*	soft
mezzo piano	*mp*	fairly soft
mezzo forte	*mf*	fairly loud
forte	*f*	loud
fortissimo	*ff*	very loud

For gradual changes of volume the following hairpin signs may be employed:

Italian	Sign	Explanation
crescendo	—	getting gradually louder
diminuendo	—	getting gradually softer

The terms below can be used to modify any of those mentioned above:

Italian	Explanation
molto	very, much
poco	slightly, a little
poco a poco	gradually
subito	suddenly
sempre	always
piu	more
meno	less

The most important articulation marking is the **slur**, a curved line, similar to a tie, running between two or more notes. This means those notes should be joined smoothly (Italian: legato), so that they make a single continuous **phrase**. (It's important

UNIT 3 | 39

to be able to distinguish a slur from a tie: if it only connects two consecutive notes on the same line or space, then it's a tie; otherwise it's a slur.)

Dividing music up into phrases gives structure to the music and helps to make it expressive – just like in speech. Knowing when and how to do this is part of what musicians call **phrasing**, which also involves being sensitive to the dynamic shaping within individual phrases.

Other basic articulation signs are:

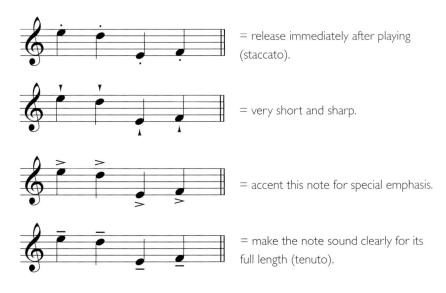

= release immediately after playing (staccato).

= very short and sharp.

= accent this note for special emphasis.

= make the note sound clearly for its full length (tenuto).

When the same articulation is required throughout a long passage of music, we give the articulation markings for the first few notes, followed by the marking 'simile' (Italian for 'in the same manner').

At the end of the next piece you will also see this sign, which concerns timing:

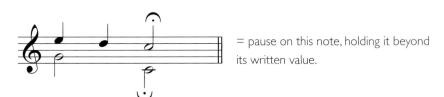

= pause on this note, holding it beyond its written value.

CD TRACK 13

CARIBBEAN SOUNDS
Caribbean music includes everything from Afro-Cuban salsa and Dominican merengue to Jamaican ska and reggae. Starting in the 1960s, reggae quickly exploded onto the worldwide music scene, thanks to its hypnotic offbeat rhythms and simple chord changes, as well as the immediacy and power of its melodic phrases and protest lyrics.

EXERCISE 3.1
To play this piece you need to catch the distinctive offbeat feel of Caribbean rhythms. Practice the right-hand chords in the first section by themselves, marking the missing strong beats with your left hand, or foot. Then practice the left-hand melody by itself. To combine them, start by just clapping the rhythm of the left hand while tapping on the strong (half-note) beats with your foot. Then try the same, but this time tap the foot off the beat, so it gives you the rhythm of the right-hand chords. Then try these two stages again, playing the actual notes in the left hand. Finally, add the actual chords in the right hand to the left-hand line. For the middle section, apply the same methods but with the relationship between the hands

reversed. Try and maintain a consistent scale of dynamic levels, and don't allow the rhythmic character of the music to make you play aggressively. Notice the different articulation markings and keep the speed relaxed throughout.

EXERCISE 3.1   CARIBBEAN SPRING

Italian	Explanation
Prestissimo	very fast
Presto	quick
Vivace	lively
Allegro	fast
Allegretto	quite fast
Moderato	moderate
Andantino	slightly faster (or slower) than Andante
Andante	leisurely, at a walking pace
Largo	fairly slow
Adagio	slow
Lento	very slow
accelerando (accel.)	gradually getting faster
ritardando (ritard.)	gradually getting slower
rallentando (rall.)	gradually getting slower
ritenuto (rit.)	hold back
A tempo	return to the original speed

KEEPING TIME

There's often a temptation to vary the speed of one's playing, as other aspects of the music can easily affect this. For example, it can feel natural to slow down for harder passages and speed up for easier ones, or to get faster when the music gets louder, and slower when it gets softer. It's important to resist this, especially in classical music. (As you can see from the last piece, non-classical styles of music tend to have a strong and repetitive beat, which makes it easier to maintain a steady speed.)

Playing along with a **metronome** can help you, but be careful: it's easy to accidentally set the metronome at a speed that is slightly too fast or too slow. Also, too much practice with the metronome can make your playing sound rather mechanical. It's more important to work out in your mind what speed you think the whole piece should go at, and to imagine how different parts of it will sound when played at exactly that speed.

Another thing to remember while learning a piece is that you'll get better results by choosing a speed that you can comfortably maintain for even the most difficult passages, so don't be afraid to practice as slowly as is necessary. (You'll often hear teachers telling their students that "the slower you practice, the quicker you learn.") That way, when you gradually bring the music up to its proper speed it will sound consistently relaxed and confident.

Musicians often use the Italian term **tempo** to refer to the speed of music, and other Italian terns are used to indicate not just the music's speed, but its character as well.

STACCATO TECHNIQUE

We've already mentioned that when we join notes smoothly it's called **legato**, and when we play them as short or detached notes with gaps in between it is **staccato**. These represent the two basic kinds of playing that are possible on the piano. However, notes can be more or less legato, or more or less staccato. In particular, what kind and degree of staccato you use will depend on many factors, including the expressive character of the music, the speed of the notes and their dynamic level. The faster the notes, the more the staccato must be produced from the fingers themselves, without assistance from the wrist or forearm. However, slower music can benefit from using the wrist to help produce the staccato effect – especially if a more gentle staccato is called for – while the forearm can be used to create a heavier, more ponderous staccato, appropriate for louder chords.

Resist the temptation to automatically play staccato notes more loudly than others, as otherwise this will give your playing a 'choppy' feel. This may also result if you allow tension in the wrist and forearm to build up, which may signal inappropriate use of the forearm in fast staccato passages or a lack of looseness in the wrist in slow staccato playing.

STRETCHING THE HANDS

By now you should have some feel for the stretch involved in reaching an octave on the piano between your thumb and little finger. If you find that you can consistently stretch an octave without looking or thinking about it too much, then you know that your 'muscular memory' is starting develop. Now's the time to start developing this further by seeing if you can consistently judge the distances when stretching all of the intervals up to an octave.

EXERCISE 3.2

Here's an exercise to develop your muscular memory for stretching different intervals. Position one hand so that the first two notes are covered by the appropriate fingers. Now try to memorize the sequence of notes and intervals, a bar or two at a time. Then close your eyes and try to play it 'blind.' (Alternatively, keep them open but don't look at the keyboard!) Only then should you try the whole exercise, with your eyes open and looking down when necessary.

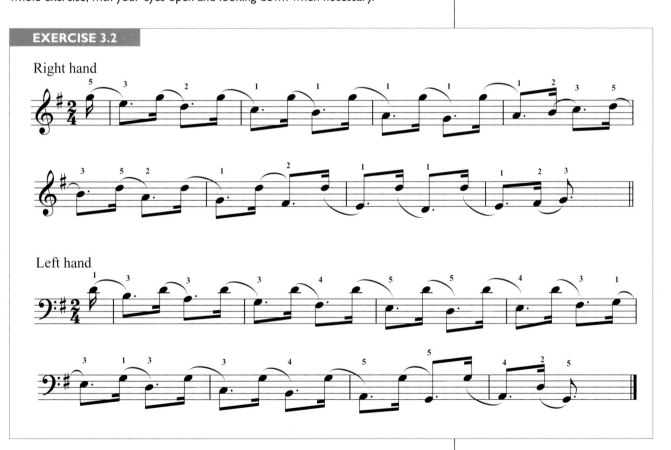

EXERCISE 3.2

EXERCISE 3.3

'Summer Song' practices these stretches with both legato and staccato playing. Notice how the hands fit together to create a continuous stream of eighth-notes, even though at the start the notes sometimes overlap, with one hand holding on while the other plays. Aim for an even eighth-note flow throughout, but note how the staccato notes in the middle actually form a single line, split between the hands, rather than melody and accompaniment. Keep the staccato light and crisp by letting the hands flick loosely up and down a little from the wrist.

EXERCISE 3.3 SUMMER SONG

EXERCISE 3.3   continued

BALANCING THE HANDS

Unlike most other musical instruments, the fact that we can play independently with both hands at the same time means that a single pianist can play music that has both a foreground and a background, or a melody and an accompaniment. This makes playing the piano infinitely more interesting and rewarding, but also more challenging, than playing most other instruments. In particular, it means that we have to be sensitive to how the two hands relate from the point of view of dynamic levels.

Achieving the right balance between the hands, or between melody and accompaniment, is crucial to any successful performance, but it can be complicated by several features. Firstly, one hand may naturally play louder than the other all the time. This is a serious fault, which you must work hard to correct. (It's usually the weaker hand – for most people the left one – and typically reflects problems associated with the build-up of muscular tension and fatigue.) Secondly, one hand may be playing material that is naturally louder than the other, because there are more notes, or because it's playing in a louder register of the instrument. You'll have to work hard to compensate for this, especially if the louder hand is playing the accompaniment rather than the melody.

CD TRACK 15

EXERCISE 3.4

This intermezzo comes from Schubert's opera 'Rosamunde.' Notice the key signature, which shows that the key is B♭ major. Because the left-hand accompaniment is in a more penetrating register of the piano than the right-hand melody, you must work extra-hard to prevent it from dominating. Sing on the right hand quarter-notes, and gently rock the left hand from side to side to help achieve the alternating pattern there. (The technical term for this is 'rotation.') Watch out for where you have to use fifth finger on a black note in the last line – you'll need to slide the left hand further into the black keys for this. Make the ritenuto effects as expressive and subtle as possible.

EXERCISE 3.4   INTERMEZZO

Schubert

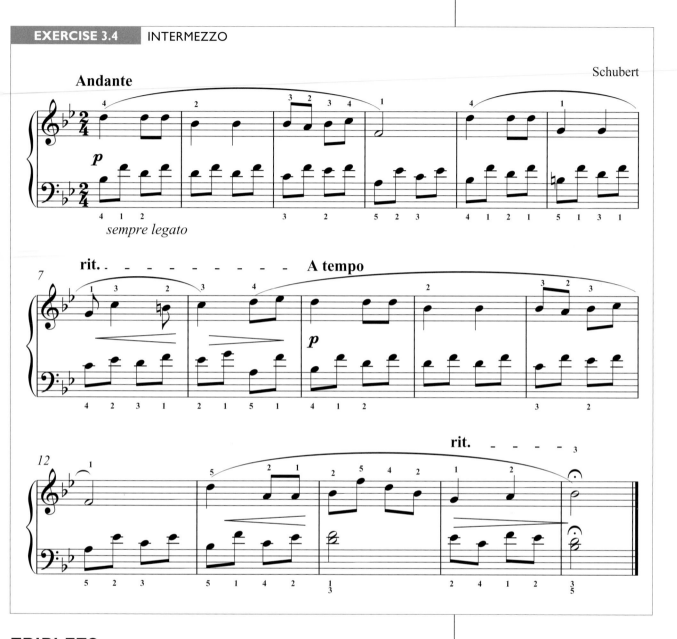

TRIPLETS

Look at the right hand in bars 8 and 16 of the next piece. You'll see groups of three eighth-notes with a figure 3 placed above or below the notes. This means we subdivide one beat of music into three equal parts instead of two, creating a **triplet**. The notes are just slightly faster than the normal subdivisions, because we're playing 'three notes in the time of two.'

three triplet eighth-notes
= two eighth-notes

CD TRACK 16

EXERCISE 3.5

This is a minuet that Mozart composed when still a young child. Notice how at the start the right hand alternates between an extended position (covering an octave) and a more contracted (five-finger) position. In Mozart's time it was common only to write slurs where necessary, and to let the character of the piece (and the note-lengths) suggest how other notes should be played. A minuet is a relaxed dance, so the remaining quarter-notes should be detached but not too short, while the half-notes should connect smoothly to the next note. Stressing the first beat of the bar highlights the dance-like character and helps to keep the triplets in time.

EXERCISE 3.5   MINUET

Mozart

Allegro

MIXING UP THE HANDS

Sometimes the two hands work independently of each other, as when playing melody and accompaniment, and sometimes they intersect to form a single texture or a single line. Some piano music switches rapidly between both of these possibilities, or lies somewhere in the middle between them.

EXERCISE 3.6

Here the hands really are mixed up. Notice how the right hand seems to form a melody by itself in the first four or five bars, but in bars 6 and 7 merges with the other hand into a single line, which also relates to what the left hand has been playing. Be careful with the time signature, which indicates eighth-note beats; sixteenth-notes are not as fast as you may think. Keep the staccato notes crisp, especially on the first beat – so they contrast with the held dotted quarter-notes, which are marked with horizontal dashes to show they must sound clearly for their full length. You'll notice a few places where the sustaining pedal – the right-hand pedal – is indicated: first learn the piece without pedal, then try adding it. Note how it's used here to add resonance to chords in the lower register, but it also helps create a join (in bars 15-16) that would otherwise be impossible.

EXERCISE 3.6   THE JOLLY MILLER

Frolicsome

Fly

continued over page

EXERCISE 3.6 continued

CHROMATIC TECHNIQUE AND FINGERING

A chromatic scale passes through every single black and white note in an octave. This means it requires a quite different fingering from major and minor scales (which are also known as diatonic scales). In fact there are two possible fingerings. The 'standard fingering' alternates between third finger on black keys and thumb on white notes in both hands, introducing the second only when we come to white notes with no black key between them. The 'alternative fingering' changes the pattern in the group of three black notes on the keyboard, to reduce the number of times that the thumb is passed under. This pattern is harder to learn, but more useful for rapid chromatic scale runs.

For chromatic scales and chromatic scale passages in music, make the fingers more rounded, allowing the thumb to move farther in to the black keys, and keep all fingers close to the keys for a smooth join.

Chromatic scales on D in standard and alternative fingerings. Play hands separately.

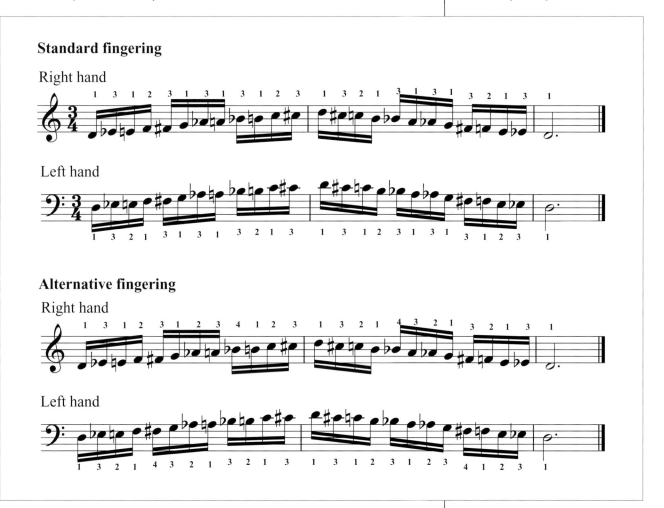

EXERCISE 3.7

This study practices chromatic scale playing. Note how the fingering uses parts of both the standard and alternative patterns, depending on the passage. (Other possible fingerings are also given in brackets – try these too.) Remember that accidentals last through to the end of the bar unless cancelled by another accidental that applies to the same pitch. You will sometimes find that the same black note is written first as a flat, then as a sharp, or vice versa – this is because the choice of notation is designed to minimize the number of accidentals in the bar.

| **EXERCISE 3.7** | CHROMATIC STUDY |

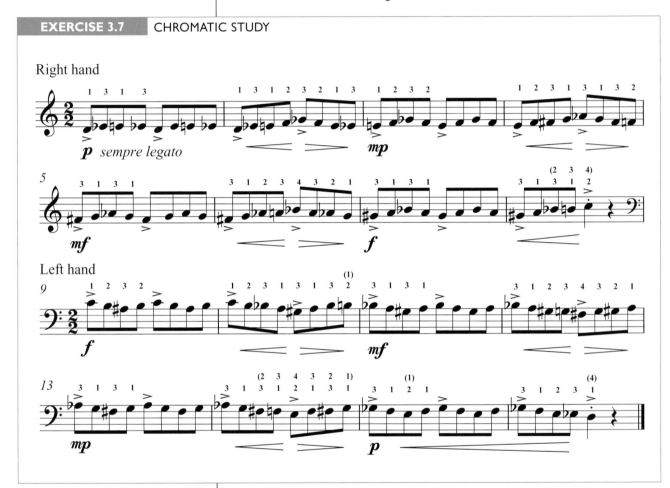

EXERCISES FOR WEAKER FINGERS

The third, fourth, and fifth fingers are naturally weaker and less flexible than the thumb and second finger. However, you can compensate for this if you regularly practice exercises for building up their muscular independence, like those given below.

EXERCISE 3.8

Play these exercises legato throughout, with a clear emphasis on both of the half-note beats in each bar. Note how the second beat corresponds to fourth finger in the second half of each exercise. This is the weakest finger, so take special care to make the stress from the finger alone, by lifting it a little more before striking the key. You must do this without moving the hand or wrist, but keeping these relaxed. Start slowly and only speed up when it feels comfortable to do so. Pay careful attention to the shape of your hand – the knuckles should be level, fingers rounded, and the wrist just a little lower than the hand itself.

EXERCISE 3.8

Suggestions for effective practicing

When learning a musical instrument it's important to work out an approach to practicing that's right for you. However, here are some good general 'rules of thumb' for the piano.

• Do give your fingers time to warm up – start off with slow and simple exercises.

• Do start your practice each time with some scales, broken chords, or other exercises.

• Do listen carefully to everything you play.

• Do be patient – Rome wasn't built in a day.

• Do check your posture while playing.

• Do make sure you're relaxed while playing, especially in difficult passages.

• Do try to imagine how the music will sound before playing it.

• Do check the time signature, key signature and tempo markings before playing.

• Do practice thoroughly hands separately before trying hands together.

• Don't keep playing when you feel tired or tense.

• Don't over-practice – this is a sign of fear.

• Don't practice your mistakes – you can't correct them by repeating them.

• Don't feel embarrassed about practicing as slowly as you need to.

• Don't forget about dynamics – they won't look after themselves.

• Don't bang.

• Don't nod your head or sway from side to side when playing.

• Don't learn music you don't like, unless there's a good technical reason.

UNIT 4

RHYTHM IN CLASSICAL AND JAZZ

SWING AND THE BIG BANDS

From the mid-1930s to the mid-1940s, young people right across America loved to listen and dance to big band jazz. Whether it was fast and brash, with an 'upbeat' feel, or slow, dreamy, and romantic, it always had a distinctive rhythmic swing. Popular tunes were 'arranged' for large bands that included choruses of saxophones, trumpets and trombones, as well as solo performers, piano and drums.

Famous jazz musicians of this period include the trumpeter Louis Armstrong, the clarinetist Benny Goodman, and the pianist Count Basie. The most important bandleaders were Duke Ellington and Glenn Miller. Many would say this was the heyday of jazz.

Rhythms tend to be written out differently in jazz from the way they are shown in classical and other non-classical music. That's because jazz has a special kind of rhythmic character, known as **'swing.'** This involves a division of the beat into two unequal subdivisions – the first longer and the second shorter. It roughly corresponds to the classical division into a triplet – ie, three equal divisions – with the first two divisions tied to create a single note worth two-thirds of the beat. (You can see this in the first line of the example below.)

However, even this isn't strictly true, because rhythms in jazz don't correspond precisely to equal divisions of the beat, but more to a kind of 'feel,' and the nature of this feel depends on how fast ('upbeat') or slow ('downbeat') the music is. The faster the music, the closer it will be to divisions of the beat into two equal parts (usually eighth-notes); the slower it is, the more it will tend towards what in classical music are written as dotted rhythms (e.g. a dotted eighth-note followed by a sixteenth-note). Because of this, in jazz we usually write swing rhythms as equal eighth-notes, or occasionally as dotted rhythms. The important thing to remember is that unlike in classical music this doesn't tell you exactly how the rhythm should sound. Instead, you must match the amount of swing to the overall character and speed of the music.

Here is a typical swing rhythm written out, first in classical notation, then in jazz notation. Notice how jazz switches to the classical notation when it wants to show an equal division of the beat into three parts, but keeps to the jazz notation for tied notes. These tied notes play an important role in jazz, because they usually correspond to offbeat accents, which are created by playing a note just before or after the beat instead of on the beat – an effect known as **syncopation**.

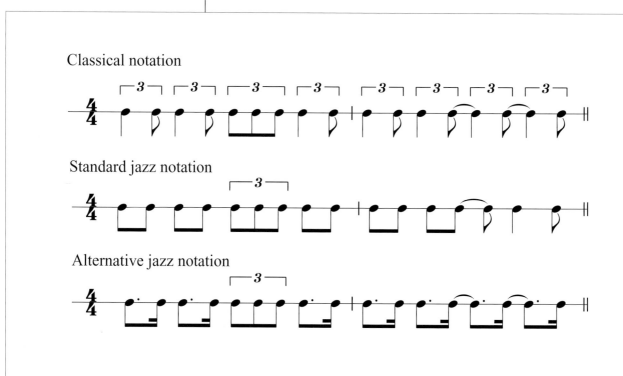

Classical notation

Standard jazz notation

Alternative jazz notation

The next piece uses swing. To help understand the rhythms, here's the opening line, written in the version of jazz notation that uses dotted rhythms. Compare it to the first line in the version of the whole piece, which uses the other kind of jazz notation, with equal eighth-notes. When learning the piece, aim for something in between what these two rhythms would correspond to when played strictly as in classical music.

CD TRACK 18

EXERCISE 4.1

'Swinging Along' explores some simple jazz rhythms and harmonies. Try to work out the rhythm of the right hand by clapping first. Be careful with the key signature of four sharps: this piece is in E major, but it also has many accidentals, because it changes key. Remember to move your hand into the black keys when playing sharps and flats, especially if you have to use thumb on a black key, as in bar 12. Stressing the first beat of each bar will help you to feel the relationship between syncopations and the underlying beat.

EXERCISE 4.1   SWINGING ALONG

EXERCISE 4.2

CD TRACK 19

In 'Soldier's March' aim for a crisp rhythm with military precision and sharply defined accents. Note that many notes are neither slurred nor staccato: this means they should be slightly held, but not joined to the next note. Playing with very rounded fingers will help you achieve a firm touch.

EXERCISE 4.2   SOLDIER'S MARCH

ROMANTIC BRAHMS

Johannes Brahms, who was born in Hamburg but eventually came to live in Vienna, was one of the most important composers of the mid-19th century – a period when classical music in Europe was dominated by the Germans. He came to be seen as something of a traditionalist as a result of his rivalry with Richard Wagner, who at the time was viewed as the leading radical composer. However, this is misleading. While Brahms was unusually active in studying and editing music of the past, and preferred traditional forms such as the symphony and sonata, his music is full of Romantic drama and lyricism, and even anticipates some features of modern music. Brahms was also greatly influenced by German folksongs.

PLAYING IN THIRDS

Because notes two steps apart in the scale sound so well together, we sometimes play a melody with each note accompanied by the note two steps lower. This interval between notes is called a '3rd,' so the effect is known as '**doubling** in 3rds.' The result is a richer, smoother texture, but this can sometimes require special fingerings, as both parts usually have to be played in the same hand.

EXERCISE 4.3

Here is a preliminary exercise for practicing playing in 3rds. Notice how we sometimes move between thumb played together with third finger and played together with second. This requires the thumb to be released a little earlier than the finger, so it can be moved into position over the new note, and played with the other new finger, just as the other previous finger is released. Try the whole exercise extremely slowly at first. If you feel the fingertips touching both of the keys you are about to play, just before pressing them, it will help you to achieve more exact co-ordination between the two parts.

EXERCISE 4.3

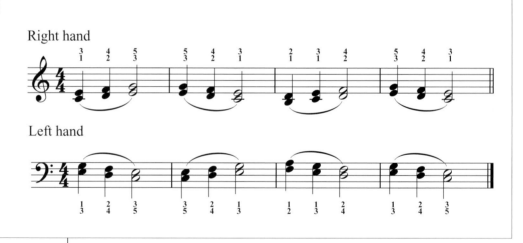

SINGING TONE

The most important ability that distinguishes a musical pianist from an unmusical one is the capacity to make the instrument sing. Remember, the piano is a percussive instrument – it produces sounds by striking the keys, with hammers. However, the notes that are produced often have a sustained quality, and we therefore expect melodies on the piano to unfold as expressively and smoothly as when sung by the human voice, or played on wind or stringed instruments. We can achieve this through keeping a legato join between notes, letting longer notes sound a little more clearly so they sustain for longer, and matching the dynamics to the rise and fall of the melody – something we naturally do when singing ourselves. This means getting slightly louder as the melody rises, and slightly softer when it falls. It also means identifying the high point or 'climax' of the melody, and letting the dynamic level peak at just this point.

EXERCISE 4.4

CD TRACK 20

This much-loved melody by Brahms is probably the most famous lullaby ever composed. It should have a gentle, rocking character, with the melody singing expressively over the accompaniment. Keep the left hand quiet throughout, and watch out for the place in bar 9 where you must change fingers while holding a note. (First play the note with the thumb, then bring second onto the note as well, before releasing the thumb. Practice this slowly by itself first.) Notice how in bar 4 the right hand plays a melody line with repeated notes underneath: the latter must be released slightly earlier than the notes in the melody, so you have time to restrike them along with the next melody note. (Keep the top part smooth here, with a good legato join.) Let the melody peak as it leaps up the octave to the F at the start of bar 10, but repeat the effect more quietly in bar 14. This will contribute to the general feeling that the music is subsiding as its end draws near, which is appropriate for a lullaby.

EXERCISE 4.4   LULLABY

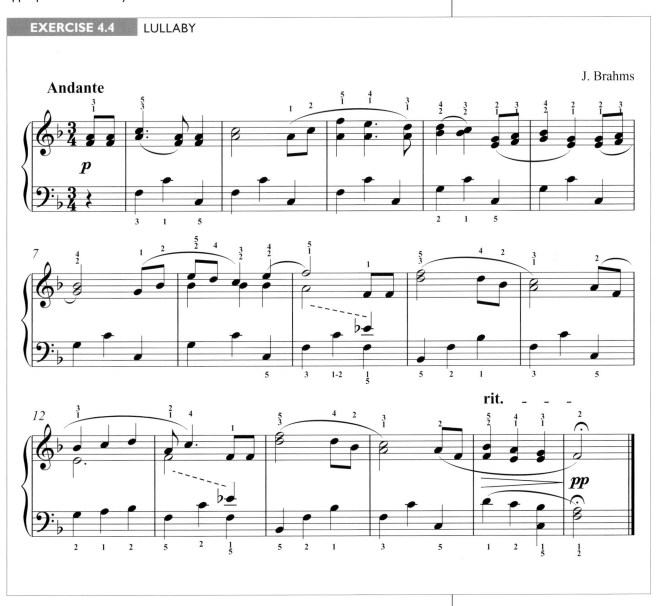

J. Brahms

SPEED AND DEXTERITY

As you progress beyond the first stages of learning the piano, you'll find you encounter more and more passages in which the fast speed of the notes demands a high degree of dexterity. This is something that must be acquired over time, through practicing scales and other exercises. It's important to resist the temptation to tense up the hand, wrist or arm in order to force the fingers to play at a faster speed than they are really capable of. Instead, keep these loose and relaxed, and build up the speed gradually, in the fingers alone.

EXERCISE 4.5
Here's a preliminary exercise that will help you to acquire the finger dexterity needed for the next piece. Practice loudly with accents first, then quietly with only a light stress on the beat.

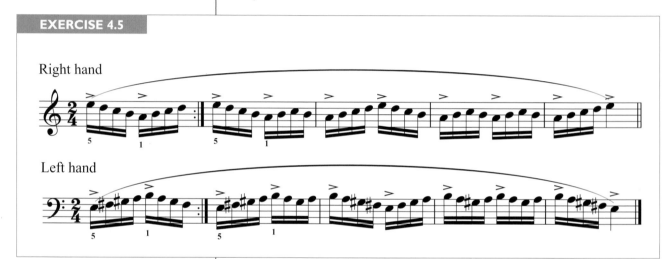

EXERCISE 4.5

Right hand

Left hand

CD **TRACK 21**

EXERCISE 4.6
In the first part of this piece, a prelude by Burgmüller, you must combine legato sixteenth-note runs with a springy staccato touch for the repeated chords. This kind of repeated staccato is produced with a light flick of the hand from the wrist, which must remain stable. (Avoid the temptation to let the whole forearm move, as this will make the staccato heavy and awkward.) In the middle section, sing on the right hand dotted quarter-notes and pay careful attention to the fingering in bar 18. 'Scherzando' is Italian for 'joky' or 'frivolous,' and 'risoluto' means that a robust, heavy touch is required. The latter is best achieved with firm, rounded fingers, leaning forward so the weight of the body presses the fingers into the keys.

EXERCISE 4.6   ARABESQUE

Burgmüller

Allegro scherzando

SCALES: TONE AND TIME

Practicing scales offers a good opportunity for developing control of tone and timing, especially if you listen carefully while playing. Because scales are so simple from a musical point of view, they expose flaws that result from the differences between fingers. It is worth spending some time focusing on dynamic levels in scales: try each scale at a variety of levels between 'piano' and 'forte'; then try playing one hand 'forte,' the other 'piano,' and then the other way around.

In addition to the scales covered in Unit 2, here are some other scales that you should know. By this stage you should be starting to get comfortable with playing scales hands together in the same direction – ie, in **'similar motion.'** However there are also some scales that are easy to play with hands moving in opposite directions – in **'contrary motion.'**

You can also apply the alternative rhythms for scales given in Unit One to all of these. This will help you to develop rhythmic evenness in your playing.

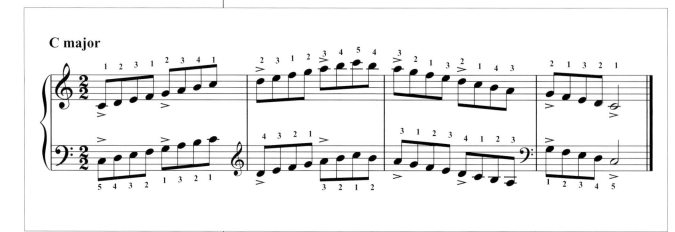

C major

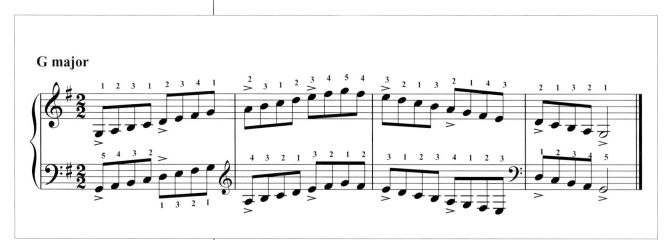

G major

D major

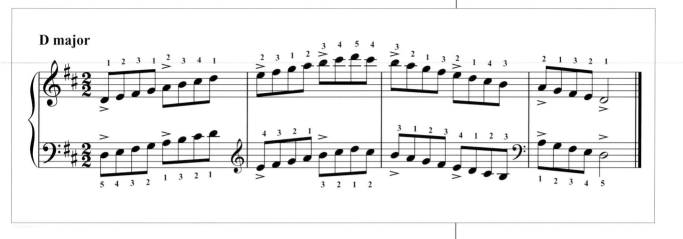

A major

Both C major and E major use standard three-four-three fingering, and are easy to play hands-together in contrary motion. This is because the C major has only white notes, while in E major the layout of black and white notes is exactly symmetrical, so black or white notes always come together. However, be careful in E major when passing the thumb under after a sharp, as the stretch to the next white note in the scale is greater for the left hand (descending) than for the right hand (ascending).

You can also try E major in similar motion.

E major (contrary motion)

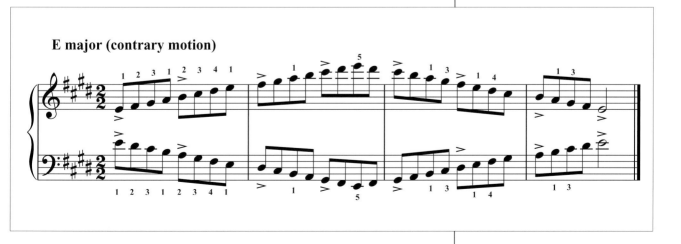

Now here's a new minor scale: B minor. B melodic minor is quite easy. Note how the ascending form resembles B major, except for the D natural (and has the same unusual left hand fingering, starting on fourth), while the descending form resembles D major.

However, B harmonic minor is much harder, as it contains a tricky stretch from G to A♯. It's worth practicing harmonic minor scales on D and then E first to get used to this, so here they are as well.

B minor (melodic)

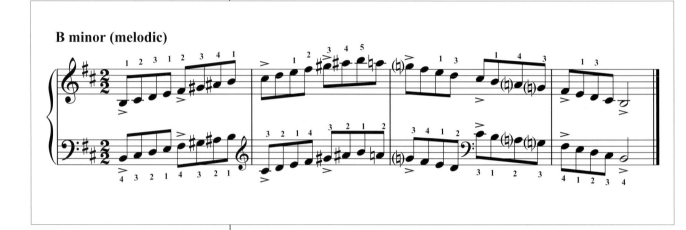

D minor (harmonic)

E minor (harmonic)

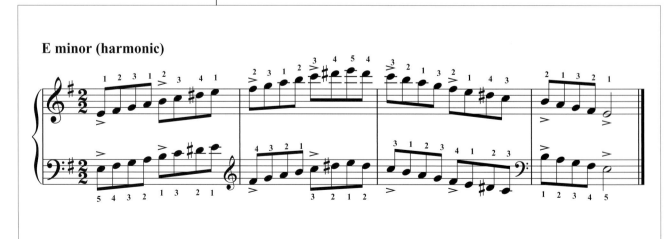

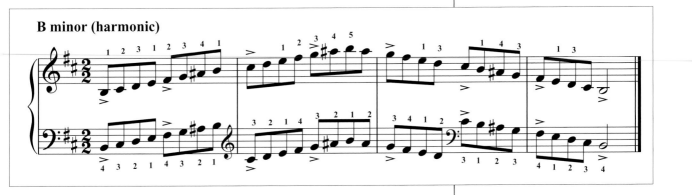

B minor (harmonic)

BASIC ARPEGGIO TECHNIQUE

An **arpeggio** consists of the notes of a chord, played straight up and down for one or more octaves. The term comes from the Italian for harp, 'arpa,' and reflects the fact that on that instrument chords are usually 'spread' rather than played melodically.

The most important feature of arpeggio technique is the use of a sideways movement of the forearm, which swings around in order to change the angle of the hand to the keyboard. Because the axis of movement is the elbow, the latter should remain fairly close to the side of your body and should not move much. This technique is known as a lateral movement. Because one-octave arpeggios form the basis for four-note broken chords, it is also used in these (see Unit Five).

We can practice each inversion of the triad as a one-octave arpeggio. Note the differences of fingering between inversions, and between right and left hand.

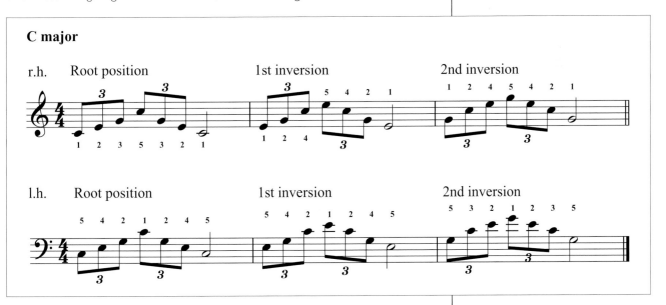

C major

These fingerings are used for all major and minor arpeggios consisting exclusively of white notes (ie, C, G, F majors, A, D, E minors), so you can familiarize yourself with all of these.

Remember, a triad consists of the 1st, 3rd and 5th of the corresponding scale. Then we just add the note an octave above the starting note to give us the four-note arpeggio.

EXERCISE 4.7

This study focuses on arpeggio technique. Keep the right hand light and flowing, and allow the forearm lateral movement to freely move with the rise and fall of the sixteenth-note arpeggio figurations. Keep the wrist loose and low.

EXERCISE 4.7 ARPEGGIO STUDY

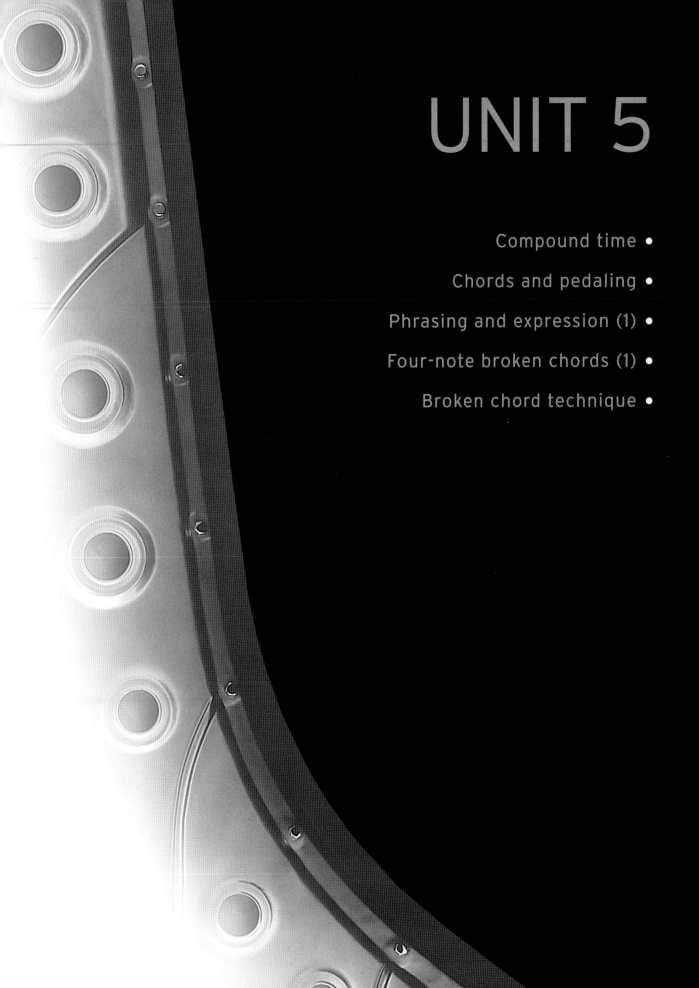

UNIT 5

COMPOUND TIME

We've already seen how triplets are used to divide the beat into thirds instead of halves. Sometimes, though, we want this effect throughout a whole piece, as the standard division of the beat. It's easier to use a special time signature that indicates this by giving the beat itself the value of a dotted note, so it naturally has three subdivisions rather than two. We express this in the time signature by showing the value of the subdivisions rather than the value of the beat (though still as a fraction of a semibreve), making this the lower number in the time signature, and putting the total number of subdivisions per bar above it. This then corresponds to the number of beats in a bar multiplied by three.

Compound duple: 6/8 = six eighth-notes = 3 + 3
= two dotted quarter-note beats per bar

Compound triple: 9/8 = nine eighth-notes = 3 + 3 +3
= three dotted quarter-note beats per bar

Compound quadruple: 12/8 = twelve eighth-notes = 3 + 3 + 3 + 3
= four dotted quarter-note beats per bar

To help you see how this works, here's a short piece, written out first in simple time with triplets, then in compound time. Try playing it from both versions – it should sound identical! Which version do you find easier to read?

CD TRACK 23

EXERCISE 5.1
Here it is first in simple time. Notice how the left hand uses arpeggio-like figures, so you can practice lateral movements and arpeggio fingerings here. Watch out for bar 12, where fifth finger and thumb both play B♭. You need to move the whole hand further into the black keys, and keep the thumb rounded so it curves in towards the fingers.

EXERCISE 5.1

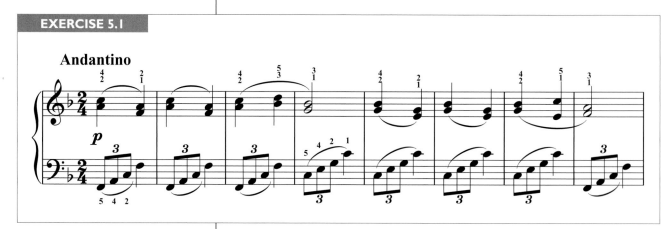

EXERCISE 5.1   continued

EXERCISE 5.2

CD TRACK 23

Now here it is again – in compound time. You must now treat dotted quarter-notes as single beats, and dotted half-notes as lasting exactly two beats. Aim for a singing right hand, with the top notes joined smoothly. When the lower note in the right hand is repeated on the next beat, as in bars 1 and 2, it helps to release it slightly before releasing the top note. This gives you a moment to prepare for re-striking it, and allows you to join it smoothly to the previous top note.

EXERCISE 5.2   LULLABY

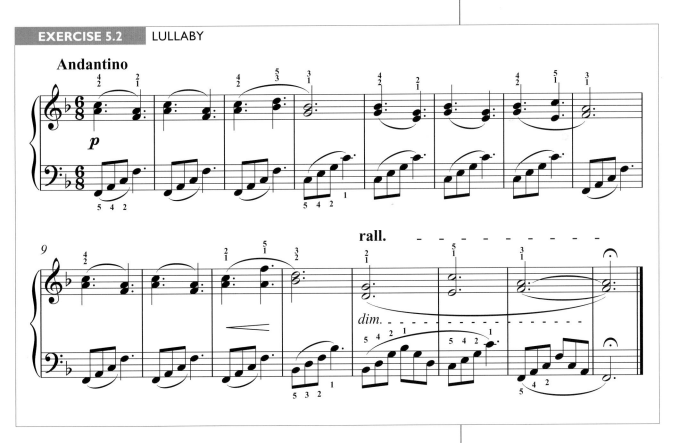

CD TRACK 24

EXERCISE 5.3

Now here's another piece, a prelude by Heller, which will help you get used to counting in compound time. The beaming of eighth-notes shows how these are grouped into threes. This can make it clearer where each new beat starts. However, remember to also count two beats in those bars where there is no music, or nothing after the first beat. Watch out for the change of fingering in the right hand, on the repeated B notes at the start. This practice was more common in the 19th century, but we still use it sometimes for clearer repetition. Note how the left hand starts in treble clef, and moves right up into the high register in bar 7. Resist the temptation to lean back away from the keyboard at this point, but make sure you're not sitting too close to the piano.

EXERCISE 5.3 PRELUDE

CHORDS AND PEDALING

An important issue when playing chords is co-ordination: all notes in the chord should sound precisely together. You can help to achieve this by preparing all of the fingers that will play, slightly ahead of actually playing the chord, so you have a moment to feel the tips of your fingers in contact with the keys you're about to press.

In Unit Three we saw how pressing down the right hand pedal (the sustaining pedal) with the right foot can add volume and resonance to chords and textures. However, it's also important to master the art of coordinating the pressing and releasing of the pedal with other aspects of the music. This means coordinating what your right foot does with what your hands are doing. Often we use pedal with a chord, but we have to make sure that we release it just before the next chord sounds, in order to avoid an audible overlap – something that may sound very messy. (This technique is known as 'direct pedaling.')

Try not to let pressing the pedal affect your playing or your posture. Keep your toes and the ball of your foot over the pedal throughout, but no more than this, and support the foot with the heel resting on the floor. The left foot should remain in its normal position, though some pianists prefer to draw it back under the seat a little as a counterbalance to the positioning of the right foot.

EXERCISE 5.4

This chord study practices co-ordination between foot and hands. Note how the pedaling comes sometimes on a strong beat, sometimes on a weak beat, and how it's often followed immediately by a staccato chord. Listen carefully to hear if the staccato chord is resonating at all in the pedal. If so, then you know your foot is too late in releasing the pedal.

EXERCISE 5.4

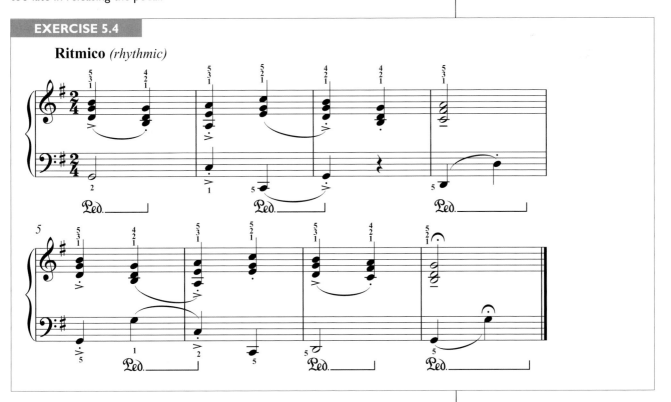

Ritmico (rhythmic)

PHRASING AND EXPRESSION (1)

MUSIC AND LANGUAGE

Just like language, music is divided into larger and smaller units, both normally referred to in music as phrases. Larger phrases are like sentences. They divide up into several smaller phrases, usually of equivalent length. These can even resemble more specific aspects of language, such as questions and answers. (Some people call this the 'grammar' or 'syntax' of music.) These phrase divisions serve as an important guide for performers when deciding how to present the music from the point of view of expressive phrasing.

It's easy to forget that to play a piece of music properly, you must do more than just accurately realize the notes and other markings in the score. Musicians spend a lot of time working on more subtle aspects of how the piece should sound: slight changes in dynamic level, or in speed or articulation, that are designed to reflect the character and structure of particular passages. We refer to the way a performer makes use of these nuances as **phrasing**. Without appropriate and imaginative phrasing, your playing will be lacking in expressive interest for others, however good you are from the point of view of sheer technique or pure accuracy. Remember, composers assume you will add these subtleties, and expect you to be familiar with any conventions that exist for how to do this. At the same time, this is where you can be creative as a performer, as often there are several different options to choose from. It is here that you have the chance to develop your individuality as a player.

Let's look at some issues connected with phrasing, as these emerge in the next piece in the book. This is the first movement of a sonatina by Beethoven. Here's the opening right-hand melody.

The small notes with slashes are **grace notes**. They are played very quickly and lightly, just before the next note. (We don't count them as subdivisions; instead we just feel how fast they should go.)

Note the detailed phrase markings (slurs). These tell us a lot about how the music divides up into phrases, but not everything. To really understand this we must perform our own analysis of the music's structure: we must 'get inside' the music. This will show us how the music was actually constructed by Beethoven, and that can also be useful if you're interested in learning how to compose or improvise music yourself. (See Unit 6 for this.)

We're going to consider three aspects: phrase-structure, contour, and arrival/departure.

Phrase-structure

Phrase-structure is the division of the music into phrases of varying length, and the way these are combined into larger units to create more extended structures.

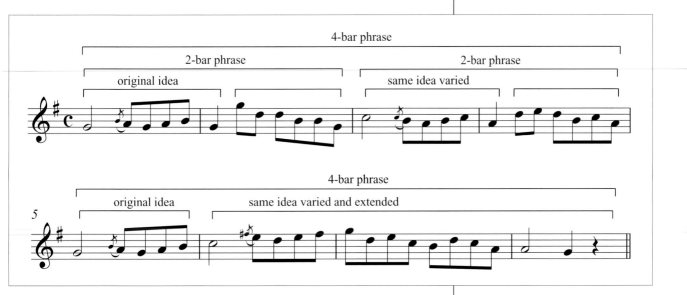

The first thing to note is that this eight-bar passage follows the most typical model for phrase-structure in music: it divides into two equal four-bar units. The second four-bar phrase appears to restate the opening musical idea or **theme**, but moves off in a new direction.

The first four-bar phrase is standard, since it divides into two equal two-bar phrases. We can tell this from the fact that the opening idea is repeated, slightly varied, in bar 3. By contrast, the second four-bar phrase doesn't divide up so simply, as the phrase markings and eighth-note movement run across the two-bar division. The eighth-note figure in bar five is repeated at a different pitch – we call this a **sequence** in music – but carries right through to the end of bar seven. Because smaller phrases and musical ideas give way to longer phrases derived from them, we have the impression that the music is growing like an organism, or developing logically.

Contour

Contour is the shape that a melody line creates as it unfolds through rising and falling pitches. Analyzing the contour of a melodic line allows us to see which notes form the underlying melodic 'skeleton', and which are merely decorative (the 'flesh' rather than the 'bones'). This helps us to grasp the underlying structure of the music more clearly.

Here are the first eight bars of the Beethoven again, with the decorative notes removed. (It's worth playing through this, with the simplified left hand, to hear how the 'skeleton' works against the chords as well.)

ORGANIC DEVELOPMENT
Beethoven was the greatest master of all at creating the feeling of 'organic growth' in music. You can hear it operating on a much more ambitious level in his symphonies and string quartets. Listening to these pieces will help you to appreciate his piano music better, so you can start to perform it with real understanding.

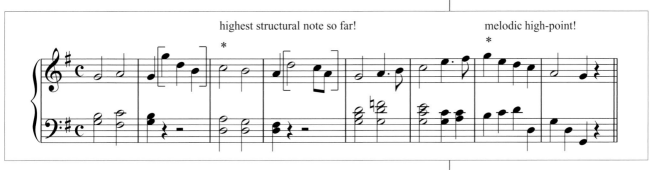

We can now see that the whole eight-bar passage has a more basic overall shape, buried beneath the surface of the music. This can inform our sense of the direction of the music, and guide our use of dynamics for expressive phrasing. (Sensitive listeners will respond to this, feeling that your performance reveals the deeper unity and form of the music.) For example, we can see that the C at the start of bar 3 represents a significant move upwards at the level of the underlying melodic shape, and we can see that the high point of the shape comes with the high G at the start of bar 7. (By contrast, the same note in bar 2 has no structural importance, as it is only part of a decorative figure linking two appearances of the opening idea.)

So now we know exactly where the expressive climax for this eight-bar phrase should come, and this tells us more precisely what Beethoven must have had in mind when he placed a crescendo sign in the bar leading up to this point. We usually match the rise and fall of the underlying shape with subtle increases and decreases of volume (sometimes called 'dynamic shading').

Arrival/departure

Another way in which analysis can shed light on phrasing and expression is through helping us to identify certain key moments in the unfolding of the music. We typically feel that the music is heading towards these, and then departing from them, and this can have implications for dynamics, and especially for tempo. To see this we may have to analyze the harmony as well as the contour, but in this passage some of these points are clear just from how the melody unfolds. Here's the next eight-bar section of the piece by Beethoven.

We can see here how the start of each two-bar phrase counts as an important arrival and departure point, with lesser points of arrival and departure located between these.

Now we're ready to begin work on learning Beethoven's piece as whole. Let's start by focusing on some specific technical points in the left hand. Here are three different passages.

EXERCISE 5.5

This first passage involves a simple alternation between pairs of notes. We use a special technique for this, called 'rotation.' This involves rocking the hand and forearm from side to side to produce the desired pattern of alternating notes. (It's rather like the way we twist our arm when turning a door handle. In this example and the next, the horizontal line dividing the fingering shows which fingers fall on each side of the alternation.) This means that the individual fingers hardly have to move to play the keys. As a preliminary exercise for this, practice repeating each pair of notes together, staccato.

MUSICAL METAPHORS

When we talk about music that unfolds or grows, about melodies that start and stop, or rise or fall, or about the music returning to where it began, we seem to be talking about music as though it were a 'thing' that 'changes', or something 'moving' through 'space'. But is this really the case, or are these just metaphors? Sometimes we also talk of musical ideas, but what kind of 'thoughts' could be expressed in music? It could be that the imagination plays a greater role in our perception of music than we normally realize.

EXERCISE 5.5

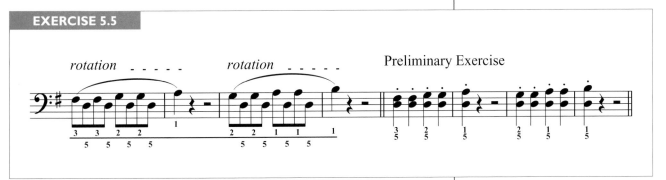

EXERCISE 5.6

Now here's a passage from slightly earlier in the piece. Here the pattern of alternation is more complex, as it involves a complete chord, but we still use rotation, this time between fingers and thumb. In this case it's better to practice each chord as a block first, so it gets prepared as a single unit.

EXERCISE 5.6

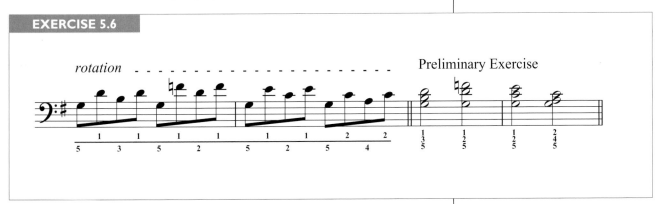

EXERCISE 5.7

Note how similar this third passage looks on paper to the one we've just been practicing. However, as soon as you try playing it you can see that there's no pattern of alternation here at all. Instead, we need to swing the hand round, using the same kind of lateral movement we practiced in arpeggios. However, the best preliminary exercise is still to first play each chord as a block, as in the previous example.

EXERCISE 5.7

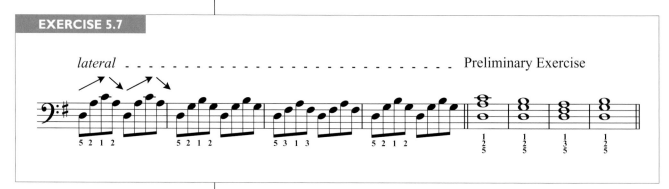

CD TRACK 25

EXERCISE 5.8

Now we're ready to try the whole of this sonatina movement. Make the grace note in the theme as light as possible, so it falls onto the next note. This will be easier if you have second and third fingers positioned so they are in contact with the keys from the start of the bar – along with the thumb. Also, notice the short, two-note phrases in the right hand in bar two: we play these by sinking in a little on the first of each pair, and drawing the hand off from the wrist on the second. Watch out for passages where the left hand plays an eighth-note accompaniment: keep it soft, and allow the right hand to sing above, especially on held notes. The whole piece should sound light, graceful and relaxed.

EXERCISE 5.8   SONATINA

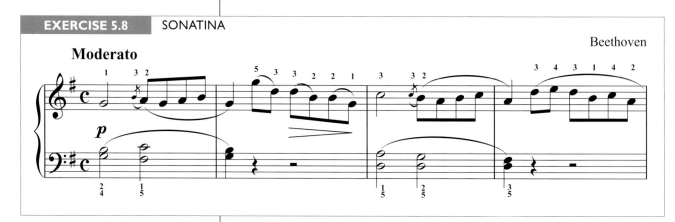

EXERCISE 5.8 continued

continued over page

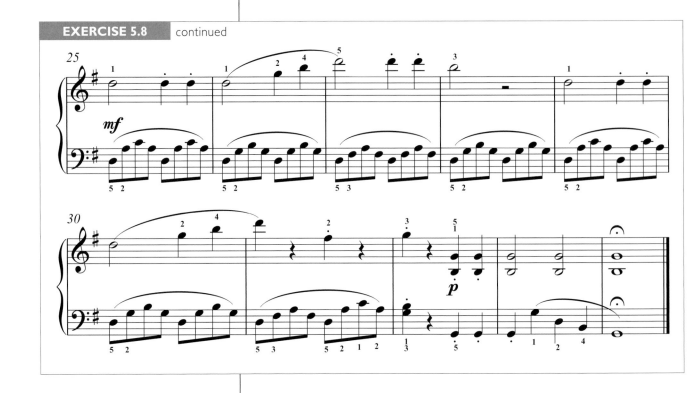

FOUR-NOTE BROKEN CHORDS (1)

These work on the same principle as three-note broken chords – we pass successively through all the positions of a chord – only this time we have four notes in each hand position. At this stage you should only try broken chords that consist entirely of white notes. Here are C major and A minor. Notice how the fingering is the same for both, so all you need to do is reproduce the same pattern starting on different notes. This goes for C, G, and F majors, and for A, D, and E minors.

C major

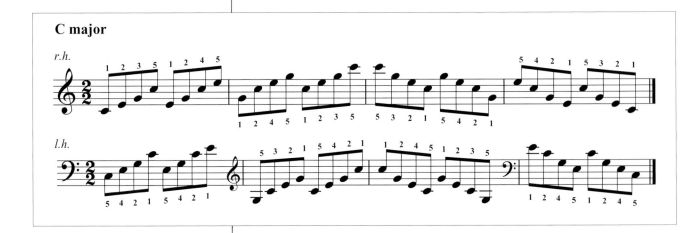

A minor

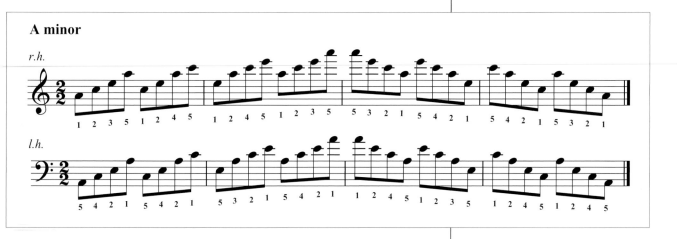

Broken chord technique

EXERCISE 5.9

Now here's an exercise to help develop greater fluency in these broken chords.
It practices the difficult move from the last note of one position to the first note
of the next. The idea is that you focus on just getting the first finger of the new
position into place, and only afterwards bring the other fingers into position.
Some lateral movement of the hand as you approach the last note of each position
and then swing back may be helpful. You can also try this exercise in the other keys
mentioned above.

EXERCISE 5.9

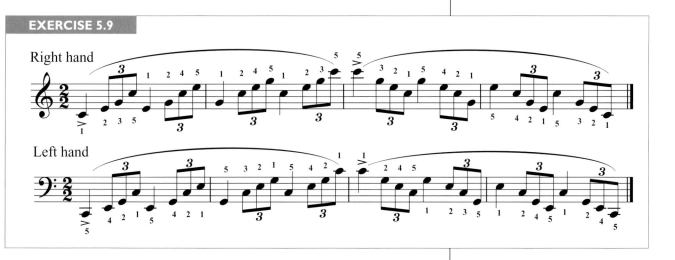

EXERCISE 5.10

This exercise practices changing the whole hand position in one go.

Here's an alternative pattern for the broken chord, which you can also try in any of the keys already mentioned. You will find that as you become fluent in this it becomes natural to use some rotation to maintain the rhythmic shape.

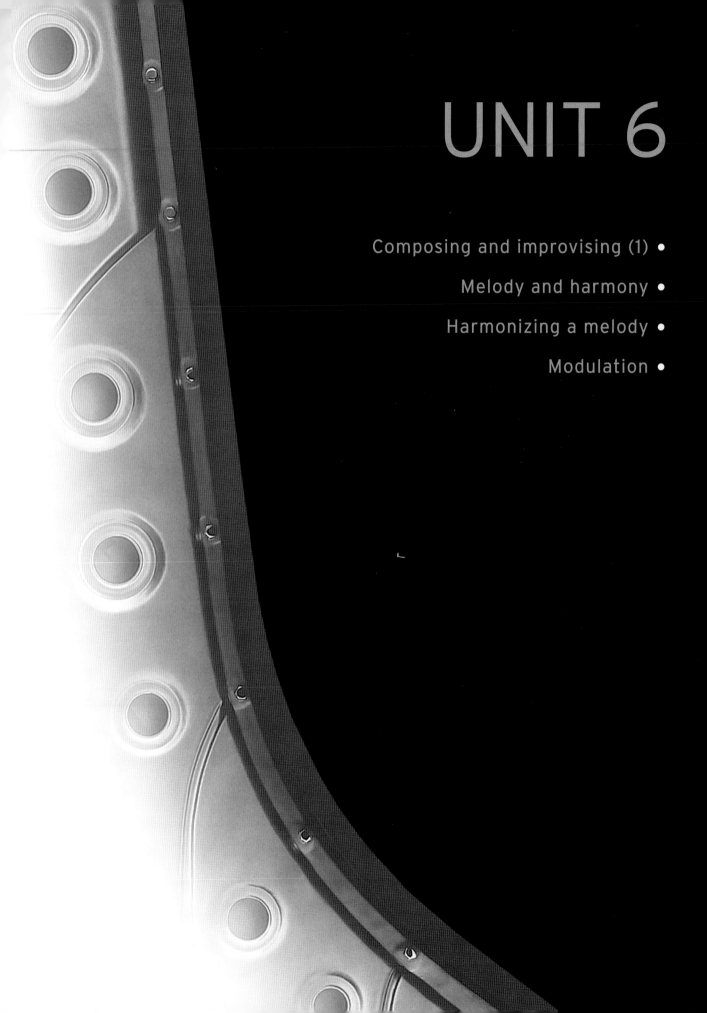

UNIT 6

COMPOSING AND IMPROVISING (1)

Composing means creating a written-out piece of music that can be performed by other people as well. Here we may use the piano because it's the instrument the music will eventually be played on, or simply as a medium for testing out musical ideas. In the latter case, the music will then have to be arranged for other instruments. (In classical music, composers usually do this themselves, but in non-classical – jazz and modern popular styles – it's often left to the performers or to an arranger.)

The piano is especially useful for testing out ideas because it allows us to hear melody and harmony at one go. That's why it became the standard instrument for classical composers to work out their compositions on. Although a lot of musicians working in modern popular styles (rock, pop, etc) are initially more comfortable with the guitar, as experienced songwriters they often switch to piano or keyboards to take advantage of the richer possibilities on offer there, especially in the area of harmony.

Improvising, on the other hand, means making up music literally as you play it. This is most typically associated with jazz, but in the past a lot of the great classical composers (eg, Handel, Bach, Mozart, Beethoven, Liszt) were also great improvisers. Nowadays, jazz tends to be less improvised, while a lot of folk and modern popular music involve elements of improvisation and composition freely mixed together, in rehearsal or in studio recordings. Some contemporary classical music also uses improvisation. If you use the piano for improvising, then of course this will also be the medium in which people hear what you do.

These approaches often get mixed together: a lot of songwriters like to improvise on the piano as a starting point for composing songs that will eventually require arranging. In this unit, we'll focus on two issues relevant to all of these approaches: how to put together a satisfying melody, and how to harmonize it with appropriate chords.

MELODY AND HARMONY

An experienced melody writer or improviser will often think up melody and harmony together. However, that skill takes time to develop, and you can't always rely on it. In practice, the melody often comes first, and you may have to figure out the chords afterwards. Other times you'll know the chords in advance, but will have to work out a melody based on them.

Melody

Like a story, poem or drama, a melody unfolds in time, playing with our expectations and emotions before satisfying them. But it also has shape and form – a kind of architecture. The rise and fall of a melody over time gives it a dynamic, expressive character, but also corresponds to a structure. Most melodies divide into phrases of roughly equal length, and some of these phrases are related, while others contrast. A good melody has to be memorable, so it must balance unity with variety, predictability with surprise.

Most good melodies display the following features:
- Variety and balance of melodic movement
- Question and answer
- Repetition with variation
- Motivic unity
- Logical phrase structure
- Direction and climax
- Surprise and fulfillment

We'll look at how these work in relation to an actual melody. Here's the opening of a well-known Irish folk tune, 'Londonderry Air.'

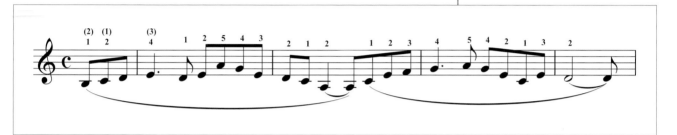

Notice how each of these two phrases has a clear rising and falling movement. Both rise towards a dotted note, decorated by alternation with an adjacent pitch, before opening out into leaps of two or three steps that finish roughly where the phrase started. A nice balance is created between stepwise movement and leaps, and between ascending and descending movement, with the second phrase opening out a little more quickly than the first. At the same time, the first phrase comes to rest on a note lower than any so far, adding an unresolved aspect to the phrase. This is resolved when the second phrase turns upwards on its second-to-last note, finishing its descent closer to the centre of the compass of the melody. This gives the two phrases the feeling of a question followed by an answer.

Now here are the next two phrases, which make up the second half of the tune's first section.

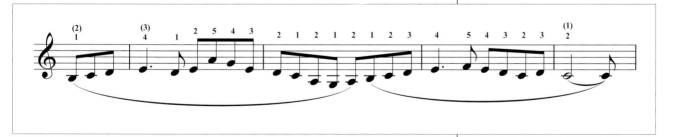

This third phrase repeats the opening phrase of the melody, but with a slight variation at the end. This increases the flow, as the eighth-notes run right through to the fourth phrase, creating momentum. That increases the sense of completion when the melody comes to rest on the held C.

At the same time, a pattern starts to emerge, thanks to the repeated use of decorative alternations with adjacent notes: we can hear these not only wherever the dotted quarter-notes appear, but also in the varied ending of the third phrase.

Overall, we have an eight-bar section divided into two four-bar phrases, each of which divides into two two-bar phrases. This gives the whole thing a nice logical architecture.

Now let's take a look at the second section. Here's the first half.

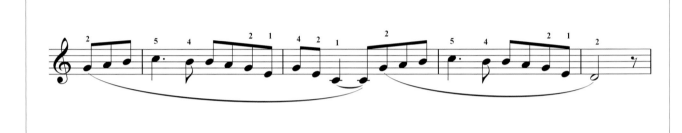

Note how it provides contrast to what has come before, both by moving into a higher register and by changing the shape of the two-bar phrase: although it begins with a rising stepwise figure, it now has a repeated note and falls more dramatically afterwards, and the second phrase repeats the effect, ending on an unresolved low note. Because this repetition takes us nowhere new, it builds a sense of expectation.

Here are the final two phrases – the second half of the second section.

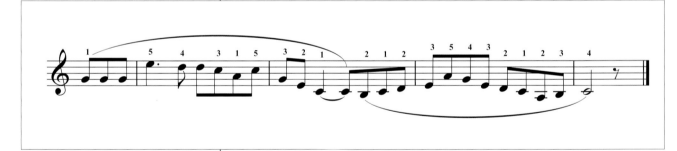

The sense of expectation is fulfilled by the leap to a high E: the largest leap and highest note so far. At the same time, the repeated eighth-notes at the start create a feeling of continuity with what came before, and the phrase descends to the same place as the first phrase of this section. Familiarity and resolution are created by the fact that the last phrase repeats the opening phrase of the melody as a whole, but with a subtle variation: this time the dotted-note figure is omitted, and this leaves room for an extra few notes.

Of course you don't need to reproduce all of these features to produce a good melody. Each melody works on its own terms, and you should trust your intuitions. Hopefully, though, this will give just a glimpse of what goes into the making of a really great tune. Knowing about these things can help, especially in those moments when your inspiration runs out.

Here are some practical tips for creating melodies:
- Sing the melody so that you feel better what ought to come next.
- Write down pitches first, rhythm afterwards.
- Experiment with different ways of continuing the same tune.
- Build new musical ideas from motives present in existing material.
- Keep in mind that your initial musical idea may not belong at the start of the melody.
- Think ahead to how your melody will unfold into a climax and an ending.

Harmony

Part of the character and structure of a melody usually depends on its relation to harmony, so making up a tune usually also requires knowing a bit about how intervals, chords and keys work. This might seem a bit theoretical, but it's information you'll find useful for a lot of other things. (It's essential for improvising, or if you want to analyze the music you're learning to play, which will make you a better interpreter.)

INTERVALS

The distances between different notes in a scale are known as **intervals**. We normally name an interval by referring to the number of scale-steps in the major or minor scale needed to pass from the lower note, treated as the first note of the scale, to the higher note. Intervals in major and minor scales are called **diatonic** intervals. They are shown here for both the major scale and the descending melodic minor scale. (However, remember that the harmonic minor scale has a raised 7th, forming an interval of a major 7th like that in the major scale, while the ascending form of the melodic minor scale has both the 6th and 7th degrees raised, so it has intervals of a major 6th and major 7th.)

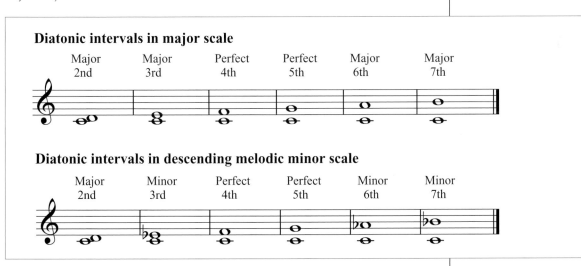

Intervals that don't appear between the keynote and another note in a major or minor scale are derived from the chromatic scale (e.g. half-steps), or treated as alterations by a half-note of the diatonic intervals: hence they are known as **chromatic** intervals. Notice how in some cases two chromatic intervals that look different on paper correspond to the same two keys on the piano. These are known as

enharmonic equivalents. (They sound the same in isolation, but the way they are written reflects how they function in the broader harmonic context, and this usually corresponds to a difference in how we hear them.)

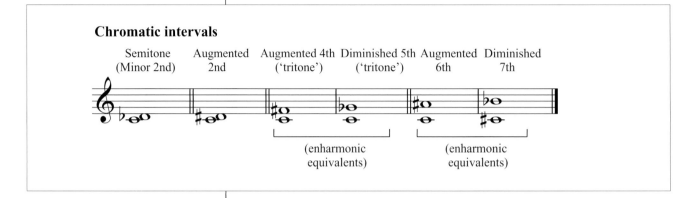

Chromatic intervals

CHORDS

We already know that the basic form of a chord, the **triad**, consists of just three notes separated by intervals of a 3rd. However, we've just seen that there are major and minor 3rds, which gives four possible combinations of interval in a triad, and four **chord types**:

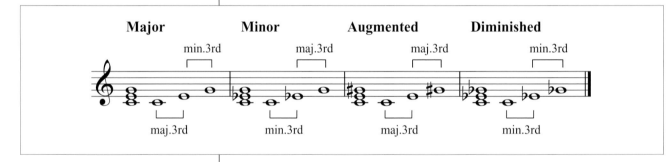

If we build a triad on each step of the major or harmonic minor scale, just using notes from that scale, then we arrive at different chord types for triads on different scale degrees. Notice that some chord types are different, depending on whether the scale is major or minor.

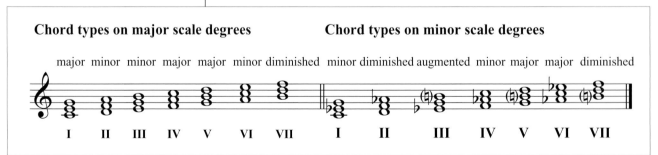

Chord types on major scale degrees   **Chord types on minor scale degrees**

Note also how we indicate the degrees of the scale using Roman numerals. These are also used to identify the chords themselves, as we typically think of a chord as being defined by the degree of the scale that it's built on.

KEYS

Chord structures in traditional classical music and modern popular music are based on the major-minor system. The harmony reflects the structure of the major or minor scale based on the note that defines the key – the **keynote**. This note, and the chord based on it (chord I), provide a centre of gravity, and the character or function of the remaining chords and notes depend on how they relate to these. This means there are two sets of functional relationships in music: **chord relationships** (that hold between chords in the same key), and **key relationships** (that hold between different keys). We often use the same terms to speak about both, but they are not the same.

Key relationships reflect the number of notes that are the same in any two keys. The greater the number of notes in common, the more closely related the keys are. This is reflected in the key signatures. We can show this by arranging the keys around a circle, in order of increasing numbers of sharps in one direction, and flats in the other.

Notice that for every major key there's a **relative minor** key with the same key signature, a minor 3rd down from the **relative major**. These minor keys can be arranged around the inside of the circle. For both major and minor this gives a series of keys, each a perfect 5th away from the next. We call this the **circle of 5ths**. It's worth trying to memorize the order of keys and key signatures in it.

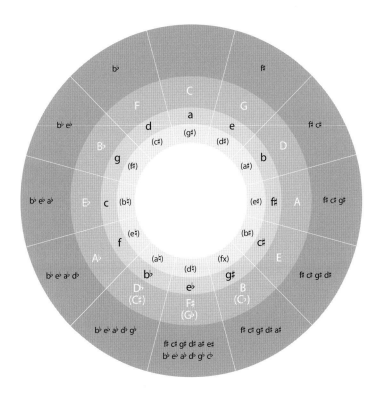

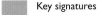 Key signatures

Major keys

Relative minor keys

Accidentals added for minor keys

HARMONIZING A MELODY (1)

To know what chords will work with a melody, you first need to grasp the basics of chord relationships. This means being aware of the functions that different chords have in a key. Here they are, listed as a table. Try learning the technical names: they are also used to describe how keys relate to the home key of a piece of music.

CHORD FUNCTIONS

Degree	Technical Term	Function
I	TONIC	**Tonal centre** (most important chord) Point of maximum harmonic resolution
II	SUPERTONIC	5th above dominant Substitutes for subdominant chord
III	MEDIANT	5th above submediant Substitutes for dominant chord
IV	SUBDOMINANT	**5th below tonic** Main source of harmonic tension with dominant
V	DOMINANT	**5th above tonic** (second most important chord) Main source of harmonic tension with tonic
VI	SUBMEDIANT	5th above supertonic Substitutes for tonic chord
VII	LEADING TONE	5th above mediant Rarely used chord

CADENCES

Cadences in music are like punctuation in writing. Perfect (V-I) and plagal (IV-I) cadences sound final, like a full stop, while an imperfect cadence (I-V) suggests the music will continue, like a comma. An interrupted cadence (V-VI) surprises the listener, replacing the expected resolution with a different, less resolved chord. The effect is rather similar to a question mark or exclamation mark.

The most important chords are the **primary triads** (I, IV, and V). In a major key these are all major triads. The **secondary triads** (II, III, and VI) are also used, but less often. In a major key these are all minor triads, and can function as substitutes for the major chords two steps higher (ie, the primary triads). Sometimes we also substitute a secondary triad for the primary triad two steps higher in a minor key. Chords usually change at a fairly consistent speed in music, eg, once every bar, or every couple of beats: this is known as the **harmonic rhythm**. Special chord progressions are used to round off a phrase or a section, and these are known as **cadences**. There are four cadences: perfect (V-I), plagal (IV-I), imperfect (I-V) and interrupted (V-VI).

Now let's take another look at 'Londonderry Air.' Here's a version with the chords marked underneath, just as triads. Note how it only uses the primary triads: I, IV, and V. Although many tunes require other chords as well, it's good to first see what you can achieve with just these. Seeing where primary triads would fit with the melody is often the best guide to the underlying harmonic structure.

Usually the first complete bar of a piece or section starts with chord I, and the last bar finishes with this same chord. Then there are two options. You can proceed from the start, and try to fit a chord to each bar or half-bar or beat of music. Alternatively you can focus on the end of each phrase or section, which is often easier to harmonize because it corresponds to a cadence, and there are only four possibilities for these (see above). In this second case, you then work backwards to find the right chords for the rest of the phrase or section. In practice we often use both methods at the same time.

LONDONDERRY AIR

Look at the melody. The key is C major. All four phrases have a note on the first beat of their first full bar that belongs to chord I. At the same time, both the first and second eight-bar sections end with the melody arriving on a held C – the keynote – and this indicates that these will require cadences that finish on chord I. On the other hand, the first and third four-bar phrases end on a D, and the only primary triad that this note belongs to is V, so we can expect an imperfect cadence (I-V) here both times.

Now let's try going from the beginning of each phrase. This gives a feel for the harmonic rhythm – the rate of chord change. Some notes in a melody are **harmony notes** (or 'chord notes'), which means they belong to the chord, while others are not.

The latter (ie, **non-harmony notes**) mostly work as stepwise decorations of the former: sometimes they are approached by step from a chord note, but the main feature is that they are almost always directly followed by stepwise movement to a chord note. (When both of these features are present, so that the non-harmony note links two different harmony notes by stepwise motion, it's called a **passing note**.) For example, in the first full bar the melody focuses on E, the 3rd of chord I, which comes on the strong first and third beats. It moves by step to D, but returns to E before leaping to A, and this is also followed by a stepwise movement to a chord note (G). This suggests that the whole bar can be harmonized as chord I.

In the next bar the melody comes to rest on a low A. This must belong to the harmony, as it is held and not followed by stepwise movement. The only primary triad with this note is chord IV. Using IV to harmonize the whole bar makes sense, even though it means that the first note in the bar is not a chord note, as this first note – the eighth-note D – can function as a passing note, since it's approached and quitted by step, and is followed by C, which belongs to chord IV. So it immediately resolves against the harmony. In the next bar the melody outlines chord I, and we also expect this chord as part of the imperfect cadence at the end of the first four-bar phrase.

In the second phrase the first two bars repeat material from the first phrase, so we can expect similar chords. (Note how a harmonic rhythm of one chord per bar has emerged by this stage.) However, this presents a problem, as this four-bar phrase is also the end of the first section, which must finish on I. If we put I in the third bar – as the E of the melody suggests – then we anticipate and so weaken the resolution onto I in the next bar. But if we increase the rate of chord change to two chords per bar here, we can fit in an extra chord between the two appearances of chord I. This won't spoil the harmonic rhythm, as a brief intensification of harmonic change just before a resolution heightens the effect of the latter. Inserting chord V here makes sense as the eighth-note E counts as a passing note, and the chord contrasts with IV in the preceding bar.

Once this faster harmonic rhythm of two changes per bar has appeared, it's a more natural option at certain points in subsequent phrases as well. The third phrase marks the start of a new section, so it's natural to expect chord I at the start, but this chord is clearly outlined at the start of the next bar too. Once again, introducing a change on the half-bar (IV) solves the problem. The same music appears in the third bar, so the same chords are used again, even though the fourth bar has a different harmony (V) corresponding to the imperfect cadence. (In this case the cadence then consists of IV-V rather than I-V.) By the fourth phrase the faster harmonic rhythm has become the norm. Chord I is implied at the start of each bar, but we must be careful not to weaken the final perfect cadence by anticipating chord V, so we avoid this chord in the preceding bars.

This only gives a basic chord structure needed for a harmonization. There are places where these primary triads don't seem quite right, or where we might expect something more interesting, and places where the chords overlap with the melody – so it's obviously not a proper piano arrangement yet. All the triads are in root position, with the notes arranged as close to one another as possible – in what we call **close position**. Some keyboard players in a rock band might be content with this, but for a solo piano arrangement we need to do a lot more to produce a satisfying harmonic texture, as we'll see in due course.

MODULATION

Take another look at the table showing the functions of different chords within a key. The technical names for these are also used to describe relations between keys. (The exception is 'leading tone,' which only describes the melodic function of the 7th step of the scale.) As we have seen, we can also use the terms 'relative major' and 'relative minor,' which refer to relations between major and minor keys with a common key signature. What's essential to realise, though, is that in addition to starting and finishing in a particular key, most music changes key at some point: we say that it **modulates**. To understand how modulations work it's essential to grasp the implications of different key relations.

A modulation to a new key usually has to be followed in due course by a modulation back to the home key (the tonic) to generate a feeling of completion. Modulating to the dominant thus represents an increase in tension, followed by a sense of relaxation when the music returns to the tonic. Modulating to the subdominant creates a loss of tension, and the subsequent return to the tonic sounds like a recovery of the music's brightness and energy. Alongside modulations to the relative major (ie, the mediant) from a minor key, and to the relative minor (ie, the submediant) from a major key, these are the most common modulations. Others are used much less often.

The key to which the music modulates will be major or minor depending on its relation to the home key. Keys follow similar principles to chords: if the chord is major when sounded using notes from the scale of the home key, then the new key corresponding to the same chord function (subdominant, dominant, etc.) will be a major key; if the chord is minor in the original key, the new key will be minor. (The exception to this is the dominant of a minor key, which can be major or minor.) It's more common for music in a major key to modulate to the dominant or subdominant – both of which are major – than to the relative minor, while it's more common for minor key music to modulate to the relative major than to the dominant or subdominant.

A modulation has to be prepared. Firstly, it must pass through a **pivot chord**: a chord all of whose notes belong to both the original and the new keys. Secondly, it must introduce notes from the new key foreign to the scale of the original key, making it clear that these now count as part of the (new) scale. This is usually done by introducing a chromatic alteration of a scale degree that has just appeared unaltered in the same melodic part. (If the alteration follows on directly from the unaltered note in a different melodic part, the effect can be unpleasant. This is called a '**false relation**,' and is avoided in traditional classical music.)

A modulation is most effective when we have a clear sense of 'having arrived,' and this most often corresponds to a cadence in the new key – usually a perfect cadence (V-I). Hence the first chord we hear in a new key is often the dominant (V).

Sometimes, though, a modulation is suggested without any sustained change of key. This is a **passing modulation**: the music appears to modulate but immediately reverts back to the original key. It means the chords of the modulation are still heard to some extent as belonging to the original key. We can think of the new dominant chord as the dominant of a chord (other than the tonic) in the home key, rather than as the dominant (of the tonic chord) in a new key. This is known as a **secondary dominant**.

Dominant harmony therefore plays an important role in regulating and signaling key structures, and it's important to know how to vary it to achieve the right level of tension and resolution. For example, we often add an extra note to the triad, above the root, 3rd and 5th, extending the chain of intervals of two steps (3rds) by adding the 7th. This produces a **dominant 7th** chord. (This process of adding successive notes a 3rd apart is taken further in late Romantic music and jazz, where it can include the 9th, 11th, and 13th.) It's important to note how this 7th resolves down by step to the 3rd in the tonic chord (see below).

Turning any chord other than the tonic into a dominant 7th produces a **secondary dominant**: ie, it becomes the dominant of the chord a perfect 5th lower. (Making this change to all of the primary triads in a major key will take the harmony in the direction of a 'blues' sound.)

A more melodramatic effect is to take a dominant 7th chord and add the 9th, in a chromatically altered, flattened form. If we then remove the root, this leaves another four-note 7th chord, this time on the 7th of the scale, known as a **diminished 7th**. In addition, we can suggest a passing modulation to the dominant, using the **dominant of the dominant** (V of V). (Indeed, any major or minor chord can be preceded by its dominant, and these secondary dominants can also be transformed into dominant 7th or diminished 7th chords.)

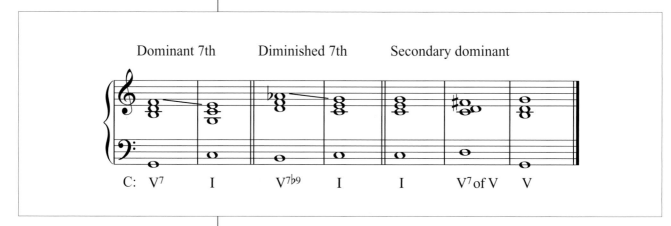

Dominant 7th   Diminished 7th   Secondary dominant

C: V^7 I $V^{7\flat9}$ I   I $V^7$of V   V

HARMONIZING A MELODY (2)

Now let's apply some of this to our harmonization of 'Londonderry Air.' Take a look at Exercise 6.1 below, which is another version of the same arrangement of this tune. (You can also learn it as a study piece.) In this case the chord functions are shown below the music as Roman numerals – the standard notation used for analyzing classical music. The same chords are also indicated above the music, in the way common for modern popular music and jazz, using letter names for the individual chords. (You'll normally only encounter the latter in sheet music, but the former is better for seeing the chord functions.)

Notice how the left hand no longer consists of just held triads in close position: many chords are now laid out in other ways, and the rhythm has changed. The bottom note or **bass note** of the chord usually sounds first, with the rest of the chord delayed so it can fill gaps in the rhythmic texture left by the melody. This is an important feature of left-hand chordal accompaniments.

Let's consider how inversions are used. The first chord of bars 4 and 15 is in first inversion: this is indicated with a small letter 'b' after the Roman numeral showing the chord function (below the music), and by a slash followed by the name of the actual bass note in popular and jazz chord notation (above the music). (That's why non-classical musicians prefer to call chords that aren't in root position **slash chords**.) First inversions add variety, as they have a less resolved feel than root positions. Here they also make for a smoother stepwise melodic movement in the bass.

The first chord of bars 8 and 16 is in second inversion: this is shown by a small 'c' after the Roman numeral, and again by slash-chord notation above the music. Second inversions are traditionally only used in very specific progressions, of which the most common, as here, involves chord V preceded by chord I in second inversion, leading to a cadence. The effect is to create a chord change over a single common bass note (called a **pedal point**), with the tension of the second inversion being released as one or more upper parts move down by step. Another second inversion effect, more common in modern popular music (especially gospel), can be seen in bar 11. Here chord I shifts to IV in second inversion and straight back, preventing the harmony from becoming too static.

Finally let's look at how the effect of dominant harmony is varied and intensified. This is achieved by adding dominant 7ths and secondary dominants. The latter can be introduced as V7 of V, immediately before the dominant (bars 4-5) or as a way of delaying it (bar 13), or before a dominant pedal (bar 15). In bar 14, the tonic (I) is itself turned into a secondary dominant (V7 of IV) through adding a flattened 7th that suggests a passing modulation to the subdominant.

EXERCISE. 6.1

Try learning to play this arrangement now, but be careful with your right hand fingering. Note how we bring the thumb up next to the fourth in the first full measure (bar 2), and stretch second over to the low A in the next one. In the left hand, try holding bass notes on while adding the rest of the chord above, and focus on joining parallel 3rds smoothly in the fingers. At the end of bar 8 note how the left hand plays two adjacent notes with just the thumb. You may also add a little pedal at the start of each bar.

EXERCISE 6.1 | LONDONDERRY AIR

UNIT 7

FREEING UP THE WRIST

In the early stages of learning the piano there's a temptation to expect that your hands will do whatever you want – to find the right notes instantly, or play fast, for example – and to force them if they don't want to. This leads to tension: in the hand, arm, and shoulders, but especially in the wrist. The wrist is crucial, because it acts as a hinge mechanism, regulating how much of the weight of your arm is brought to bear on the piano keys via your hands and fingers. This weight is important not just for controlling dynamic levels, but also for ensuring a good smooth join between notes, and creating a singing tone.

Put one hand on the keyboard in the normal playing position and try raising or lowering the wrist while keeping the fingers in contact with the keys. Note how this changes the angle formed by the forearm and hand. Now try playing and holding a note with the second, third, or fourth finger. Let the wrist relax so that it lies below the level of the hand, with a gentle upwards slope to the knuckles, and feel the arm weight being transmitted directly to the finger holding the key down. Now let the wrist gently move up, keeping the key held, and note how this movement automatically forces the weight to be withdrawn from the hand. In effect, you are controlling weight through movement. This means that we can use the wrist to control rhythmic stress and accentuation, and to integrate these with other aspects of articulation such as legato and staccato, which often also involve wrist movement.

This aspect of what the wrist does is central to many aspects of piano technique, but is seriously impeded if your wrist is tense and tired. That's why you should never force your hands or fingers, but should always practice at a speed that is comfortable, taking regular breaks or switching between hands. (It's also a good idea to divide the music into small phrases, preferably overlapping, and practice these separately, before linking them up.) For this reason, it's worth spending some time focusing on getting a feel for how your wrists ought to be working.

Now look at the exercise below. Note how the music is phrased as slurred pairs of notes. These are known as couplets. In piano playing they normally correspond to a use of the wrist to control accentuation and legato or staccato with a single complex action: as we play the first note of each pair we let the wrist sink down, so weight is transmitted into the hand and finger (and key). This produces a small accent and ensures a smooth join to the next note. (This is because it makes the fingers more reluctant to release keys, as this involves moving upwards, in the opposite direction from the flow of weight itself: hence the slight overlap between notes corresponding to a legato join is increased.) Then, as we play the second note, we let the wrist move up gradually so that the weight is taken off just as the second note is sounded. This means the second note is softer than the first. At the same time, this lifting of the wrist is continued or 'followed through,' leading to the release of the second note just after it has began to sound, producing a staccato effect.

EXERCISE 7.1
Start by practicing this exercise very slowly, then gradually speed up. First check your wrists are loose by flapping your hands. Notice that after releasing the second note of each couplet you can let the forearm drop from its raised

position to sound the first note of the next couplet. This keeps the wrist loose and relaxed, while contributing towards a slight accentuation of the note that begins the next couplet.

EXERCISE 7.1

This combination of legato-staccato and strong-weak within a single gesture occurs with great frequency in music, especially in music from the late 18th century. It's also worth noting that sometimes we play two or three notes legato before arriving at the final release, but the underlying action of the wrist is the same. (In this case all the notes except the final one are played with a lowered wrist, and the 'tailing off' – the lightening and shortening achieved by lifting from the wrist – is reserved for the final note.)

Occasionally, the relationship between length and volume is reversed: the first note is softer, and is joined to a second note that is shorter but stressed. In this case we kick in with forearm as we lift the wrist, so the hand and finger are propelled into the key: here too, the wrist enables us to control and coordinate volume and length with a single physical movement.

CD TRACK 27

EXERCISE 7.2

In the first section of this couplet study, try to coordinate the release of each left-hand chord with that of the second note of each right-hand couplet. (The wrists should lift and fall together.) Pay careful attention to the changes of clef in the left hand, and note the accented weak beat and phrasing across the barline in the right hand in bars 17, 21, and in the left hand in bars 25 and 29.

EXERCISE 7.2 COUPLET STUDY

EXERCISE 7.3

The next complete piece – Exercise 7.4 – uses couplets in a more advanced way. Here is a preliminary exercise for practicing the left hand. The idea is to link the lower note of each pair into a legato bass line, while releasing the repeated Middle C early in order to have time to restrike it. It's important to make sure that the thumb doesn't dominate, so try to keep the volume of the repeated notes below that of the bass line itself.

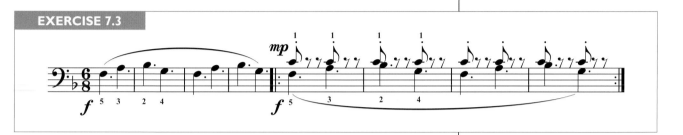

EXERCISE 7.3

EXERCISE 7.4

CD TRACK 28

Now here's the whole piece: 'The Pipers' by Gounod. It's in compound time, so the rhythm is more complex. Also, the slurred pairs of notes in the right hand finish on the beat, so the accent comes with the shortened second note of each pair. You must therefore kick in slightly with the forearm as you lift the wrist, as described above. Note how the slur sometimes includes several legato notes before the final release, so the final 'tailing off' is delayed, with a gradual lifting of the wrist over the course of a short four-note phrase. Aim for a consistent quality of articulation with right-hand phrasing throughout, and pay careful attention to fingering in the scale passages in bars 26-29.

EXERCISE 7.4   THE PIPERS

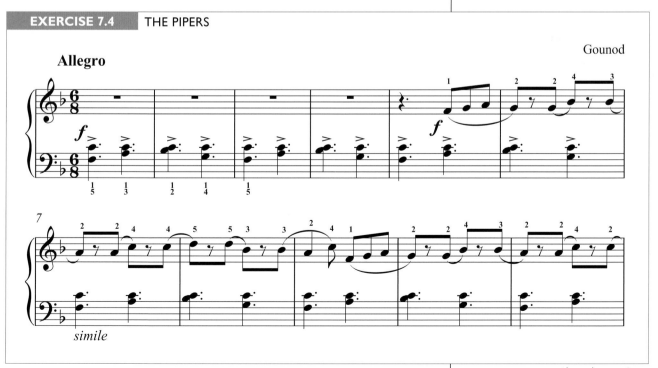

continued over page

EXERCISE 7.4 continued

EXERCISE 7.4 continued

RHYTHM AND STRESS

Rhythm is not just about timing or duration – how fast or slow you play, or how long you hold notes. Stress – or accenting – is also an essential aspect of rhythm, as it helps to define rhythmic patterns. These patterns typically reflect the normal patterns of stress implied by the music's meter (or time signature), but they also work against these. (You'll find the same is true of poetry.) The most important aspect of metrical stress is the emphasis on the first beat of the bar: how strongly you emphasize this will depend on the style and feel of the particular piece you are playing. Dance music usually emphasizes the first beat more strongly than lyrical song-like compositions, and this leaves more room for emphasizing offbeats (notes that do not fall on the beat) as well, without undermining our underlying sense of meter. In a moment we'll look at a piece by Beethoven in which these points are well illustrated.

EXERCISE 7.5
Here's a preparatory exercise for the Beethoven piece below. In this case you are practicing chordal patterns in blocks, to help to achieve fluent changes of position. This will then allow you to concentrate on rhythmic precision and stress, without interference from shifts of position.

EXERCISE 7.5

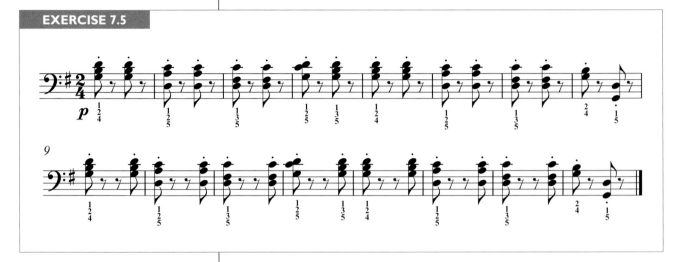

EXERCISE 7.6

This is another preliminary exercise for the same piece, this time practicing left-hand staccato octaves. These appear in the left hand in the middle section of the Beethoven piece. They involve rapid shifts of position for the fifth finger, and require both fifth and thumb to move up onto black notes and back again. Because the weaker fifth finger plays on the beat, and the heavier thumb off the beat, you will need to emphasize the fifth and restrain the thumb. In the latter case you can accomplish this by bringing the thumb into position over the key just before it actually plays.

EXERCISE 7.6

CD TRACK 29

EXERCISE 7.7

Écossaise means 'Scottish Dance' in French. In the first section you must control stress independently in each hand, so right-hand offbeat accents work against the metrical pattern of the left hand, and do not interfere with the latter. (A similar relationship between the hands is a feature of many modern popular styles, especially ragtime and jazz.) Practice each hand extensively by itself before combining them at a slow speed, and listen carefully to check that you've preserved the stress pattern in each hand. Be careful with the repeated 3rds in the right hand in bars 10 and 12 – these must express the metrical stress pattern clearly if they are not to sound pedestrian. (As with the left hand at the beginning, this means a strong accent on the first, and a weaker accent on the second beat.) In bars 14 and 15 the slurring suggests that the offbeat accent is applied in both hands. Aim for clear and consistent differences of dynamic level throughout. Don't let offbeat accents make the overall texture louder than it would otherwise be.

EXERCISE 7.7 ECOSSAISE

Allegretto

Beethoven

Direct pedaling

When we talk about pedaling on the piano, we are normally referring to the right-hand pedal, or **sustaining pedal**. This can affect the music in a number of ways. Depressing it – which is always done with the right foot, supported with the heel on the ground – disables the mechanism that makes individual notes cut off as you release their keys. It does this for all notes simultaneously, as long as the pedal is held down. (Steinway pianos have a special middle pedal, the sostenuto pedal, which enables you to apply the same effect exclusively to the notes whose keys you are holding down at the moment you depress the pedal. This is used in contemporary classical music, but did not exist as an option for traditional classical composers, who expected their music to be pedaled using just the right pedal.)

The most important consequence is that notes can be held on in the pedal when the corresponding keys have been released. This allows for sounds to accumulate and produce richer textures, especially in accompaniments. It also increases the volume of the texture, and changes the tone color of notes, which sound more resonant due to the phenomenon of sympathetic resonance.

The most straightforward way of using the pedal is known as **direct pedaling**: in this case the pedal is depressed at the same time as a note or chord is sounded. It can then either be released at the same time as those keys, or held down while other notes are sounded, and released along with the last of these. The principal alternative to this is **legato pedaling**, which we will explore in due course.

Look at Exercise 7.9 (over the page). Note how the pedaling is indicated below the notes for the left hand, and tends to coincide with places where the left hand is active. In this case it is being used to hold bass notes on while the hand jumps up to play chords that should sound over them. This is a common technique, especially in 19th-century classical music.

An important rule is that we generally try to practice music to the point where it is fluent *before* adding pedal. It's tempting to use the pedal to compensate for other technical insecurities, but remember, if the music has not been mastered independently of the pedal, this will be apparent to a listener even when pedal is added.

EXERCISE 7.8

This exercise prepares you for practicing the left hand by focusing on the changes of hand position required for the chords themselves. Try to position all the fingers for each chord over the keys they are about to play, just before you play them, moving them into position as quickly as possible. Afterwards try practicing the left hand as it appears in the piece, but without pedal. Only then practice the left hand with pedal.

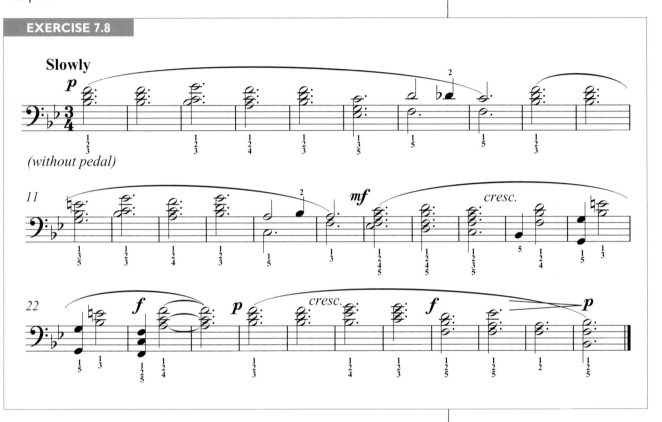

CD TRACK 30

EXERCISE 7.9

It's important to maintain a careful balance here between the three elements of melody, bass line, and chords. The melody should sing out clearly above the left hand – especially on longer notes – but should still sound delicate and lyrical. At the same time, the left-hand chords should be restrained, so they don't appear heavier than the bass notes. Try to let dynamic levels follow the rise and fall of the melody, and use lateral movement to assist the left hand in bars 17-23. Notice that in the principal theme the pedal must be released as soon as the second melody note in each bar is sounded, to avoid an unpleasant overlap. Try to avoid an uncontrolled accent every time you press the pedal down. Do not swing forwards with your body as you depress the pedal, or backwards when you release it. Keeping the left foot firmly on the ground in front of you rather than over the left pedal will help to stabilize your body weight.

EXERCISE 7.9   SONG

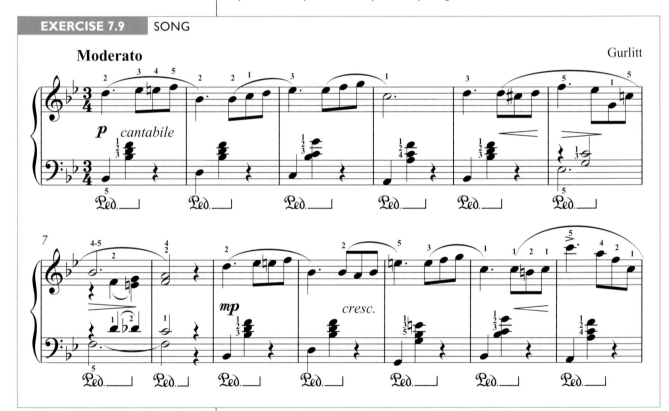

FOUR-NOTE BROKEN CHORDS (2)

Now it's time to look at some four-note broken chords containing black notes. In the triads of D major and B minor there's only a single black note, while in those of B major and E♭ major there are two. Don't be afraid to let the hands play right into the black keys, but make sure that when you do this you don't tense up the wrist or flatten the fingers – especially when playing with thumb or fifth on a black note. Tensing or flattening won't help to avoid slipping off the black keys, and actually makes it harder to get used to playing in this position.

D major

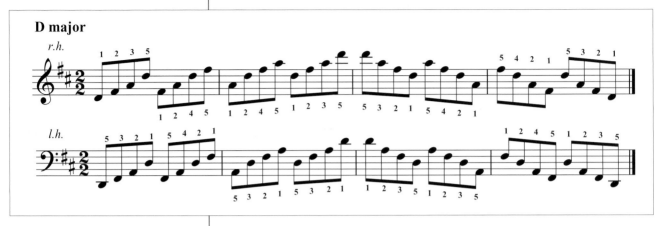

B minor

B major

E♭ major

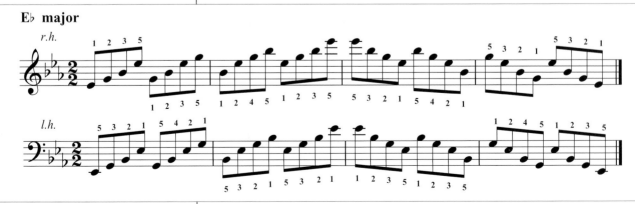

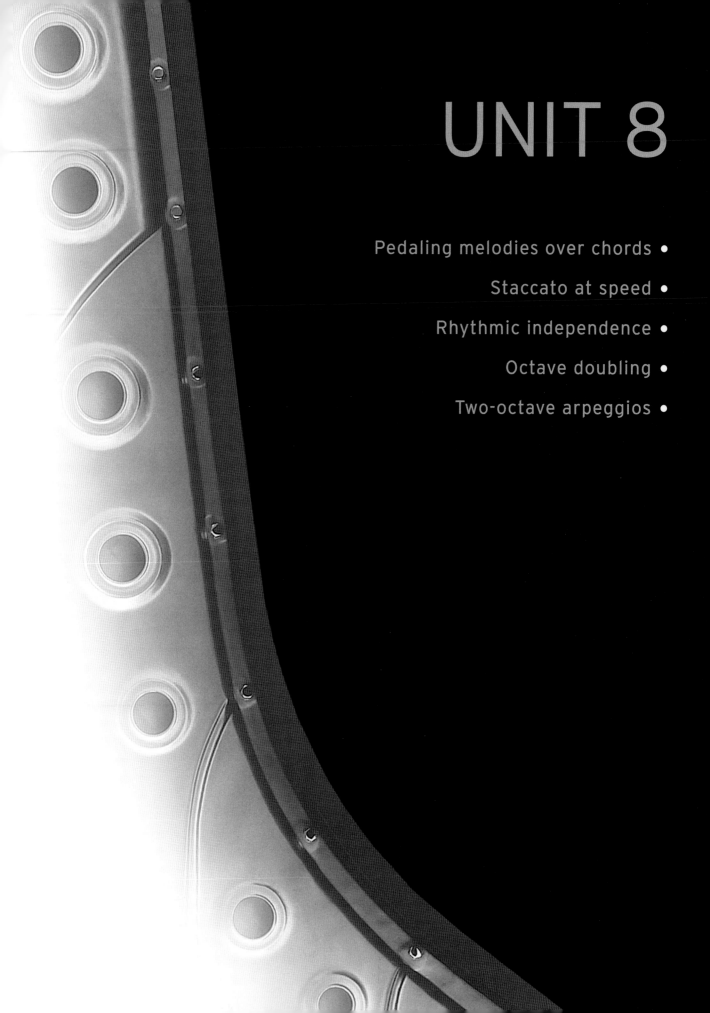

UNIT 8

PEDALING MELODIES OVER CHORDS

In the previous unit we looked at **direct pedaling**, where the pedal is depressed just as a note or chord sounds, and is released when a note or chord is released. This makes for a straightforward pattern of co-ordination between what your hands and your right foot are doing.

The alternative – known as **legato pedaling** – involves a more complex form of co-ordination. In this case, we put the pedal down with the first of a series of notes or chords, and then use it to create a legato join between them. We do this by quickly releasing the pedal just after each new note or chord is sounded, and immediately pressing it back down again. This is known as 'clearing the pedal.' The pedal is therefore down, and the previous note or chord is held on, while our fingers prepare to play the next note or chord. At the same time, as soon as the new note or chord is sounded the previous one ceases, thanks to the quick release of the pedal. (The old note or chord is 'cleared.') Putting the pedal straight back down again in this way allows the new note(s) to be held in the pedal, which means that the fingers are once again free to move into new positions to play subsequent notes or chords, without sacrificing continuity of texture or line. So we release the pedal just after we play notes, and depress the pedal when we have already played the notes and are now just holding the keys down. This makes for a more complex relationship of co-ordination.

Unfortunately the principles for when to use legato pedaling, direct pedaling, or no pedaling at all, are not easy to grasp. You'll encounter a lot of music in which no pedaling is indicated, but it's assumed it will be used, or where there is only the general instruction 'with pedal' (Italian: Con pedale).

Basically we use direct pedaling to add resonance (and sometimes volume) to individual sounds and to accumulate sounds into a richer texture, while we use legato pedaling to join notes or chords smoothly without accumulating any such texture. However, where there is a change of harmony, or the melody moves by step, and we want to use pedal to add resonance, we must use legato pedaling, even if we can join the notes in the fingers. This is because we still need to 'clear' the previous chord or melody note to avoid an unpleasant overlap.

If we are pedaling a melody which ascends from one harmony note to another belonging to the same chord, we don't need to clear the pedal, as we can allow the first note to continue sounding as part of the chord, beneath the next one. But the same logic doesn't apply when the melody descends through harmony notes. If these are allowed to accumulate the effect will be something more like a texture than a melody line. (An exception is certain types of piano music from the late 19th century onwards which deliberately blur the boundary between melody and texture, as we'll see later.)

The place where legato pedaling is least used is at the very end of a phrase, as this is normally marked by a small gap in the texture. Even when the overall texture of the music is sustained, these small gaps introduce a vital element of contrast – what pianists sometimes call 'daylight' – and help to articulate phrase-structure.

It's important to also remember that these constraints may apply more or less strictly depending on the style. Music that emphasizes clarity of melodic unfolding, such as classical music from the 18th and early 19th centuries, tends to follow these guidelines more strictly, whereas music with impressionistic textures such as late

Romantic and early 20th-century music does not. Non-classical styles such as rock and pop and jazz also tend to apply these rules a bit more loosely, on account of their freer approach to how melody and harmony relate to each other.

EXERCISE 8.1

This preliminary exercise prepares you for the changes of hand position in the first eight bars of the piece below, and practices the relationship between harmony and legato pedaling in a simplified form.

EXERCISE 8.1

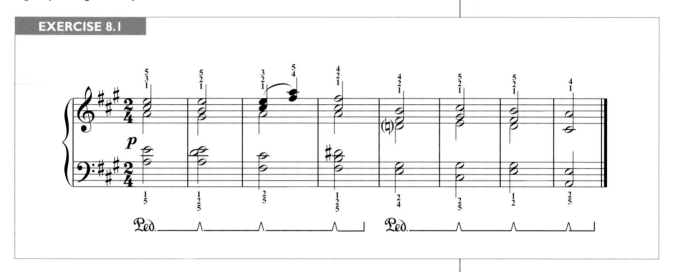

CD TRACK 31

EXERCISE 8.2

This early Romantic miniature by the American composer MacDowell requires a delicate touch, as well as precise co-ordination of notes in chords. It illustrates many of the subtle choices to be made when deciding how to pedal a piece. At the start we use legato pedaling with one change per bar, as the first note of each phrase provides harmony for what follows. In bar 3 we hold the pedal through the stepwise melodic ascent, as the E counts as the 7th of the chord. In bar 4 we release the pedal to mark the end of a four-bar phrase. This is to anticipate the fact that we must do this at the equivalent halfway point in the next eight-bar phrase, to avoid an undesirable overlap when the melody resolves downwards by step (in bar 10). (Note how the end of each eight-bar phrase is also marked with a break in the legato texture.) In bars 19, 22 and 24 the pedal is held over the barline for a moment – as it would be for legato pedaling – but is not depressed again. This helps to maintain continuity of sound, even though the stepwise movement in the melody in the next bar is not pedaled. In bars 25-28 the pedal is used to accumulate harmony, while in bar 41 the change of pedal that should accompany the chromatic descent from C♯ to C-natural is omitted so that the bass can sound through. (Once you reach the B or the A, you should be able to take over the bass note in the fifth finger silently, freeing up the pedal for the changes.) In bar 49 we can delay the return of the pedal slightly, so that it does not catch the F♯. This way the final chord is a pure major triad and sounds more resolved.

EXERCISE 8.2 TO A WILD ROSE

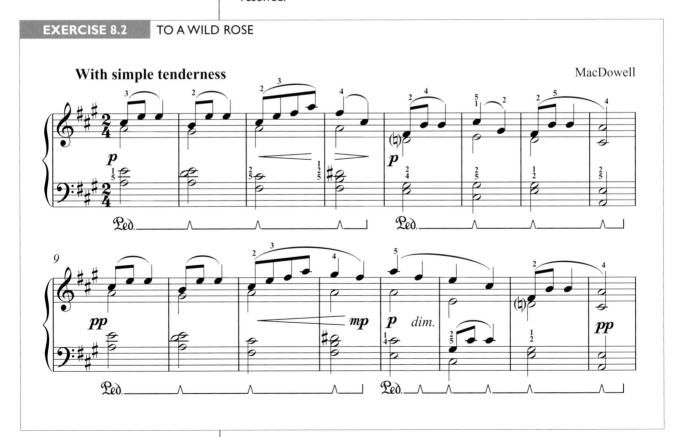

EXERCISE 8.2 continued

STACCATO AT SPEED

Staccato playing is a common source of tension and other technical problems. This is because it's tempting to assume that all staccato notes are produced in the same way, as initially they may appear to sound the same. In fact, we use different techniques for producing staccato, depending on the speed and volume of the notes, and these give rise to different qualities of attack. A single isolated note played staccato will normally be performed by releasing the finger quickly just after the note sounds. A single chord, played loudly, may be given a very sharp, 'snappy' staccato character by suddenly withdrawing all the fingers from the keys into the hand, with a sudden and brief clenching movement. Alternatively, it can be given a slower, ponderous character by releasing the hands with a movement of the forearm or entire arm similar to that used in couplets. This simultaneously generates the force of the attack by 'digging in' to the keys and, when followed through into a lifting movement, produces a release that is really a slowed-down staccato.

However, in most cases the quality of staccato depends on the character of a succession of notes, and especially on their speed. Moderate or relaxed staccato passages tend to be performed using a similar movement to couplets for each individual note. Because this movement comes from a lifting of the wrist it is referred to as **wrist staccato**.

Faster and lighter staccato passages are produced by holding the wrist in a slightly raised position (so that the back of the hand slopes down from the wrist towards the knuckles, rather than up), supported from the forearm. The wrist is kept loose, so that rapid moving of the forearm up and down causes the hand to flap slightly onto the keys. At the same time this movement is controlled so that only individual fingers actually strike the keys. (This combination of a loose overall movement with control of which fingers actually play requires considerable practice to master.) Because the movement that gives rise to the staccato is the flapping movement of the hand, this is known as **hand staccato**. This technique is also useful for practicing scales with staccato.

EXERCISE 8.3
Here's a preliminary exercise for the piece below, which features hand staccato in the right hand. A good way to practice such passages is to rewrite them so that each note is repeated once. This simplifies the relationship between fingers and hand movements. The challenge is to achieve a similar degree of looseness without the repetitions.

EXERCISE 8.3

EXERCISE 8.4

This exercise practices the awkward left-hand chord patterns in the second section of the piece below. Note how the notes that change in the bass are emphasized more clearly than those that do not. Also, notice how the texture has been split into two layers that are first practiced separately before being combined. This is an indispensable practice technique.

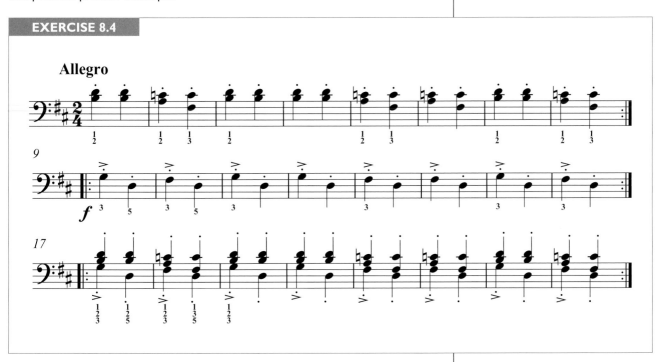

EXERCISE 8.4

Allegro

EXERCISE 8.5

This well-known tune from an opera by Offenbach was used to accompany popular theatrical dancing and circus entertainments in the 19th and early 20th centuries. In the first section, accenting the first right-hand note of each bar will help to achieve good rhythmic control of the hand staccato. The left-hand leaps will also require practice, and you'll need to use lateral movement to reach past the middle of the piano with your left hand. The fortissimo passages should be played with arm weight, but the eighth-notes should still be staccato. Note the marking 'D.C. al fine' at the end: this stands for 'Da Capo,' which means 'repeat from the start,' while 'al fine' means that you finish the second time round at the place marked 'Fine' (which is Italian for 'end').

CD TRACK 32

MUSIC AND THE THEATRE

Music has always been closely connected to theatre. Greek tragedies would pause to use music and movement to comment on the drama. In 17th century Europe opera emerged as an art form in which music and drama were even more closely intertwined, influencing the way in which composers have written melodies ever since. In the 19th century the composer Richard Wagner treated opera as a medium for a 'total work of art' in which music, text and drama would be unified. Wagner's music provided the model for the classic film scores of the 20th century, while in our own day musicals have explored the popular potential of the relationship between music and theatre. Films and TV tend to use music as little more than a background, but music has recovered a theatrical aspect in rock concerts.

EXERCISE 8.5 CAN-CAN

Offenbach

RHYTHMIC INDEPENDENCE

One of the main challenges of piano playing is acquiring rhythmic independence between the hands. In classical music the hands tend to work together in a fairly straightforward way, as they normally involve regular subdivisions of a common beat. However, in non-classical music the rhythmic relationship can be different. A great deal of modern popular music and jazz is influenced by Afro-American rhythms, in which accents often occur off the beat, creating a tension with an underlying pulse that is itself more strongly felt than in classical music. This is known as **syncopation**, and it explains why such music has a more powerfully rhythmic character than traditional European music.

Take a look at the piece below: in the complete version you can see how syncopation is consistently used in the right hand, which stresses the second quarter-note subdivision of the first half-note beat, and then also the second quarter-note subdivision of the second half-note beat. Because this is difficult to master, you should first practice the piece without these subdivisions, as shown in the simplified version given as a preliminary exercise. Then practice just the rhythm of the two hands, tapping both hands together, but away from the keyboard (eg, on your legs). Finally, try combining the notes and rhythm at a slower speed, before bringing the music gradually up to tempo.

EXERCISE 8.6

Practice this simplified version of a song by Gershwin very slowly at first, and allow yourself lots of time to get familiar with the right-hand chords. Read the accidentals carefully in the middle section, and try to highlight the top notes in the right-hand chords there, using a firm fifth finger. Note the 'question-and-answer' character of the phrases. You may find it easier to spend a few weeks playing just this version, before proceeding to the actual song.

THE GERSHWINS

In scores such as *Rhapsody In Blue* and the opera *Porgy And Bess* the American composer and virtuoso pianist George Gershwin perhaps came closer than anyone else in the 20th century to bridging the gap between 'serious' classical music on the one hand, and jazz and blues on the other. He also formed one of the most successful songwriting partnerships ever, with his brother Ira Gershwin. Many of the resulting songs became Broadway hits. At the same time their elegant harmonic and melodic construction made them ideally suited to being used as jazz 'standards' that provide the chord structures and melodic outlines explored by other improvising jazz musicians.

EXERCISE 8.6

EXERCISE 8.7

Here's the actual song, with a highly syncopated right-hand. Don't try to play this version until you've first practiced the syncopations away from the piano. Note how the rhythm changes to even quarter-notes in the left hand for the middle section. The switch back to two left-hand notes per bar in measure 17 may require practice, as this change may momentarily disrupt your sense of how the hands relate rhythmically. Note that the right hand chords are accented, even though they fall off the beat. The left hand should counterbalance this with strong accents on the first beat of each bar, and in the middle section the second half-note beat should be stressed in the left hand.

EXERCISE 8.7 | I GOT RHYTHM

Gershwin

OCTAVE DOUBLING

Sometimes a melody is doubled at the octave, with both parts played in the same hand. This is especially common in Romantic piano music, where it is often needed in order to ensure that a melody or bass line penetrates through rich textures. Practicing octave doubling will help to strengthen your hand and increase your ability to cover larger stretches, but be careful not to overstrain the muscles, as this can lead to permanent physical damage. Octaves are normally played using a hand staccato, with the wrist raised even more than usual.

The normal fingering for octaves consists of thumb and fifth. However, if there are not too many black notes, and your hand can manage the extra stretch comfortably, you may prefer to use thumb and fourth on the black notes, and thumb and fifth on white notes only. This introduces a greater sense of pattern into the fingering, making accidental slips less likely.

Compare the two scales below. In B♭ major we might well opt for fourth on black notes, but in B major most notes are black, so using fourth finger would not be such a good idea; it's the weakest finger of the hand and will quickly get tired – unless you are an advanced pianist with well-developed fourth fingers.

Scale of B♭ major

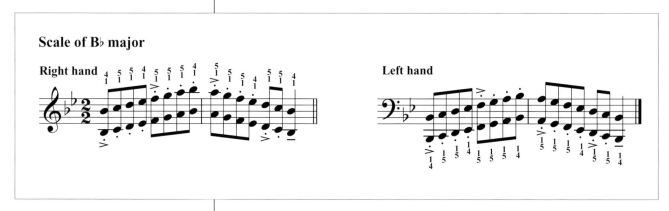

Scale of B major

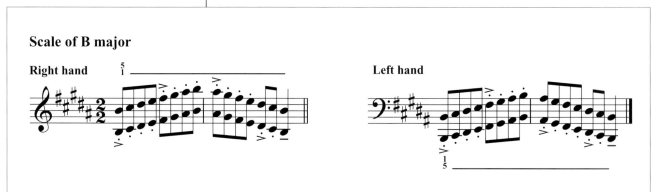

EXERCISE 8.8

Notice how in this octave study the choice of fourth or fifth finger depends on more than just whether the notes are black or white. If a strong accent is required, we tend to prefer fifth even on a black key, but we also try to maintain a regular pattern of fingering, as in bars 10-11 in the left hand.

EXERCISE 8.8   OCTAVE STUDY

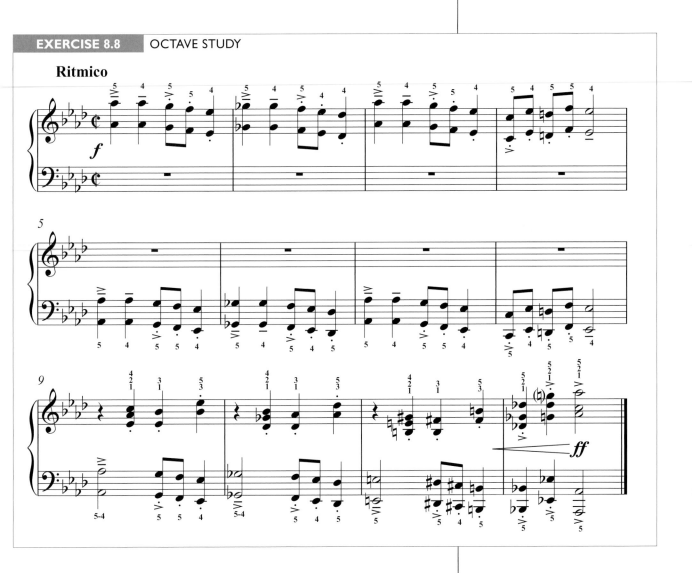

TWO-OCTAVE ARPEGGIOS

Arpeggios spread over two octaves are important, both for developing flexibility of the wrist and for acquiring control of difficult stretches of the sort required when passing the thumb under, or third or fourth finger over, to move into position for a new octave.

C major is given below to remind you of the standard fingering, which also applies to other arpeggios with just white notes (ie, F and G majors, and A, D and E minors).

In addition you should become familiar with arpeggios that contain a sharp as the second note. An example is D major. (A and E majors follow the same pattern.) This kind of arpeggio uses third instead of fourth in the left hand. Note how B major does the same, even though the third note is a sharp as well. By contrast, B minor uses the same fingering as C major, as the second note is a white note, even though the third note is still sharpened.

A third group of arpeggios contains a flat as the second note. These are usually minor key arpeggios starting on white notes, as with G minor. (C minor and F minor follow the same pattern).

Aim for a loose wrist as you pass between octaves, keeping the elbows reasonably close to the sides of your body. Listen carefully to check whether you are achieving a legato join as you stretch under or over, and try not to let this difficult movement result in uncontrolled accents

C major

D major

B major

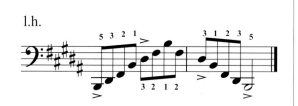

B minor

G minor

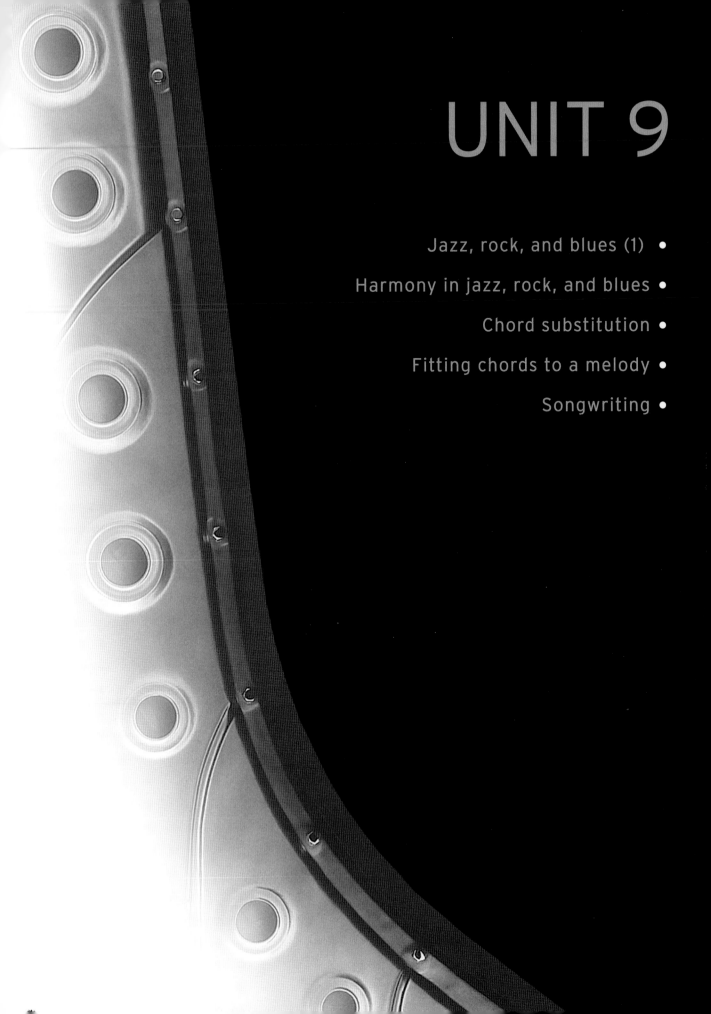

UNIT 9

JAZZ, ROCK, AND BLUES (1)

The main difference between classical music and non-classical styles, like jazz, folk, rock, blues, and country, is that the latter treat rhythm very differently. In classical music, rhythm is one element of a more complex overall texture, and is always defined by how it relates to melody and harmony. This reflects the fact that Western classical music evolved under the influence of Church music, in which rhythm played a marginal role. By contrast, modern non-classical styles reflect a fusion of influences. The harmonies of European settlers in America were combined in various ways with the rhythms, scales, and forms of African music. The slaves brought these with them from Africa, and developed them into new musical genres, such as the spiritual and blues, to express themselves in the conditions of slavery.

When slavery was abolished, many Afro-Americans headed for the cities: at the end of the 19th century, as they sought work in bars as musical entertainers, styles such as ragtime developed quickly. Jazz emerged from another fusion, as Afro-Americans came into contact with French and Central American influences in places such as New Orleans. As jazz developed through the 20th century it became more sophisticated and less improvised, but other American folk styles such as gospel and country have preserved their simplicity and directness. In the middle of the century a renewed interaction of jazz and blues produced rhythm & blues, and then eventually rock'n'roll, leading to the many modern rock and dance styles that make up the mainstream of popular musical culture today.

All these non-classical styles have one thing in common: unlike classical music, they treat rhythm as central, and as an element of music defined independently of its relationship to melody and harmony, even when it interacts with these. Jazz and rock ensembles typically have a **rhythm section**, consisting of bass (double bass or bass guitar) and drums, and this plays a pivotal role, defining a basic pattern of rhythm and metre, known as the **groove**, and linking this to a melodic bass line that marks the underlying chord structure of the music. This pattern allows for a great deal of variation of harmony and rhythm, and free melodic embellishment, without undermining the underlying **feel** (the rhythmic character) and structure of the music, giving greater opportunities for improvisation than in classical music.

Hence an important part of these styles consists of learning to play 'around' the beat in the appropriate way, playing just before or after it (ie, **pushing** or **leaning on** the beat respectively), and in learning to embellish a basic chord structure with more complex chords and improvised melodic figures.

Syncopation plays a much greater role in these styles of music, and solo piano styles often try to use the division between the hands to reproduce as many elements as possible of the multi-leveled approach to rhythm, harmony and melody typical of jazz and rock groups.

A good starting point is to learn to distinguish the different non-classical styles in terms of how they use meter and rhythmic subdivision. (We'll look at harmonic differences later.)

Blues tends to have two beats per bar, usually divided into thirds to produce a long-short **shuffle** rhythm; the same rhythm also appears in speeded-up form in some boogie-woogie styles.

In jazz, the same two-beat metre is preserved, but the rhythm works more flexibly, mixing divisions of the beat into halves, thirds and quarters. The rhythmic subdivisions of jazz often inhabit a grey area between two equal divisions of the beat and a longer division followed by a shorter one, similar to that found in blues and boogie-woogie. This effect is known as **swing**, and it's simpler to write these rhythms as 'classical' divisions into two or four and leave it to the performer to introduce the amount of 'swing' appropriate to the feel and speed of the music (see below).

Rock styles tend to use a straight four beats per bar, but with the second and fourth beats strongly accented, instead of the first and third as in classical music. This effect is called a **backbeat**. (The stronger the backbeat, the 'heavier' or 'harder' the rock groove.)

Gospel often has three beats per bar, and can be 'rocked up' by introducing a shuffle rhythm, either as triplets or compound (9/8) time.

Soul music mixes elements of rock and blues and gospel, while funk and fusion styles introduce **halftime** grooves, in which the beat is divided into quarters instead of halves, doubling the amount of potential syncopation per beat.

Here's an example of how a jazz rhythm would be written, and how it might be played in practice.

The next way to distinguish these styles is in terms of how they use different scales as a basis for both melodic improvisation and chord structures. The examples over the page show the most commonly used scales in non-classical and popular styles. Notice that they are grouped in terms of whether they relate primarily to the major or minor scale of traditional Western music. In non-classical music theory, we normally refer to the structure of the scale by thinking of it as a series of alterations from the major scale. (Even so, the minor scale is also an important reference point for some of these scales.)

At the same time all of these scales, including the major and (melodic) minor scales taken from classical music, tend to be regarded as based on a more basic five-note scale known as the **pentatonic scale**, which appears in nearly all primitive musical cultures across the world. This scale, which can be seen as having two versions, one closer to the major scale and one closer to the minor, plays a much more prominent role in folk-based styles such as blues and gospel, and even in jazz and rock, partly as it allows for much freer melodic improvisation over chords without resulting in clashes between melody and harmony.

Major-derived scales

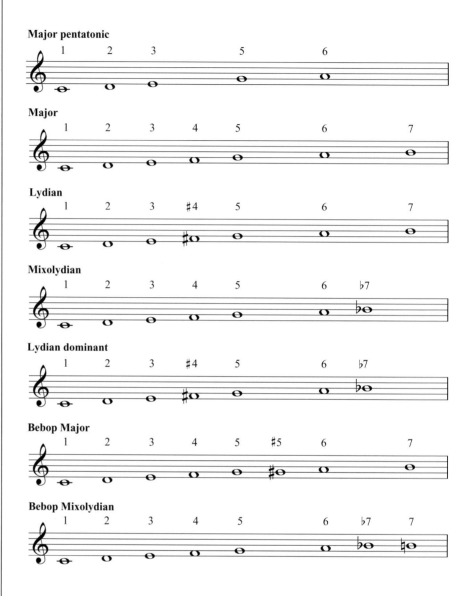

You should note that properly speaking, the Lydian, Mixolydian and Dorian are **modes** rather than scales. This is because they are derived from major or minor scales, whose notes they use — but starting and finishing on different steps. These modes were first used by the ancient Greeks, and were the basis for early European church music. They also play an important role in jazz, as we'll see later in the book.

From the point of view of scales, country, gospel and rock are the most straightforward styles. Country music tends to stick to major scales, with the occasional use of the Lydian mode for a sweeter, more 'upbeat' effect. Gospel does the same, but may also include elements of blues-scale harmony.

Rock makes extensive use of both the major scale and the 'natural' minor (which is also known as the Aeolian mode), though it may also use the Dorian mode as a less dark alternative to the latter.

Blues makes use of the blues scale, of course, but it's important to note that it does so over major key harmony — even though chords may also be voiced to include the flattened **blue notes** of the scale as well.

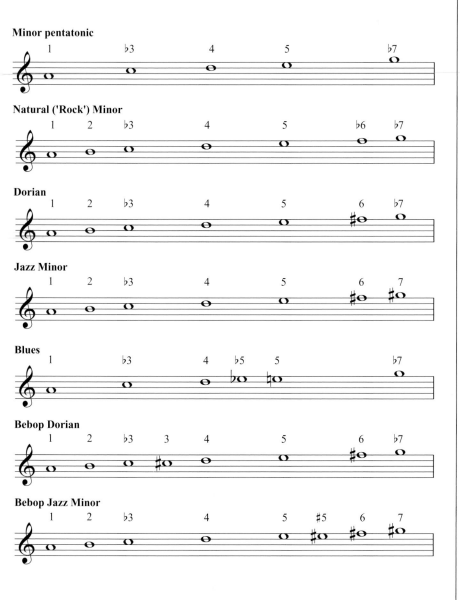

Meanwhile funk and soul combine elements of rock or gospel (e.g. the Dorian mode) with the blues scale to create a synthesis of these styles.

Jazz covers a wide spectrum of scales that reflect different stages in its evolution and different musical influences that may be more or less strongly emphasized. The simplest approach is to think of jazz as starting out from the major and jazz minor scales, deriving other scales, such as the Dorian, Lydian, Mixolydian, and Lydian Dominant from these (as modes – see above). (Note that the first three of these are derived from the major scale, whereas the Lydian Dominant is derived from the jazz minor scale). In jazz the choice of scale or mode for melodic improvising will often reflect a particular chord or chord structure sounding at the same time. Moreover the chord structures themselves – what jazz musicians call the **changes** – will tend to be derived from well-known songs, known as 'standards,' that use traditional major-minor harmony, though sometimes with freer modulation than in classical music.

Jazz can also reflect blues influences, or be fused with rock elements that introduce more straightforward major or minor scales as melodic material. Bebop scales are named after a style of jazz that emerged in the late 1940s and early 1950s, in which greater emphasis was put on freer styles of melodic improvisation. As a result it became useful to add an additional note to existing jazz scales, to make a total of eight different notes per octave. This allows for a more regular relationship between melodic patterns and meter. We'll be learning about all of these aspects of jazz in more detail later.

HARMONY IN JAZZ, ROCK, AND BLUES

The third way to distinguish different non-classical styles from one another is in terms of the kinds of chord they use. This is partly a question of which scales their chord structures are based on, but in some cases – especially jazz – it's also a question of how extra notes are added above and beyond those that naturally belong to the chords by virtue of their position in the scale; these extra notes have the effect of increasing the range of available harmonies.

In classical music, as we saw in Unit 6, this is mainly done through the occasional use of dominant and diminished 7ths, chromatic alterations of existing chords, and through introducing secondary harmony such as V of V. In blues and jazz, we use 7th chords much more freely than in classical music, but in rock, country and gospel, we are more likely to make use of simple triads in which the 3rd is replaced with either the 2nd or 4th – creating an effect similar to an unresolved suspension in classical music. (A **suspension** is where a melodic note is held over, so that it sounds as a dissonance against the next chord, before resolving the dissonance by stepwise movement to a note that belongs to the new chord.) Hence these are known as **sus chords**. Alternatively we may simply add an extra note to the chord – usually the 6th, or occasionally the 9th or 11th, making an **added-note chord**. (In contrast to sus chords, with added-note chords the extra note sounds alongside the existing notes of the triad rather than substituting for one of them. Note that unless the chord is minor we normally sharpen the added 11th, to avoid a clash with the 3rd, while an added 13th would be the same as an added 6th.)

Sus chord and added-note chord voicings

Rock, country and gospel also make use of **slash chords** to vary the harmonic texture. These are similar to chord inversions in classical music, with the note after the slash indicating the bass note independently of the chord above it. Slash-chord notation is sometimes used in non-classical styles to indicate more complex added-note chords.

Slash chord voicings

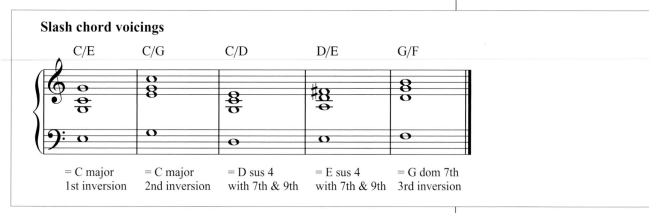

C/E	C/G	C/D	D/E	G/F
= C major 1st inversion	= C major 2nd inversion	= D sus 4 with 7th & 9th	= E sus 4 with 7th & 9th	= G dom 7th 3rd inversion

In jazz these more complex chords are understood differently, as having been derived through a process known as **chord extension**. Chord extension adds notes to triads by continuing the stacking up of notes on top of each other a third apart that gives rise to the original triads themselves. This means that a chord can be thought of as containing not only a root, 3rd and 5th, but also a 7th, 9th, 11th, and 13th. Hence a single chord can, in principle, be seen as containing every note of the scale. That's a striking development, as it allows jazz musicians to think of chords as no longer defined by which notes of the scale are included or excluded, as in classical music, but instead simply by which scale the notes of the extended chord correspond to.

Chord extensions

Open position voicings   Close position voicings

triad 7th 9th 11th 13th | 7th 9th 11th 13th | 7th 9th 11th 13th

As we shall see later, this way of thinking of a chord as corresponding to a scale is central to advanced jazz styles such as bebop. However, in the earlier stages of learning to play jazz, and for less advanced styles, it is more useful to think of jazz chords as being defined by the kind of 7th chord that appears on each scale degree. There are four different kinds of 7th chord, which we can think of as being derived by a process of successive chromatic alteration.

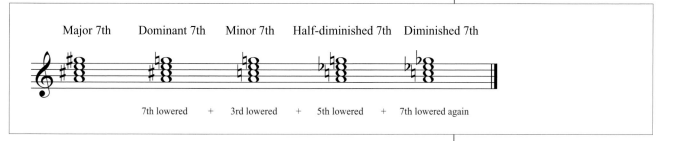

Major 7th   Dominant 7th   Minor 7th   Half-diminished 7th   Diminished 7th

7th lowered   +   3rd lowered   +   5th lowered   +   7th lowered again

This makes it easier to relate the different chord types to the chord functions of classical harmony, which tend to appear in standards. Just think of each chord-function as automatically implying one of the four different 7th chord types. (Where the chord has a major 7th we sometimes substitute a 6th for the 7th for a more resolved effect.)

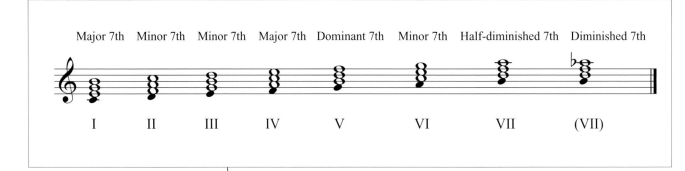

HARMONY AS LINE

As jazz evolved away from the more traditional styles of the 1920s and 1930s towards new styles such as bebop, its emphasis shifted from the embellishment of well-known tunes towards free melodic improvisation based purely on their chord structures. Thinking of a chord as extendable, so that it contains all seven notes of the scale, changed the way musicians thought about melody. Instead of thinking of melody and harmony as distinct but complimentary, jazz soloists began to treat melodic lines simply as projections of the harmonic character of particular chords into linear form.

Something similar happens in blues, though for different reasons. Here the tendency is to treat all chords as dominant 7ths; the dominant 7th usually introduces a flattened note equivalent to a blue note. (Have a look at the chord chart in the next section if you want to see how this works for the standard 12-bar blues chord changes.)

We may also introduce the flattened 9th as well. This can be heard as a blue note too, though it tends to be reserved for chord V, as it produces a powerful dissonance with the root. As in classical harmony, we generally prefer to omit the root, leaving a diminished 7th chord (on VII), which is less dissonant. This is also common in traditional jazz harmonizations, because diminished 7th chords have a special characteristic that makes them beloved of improvisers: the same chord belongs in four different keys, and can be used to move between four otherwise unrelated chords, with a neat stepwise chromatic movement in the bass that is easily remembered when improvising. The example below shows the diminished 7th chord in two-handed voicings, with different inversions moving chromatically to four different resolutions.

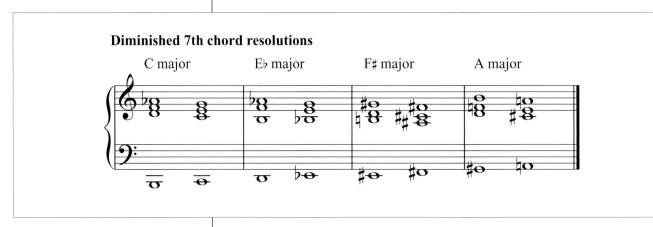

You should become familiar with the symbols used to indicate different chord types in non-classical music. Unfortunately these vary, and in advanced jazz you will sometimes find that the 7th is not indicated at all, as it is assumed. The table below shows the most common notations.

CHORD SYMBOL NOTATIONS

CHORD TYPE	NOTATION
Major triad	C or C$^m\Sigma$
Major 7th	Cmaj7, CM7, C^{m}7 or C^m
Dominant 7th	C7
Minor triad	Cmin, Cm or C–
Minor 7th	Cmin7, Cm7, C–7 or C–
Diminished triad	Cdim or C°
Minor 7th, flat 5th ('half-diminished 7th')	Cmin7♭5 or C^{ø}7
Diminished 7th	Cdim7 or C°7
Augmented triad	Caug, C♯5, C$^+$ or C$^+$5

CHORD SUBSTITUTION

An important element in jazz and blues harmony is the substitution of different chords for those we are familiar with, when a familiar sequence of chords is being repeated, as often happens in these styles. Only certain substitutions work. That's because they don't undermine the underlying functional character of the progression. We've already seen some examples of this technique in classical harmony – for example the use of chord II as a substitute for IV, or VI as a substitute for I (as in interrupted cadences, for example). Another kind of substitution in classical music replaces a chord with another in exactly the same inversion, on the same scale degree, only chromatically altered. For example in minor key music it is common to precede chord V with IIb – a diminished triad which sounds better in first inversion. Lowering the root by a semitone changes this to a major chord on ♭II, with an exotic lustre, and a tritone away from the dominant, so that it makes the ensuing progression much more striking. This is known as a **Neapolitan Sixth** (see below).

(First inversion chords in classical music are traditionally referred to as '6th chords,' and second inversion chords as 'six-four chords.' These names reflect the numbers used in **figured bass** – a system of notation used in the 17th and 18th centuries. In figured bass, only the bass line would be notated, with numbers indicating the types of chord to be used, leaving it open to the player to decide how to realize these as a keyboard texture.)

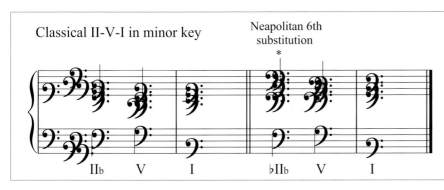

Whereas in classical music we would tend to think of a II-V-I progression like that in the above example as substituting the secondary triad II for the primary triad IV, in jazz we approach it in a different way. Here what is important is that both II-V and V-I involve the root moving to another root a perfect 5th lower (or perfect 4th higher). This movement 'down' the circle of 5ths is central to jazz harmony, and can be carried on endlessly. However, it's primarily defined as corresponding to the II-V-I progression, so many other progressions get treated as variations on this. (In a major key, II is a minor 7th chord, V is dominant 7th chord, and I is a major 7th chord, and it becomes easier simply to equate these chord types with the chord functions of II, V and I, wherever they occur.)

In jazz the most common technique of chord substitution is **tritone substitution**. Here we replace one or more of the elements of the II-V-I with a chord of the same type but built on a root a tritone (ie, augmented 4th or diminished 5th) away, as in the examples below. Note how this changes a progression to a root a perfect 5th lower into one to a root a half-step (semitone) lower. This focus on root progressions that either follow the circle of 5ths or move downwards chromatically by step is an important feature of jazz. In the example below, note the voice leading in the three

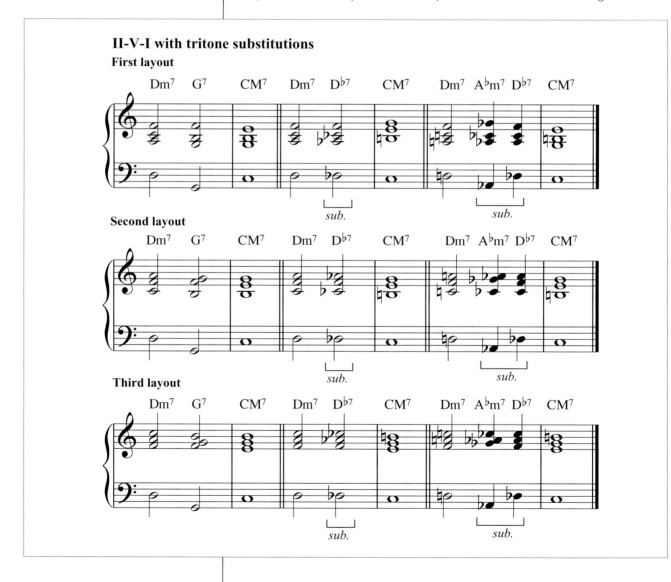

II-V-I with tritone substitutions
First layout

Second layout

Third layout

possible layouts of the original progression. This voice leading is typical of jazz, and you should aim to be able to reproduce it from memory in as many keys as possible.

In blues, tritone substitution is also used extensively. Blues tends to follow a fixed harmonic pattern, which is repeated with harmonic variations. In its most common form this lasts for 12 measures, and is therefore known as the **12-bar blues**. Look at the two chord charts below. The first shows the standard chord pattern for 12-bar blues. (Note how this already uses dominant 7th chords.) The second shows how this might be **reharmonized** by using alternative chord extensions or added notes, and/or chord substitutions, where appropriate.

Standard 12-bar blues (in C)

	C7		C7		C7		C7	
	F7		F7		C7		C7	
	G7		F7		C7		C7	:|

12-bar blues with chord substitutions:

	C7		F7		C7		Gm7 C7	
	F7		F#°7		C/G		C7	
	G7		F7 E7		Am7 A♭m7		D♭7 G7	:|

Note how bar 4 is reharmonized to give a II-V-I progression finishing on the F7 chord in bar 5, which marks the start of the second of the three four-bar sections of the blues. The diminished 7th chord in bar 6, followed by a second inversion (slash chord) of C in bar seven, implies a nice chromatically ascending bass line.

In bar 10 the chord shape is dropped by a semitone from F7 to E7. (This is a common technique, derived from the guitar, where it is natural to slide the hand down the fret board, keeping the fingers locked into a single chord shape.) Because this chord is inserted between the F7 chord and the next one, we call it a **passing chord**.

This opens the way for the roots to pass through a series of descending 5ths, from III to VI, to a nice II-V-I, taking us back to the opening, for a repeat of the whole cycle. In this case tritone substitutions have been introduced for the II chord and the first half of the final V chord, substituting A♭m7 for Dm7 and D♭7 for G7. (Notice how the tritone substitution can either replace the original chord completely, or be introduced in front of it, as in bar 12, which would otherwise consist entirely of chord V – itself a substitute for the final chord I of the original blues.) Note also how the II-V-I progression in bars four to five could be treated in a similar fashion, substituting chords a tritone away for the Gm7 and C7 chords.

Indeed, there are endless possible reharmonizations of this simple chord sequence using these techniques. It's worth memorizing the original blues sequence, as experimenting with this together is a popular way for musicians to get acquainted with each other musically.

The **chord charts** shown above are typical of those used by jazz and blues musicians. Often, they show only the basic chord structure, which musicians are expected to then vary themselves. **Lead sheets** are similar, except that they usually include the melody line, and sometimes a few other important melodic or rhythmic ideas as well.

FITTING CHORDS TO A MELODY

Compare the version below of the opening of 'Londonderry Air' with the one we studied in Unit 6 (Exercise 6.1). Which sounds better? Which is easier to play?

The earlier version had just the melody in the right hand, with the left hand playing both bass and harmony. This version is the opposite: the right hand takes over harmony as well as melody, while the left sticks to the bass notes. (We must adjust the fingering of the right-hand melody, and makes us more dependent on the pedal for legato texture.)

These are the two basic options for the layout of chords beneath a melody. Having the chords in the left hand frees up the right to concentrate on giving an expressive rendition of the melody, and is the only option if the melody has some fast or complex passages. However, it can mean the harmony gets pushed down into the lower registers of the piano, closer to the bass notes, and this can make the texture muddy and dark. On the other hand, putting the chords in the right hand with the melody can mean they get pushed into the higher register, where the sound is thinner, so they may no longer give proper support to the melody. Yet this frees up the bass line, which now moves further down into the low register, giving more sonorous support to the whole texture. Often the nature of the melody itself will decide which approach is more appropriate, but it can also be useful to mix them.

Here's a more sophisticated version of the song, with chords laid out flexibly between the hands. Note how this allows us to move more of the harmony onto the first beat of each bar, making the texture more continuous, and creates more options for both harmonic layout and chord extensions such as 7ths and 9ths. (Note the chord substitution at the start of bar 13, and the chromatic descent in the bass in bar 15.) Try learning this version, and compare it to Exercise 6.1. (You can also flick between the two versions recorded on the CD.) Afterwards, why not try creating your own harmonization? And why not apply these techniques to some other well-known tunes?

EXERCISE 9.1

Notice how the fingering of the melody has changed in some places, compared to Exercise 6.1, so that you can accommodate harmonic material in the right hand as well. This makes you more dependent on the use of the sustaining pedal to achieve a legato feel, so be prepared to use legato pedaling at quite a few points in this version.

CD TRACK 35

EXERCISE 9.1	LONDONDERRY AIR

SONGWRITING

Form

There's no magic formula for composing a hit song, but songs that catch on tend to have something distinctive and original that's also memorable – often to the point of contagiousness. In modern times that's often a particular short musical figure, combined with a line of text in such a way as to have connotations that are suggestive in one way or another. To be effective, such a figure must come at just the right moment, and be supported by the right verbal narrative, rhythmic, and harmonic background, and build-up and release of energy or tension. The form of popular songs tends to be oriented towards achieving this.

A typical song will have three principal sections, the **verse**, **chorus**, and **bridge** (also known as the **middle-eight**).

Traditional classical and folk songs, as well as hymns, were based on **strophic form**. This alternates between a verse (or strophe), in which the music remains the same but the words change with each repeat, and a chorus, in which both words and music return unchanged with every repeat. This sets up a contrast between a developing narrative (the verses) and something predictable (the chorus) that distils the emotional significance of the song into a simpler, more direct utterance. (Originally, the 'chorus' was a character or group of characters in ancient Greek theatrical drama whose role was to comment on the action of the play as it unfolded.)

Popular songs use the same idea, but more emotional weight is thrown on the chorus, with the verse being used to build up tensions that are usually only released as the music enters the chorus. Hence the strongest ideas tend to be saved for the chorus, which uses simpler material for a more immediate effect. Once a song as been through two or three cycles of verse and chorus, it's usual to introduce a short section consisting of new material, which can lead back to another verse or take us to a final appearance of the chorus. This is the bridge.

If the purpose of the verse is to prepare the ground – musically and psychologically – for the chorus, the purpose of the bridge is to offer us a momentary change of perspective, in terms of both musical content and lyrics. This is often a good moment to throw in that extra musical idea that didn't seem to fit in the verse or chorus, but seemed too good to waste. It can often involve a change of key or shift of focus, or feature an instrumental solo or a different configuration of instruments alongside the voice. (If the accompaniment is solo piano, it might be a chance to explore some unfamiliar textures and registers.)

In addition to these elements, many songs have additional sections, such as an **intro** and a **coda**. They may also have short **linking passages** between sections, or intersperse longer instrumental **solos** to break up the alternation of verse and chorus. An intro will 'set the scene,' perhaps tentatively anticipating a few of the harmonic or melodic figures that emerge fully later on, and will focus on establishing the right atmosphere. A coda is an additional section placed after the final chorus, sometimes introducing new material to suggest a last-minute development or change in the narrative. It may bring the song full-circle by repeating elements from the introduction, or present a simplified version of the chorus as a background to a solo. Many songs recorded specifically for albums don't need a coda as they end by repeating the final chorus as part of a gradual **fadeout**.

Jazz standards often follow a different form, as they frequently dispense with the chorus, but still make use of the idea of a bridge (or 'middle eight'). (Some early Beatles songs do the same.) They do this by playing the first section and straightaway repeating it once, then passing through the bridge, and then repeating the first section once again. (This can be summarized as an 'AABA' pattern, where A is the first section and B the bridge.) This whole pattern will then be repeated to form the basis for embellishment and improvisation.

Chord structure

In Unit 6 we considered the ingredients that go to make a satisfying melody, and looked at the theory behind chords, scales and keys. But when you come to actually write a song, it's not just enough to have a good tune and know about these. You must also be able to construct chord sequences that make musical sense, and that have the right character for the effect you want to achieve in the song you're working on.

As we've already seen, music is divided up into regular divisions, which usually correspond neatly to sections of 4, 8, 12, or 16 bars in length. It's good to start by getting to grips with the typical ways in which basic chord sequences can map onto these. Let's see what we can do with just our three **primary triads** (I, IV, and V). (Remember, more complex chord structures often boil down to just being variations on structures using I, IV, and V.)

The simplest structures of all use the three primary triads over the course of an eight-bar section, repeating one of the chords in each four-bar phrase. (These structures work in both a major and a minor key.) In the example below, notice how V is used at the end of each four-bar phrase, as a more dramatic contrast with I, which it leads nicely back to, while IV is used as a more moderate counterbalancing element. (Another way to look at this is that chords I and IV swap positions between the two phrases, while V remains constant.)

```
| I          | IV         | I          | V     |
| IV         | I          | IV         | V    :||
```

Here's a standard 12-bar pattern with the same three chords. Once again, IV offers a basic contrast: note how it gets emphasized at the start of the second four-bar segment. V is used to 'cap' the structure, as it's saved for the third four-bar segment and used at the very end to lead back to I for a repeat. You should recognize this sequence by now: it's the same as the 12-bar blues we looked at earlier.

```
| I          | IV         | I          | I     |
| IV         | IV         | I          | I     |
| V          | IV         | I          | V    :||
```

Once we move up to 16 bars, more choices become possible, even when we're confined to three chords. At its simplest, a 16-bar section will consist of the same four-bar phrase repeated four times, but a more interesting option is to make one of the four phrases different. This is usually the third or fourth phrase, producing a pattern along the lines of AABA or AAAB. Here's an example of the former:

I		IV		I		V	
I		IV		I		V	
IV		I		IV		V	
I		IV		I		V	:||

These are just about the simplest kinds of chord structure that might serve as a basis for a song. In fact they're so simple you're unlikely to encounter them outside of the most straightforward rock and pop songs. However, it's a good discipline to start with as few chords as possible. You'll be clearer about the workings of the basic chord functions associated with I, IV, and V, and when you introduce other chords they'll make a bigger impact.

Note how the chord sequences above feature a direct move down from V to IV. This root progression is central to rock and blues, but is avoided in classical music, where it conflicts with the slightly different relationship that exists between subdominant and dominant within a major or minor key.

Now let's run through some of the more common harmonic variants you can use to make structures like these more interesting. You might like to think of this as a kind of elementary 'chord phrasebook' that you can refer back to whenever you need to.

COMMON HARMONIC VARIANTS

Primary triads: these are the chords we've just been looking at. Remember that V leads back most effectively to I, while in popular and jazz styles IV functions as the main counter-pole to I – at least in a major key. (In classical music, however, V tends to play this role more often than IV.)

Secondary triads in a major key: these are the most common source of harmonic contrast, as II, III, VI are all minor chords, so they introduce a sad feel. VI is the most common, and is darker and sadder than II, while III is used less often and sounds brighter. (Juxtaposing III with IV in a major key evokes Arabic and Hispanic flavours.) Remember that VI can substitute for I, and II frequently substitutes for IV (but is often in first inversion so the bass is the same), and leads nicely to V. Secondary triads also sound good just after the primary triad they substitute for.

Secondary triads in a minor key: these also add contrast. In a minor key VI is one of the few major chords – the other being V – so it offers a chance for a temporary emotional uplift. II is diminished, so it tends to be associated with dramatic tension, and is usually used in first inversion. As in a major key, it can substitute for IV (which in a minor key is a very gloomy chord), and leads nicely to V. In classical music, III is an augmented triad, as its 5th is the 7th of the scale, which is sharpened. This gives the chord a dreamy, impressionistic, and rather sophisticated feel. In rock it's often treated instead as a major triad, that sounds bright and positive.

VII in a major key: like chord II in a minor key, this is a diminished triad, so it tends to be used in first inversion; however in this case it is rarely used. Its main use is in a chain of root progressions falling by a 5th each time (e.g. I-IV-VII-III-VI-II-V-I) – a very common effect in Baroque music, sometimes copied in jazz and occasionally in rock.

VII or ♭VII in a minor key: in classical music VII is the same as in a major key, as it is based on the sharpened 7th of the harmonic minor scale. However it's more likely to be changed into a diminished 7th, intensifying the feeling of unresolved drama and tension. In rock it's usually built on ♭VII, as this corresponds to the 7th of the natural minor scale and the Dorian mode, and will be a major triad, either resolving up by step to I, or down to ♭VI, or falling a 5th to ♭III. Its modal character is useful for establishing a 'hard rock' atmosphere.

Inversions: inversions appear less often in modern popular styles than in classical music, but they can still play an important role in varying the texture of a song, or in establishing a smoother bass line movement. First inversion makes major chords sound ever-so-slightly minor, and minor chords ever-so-slightly major. Second inversion sounds closer to root position in this respect, but makes the chord less resolved than either root position or first inversion, and in piano textures this tension normally has to be resolved by moving to a root position chord over the same bass note.

Major 7th chords: these usually come on I or IV in a major key, or VI in a minor key. The effect is one of gentle sweetness. Be careful not to overuse them, as it may sound sickly sweet and sentimental. In jazz the major 7th can sometimes be felt to be too dissonant, and is replaced by a major 6th.

Dominant 7th chords: here the 7th adds tension to a dominant chord, and in classical music this requires immediate resolution to I (or its substitute, VI). However, in jazz and other non-classical styles it need not always be resolved, and in that case will be more suggestive of blues, especially when chords other than V are also treated as dominant 7ths. In jazz a further variation consists of flattening the 5th (shown as V7♭5). This makes for a more ambivalent and chromatic feel, and is often associated with tritone substitutions.

Minor 7th chords: these give minor triads a fuller, fruitier sound, which is especially useful in jazz.

Half-diminished 7th chords: both VII in major and II in minor (but not Dorian) offer the possibility of 7th chords with a minor 7th but a diminished 5th. These have a wistful quality and were popular in 19th century Romantic music. In first inversion this is the same as playing a minor triad and adding a major 6th, and you're more likely to see it in this form.

Diminished 7th chords: these substitute for chord VII (see above), and are useful for modulation as the same chord allows multiple resolutions into keys a minor 3rd apart.

Minor subdominant: changing IV in a major key into a minor chord is a highly emotive device, suggesting tragic feelings. It was popular in early Romantic music (for instance, Schubert), and in modern popular songs tends to be reserved for 'heavy' emotional statements.

Major triad with added major 6th: this produces a very warm sonority, and contains a mild dissonance that need not be resolved outside of traditional classical music.

Minor triad with added major 7th: this chord only makes sense with reference to chord I of the harmonic minor or jazz minor scales. It's rarely used in classical music, however, but may appear in jazz, often as a result of sounding chord I and then lowering the note an octave above the bass by a semitone.

Minor triad with added major 9th: adding a 9th with no 7th heightens the melancholy character of minor triad, introducing an expressive dissonance. (Adding the 9th and 7th together is also extremely effective in jazz.)

Here are two other harmonic devices that can contribute to effective chord structures:

Stepwise descending bass: a strong support for a chord sequence is created whenever the bass line moves down by step, which it may do either diatonically or chromatically, in a major or minor key. This is made more effective by using a mix of root position chords and inversions (slash chords), so the chords remain closely linked. Here are some examples:

| C | G/B | Am | Em/G | F | C/E | Dm7 | G7 ||

| C | G/B | B♭ | F/A | Fm/A♭ | C/G | D7/F♯ | G7 ||

Pedal (point): this is created by holding the bass note on while chords change over it, and the effect is to accumulate tension as we await a move in the bass. Tonic pedals can build up suspense at the start of a song, as we wonder why the bass line is not moving away from the keynote, but the most common variant is a dominant pedal, with the 5th of the scale persisting beneath a succession of chords ending with chord V and a final cadential resolution of harmony and bass to chord I (with the keynote in the bass).

UNIT 10

GREAT INTERPRETERS

Great interpreters are more than just great performers: they must show an especially deep intellectual understanding of the music, which is often only achieved after careful analysis of the score and study of the historical context of the music. They must also possess an exceptional sensitivity to its emotional, poetic and sensual qualities – something that requires an active and precise imagination, and maybe emotional maturity as well. Can one be an interesting interpreter if one has not lived an interesting life? I doubt it!

INTERPRETATION MATTERS

Playing a piece of music is never just a matter of learning notes so you can reproduce them accurately. Even if you carefully follow all the instructions in the music telling you how loudly or softly to play, how fast or slow, it's still not enough. Why? Because the score is only a starting point for developing a musical performance. Many of the most important instructions that it contains are open-ended, and it is up to you to work out what they really mean in practice.

For example, tempo markings are rarely precise. (OK, its true, some composers give metronome markings, but did they always expect musicians to follow them precisely? It's unlikely, as in the 19th century there was no way to ensure that everyone's metronomes ran at the same speed.) Expressive markings also mean little unless you're prepared to think about what it means to experience the feelings to which they refer. A composer can mark a piece 'sad,' but there are as many different experiences of sadness as there are sad people, sad faces, and sad pieces of music.

What all this is building up to is this: it's only when you commit yourself imaginatively, by getting involved in the emotional world of the music you're playing, that you can really judge what's appropriate for a particular passage. In today's culture it's easy to get to hear classical musicians with a perfect technique, with all the right notes in the right place, never making a mistake, and so on. But outside of vintage recordings, performances with real imagination and personal vision are proving harder and harder to come across.

This is all connected with what musicians mean by **interpretation**. To interpret music is to first reach an understanding of what the music 'is about' – what its important features are, what it expresses, why it's worth hearing. Then we try and communicate this through playing. If we achieve this, listeners will feel we've done more than just present the music – we've also given them special insights that maybe they couldn't have got elsewhere.

Sometimes that listener is also you: the player. It's easy to forget that you can get musical insights from listening to your own playing, as you play.

Interpretation also means balancing creativity (and personal involvement) with respect for the score. But that's not easy. When learning the piano it's natural to focus on solving technical difficulties, yet this tends to encourage a one-sided approach: you may start to become deaf to just those aspects of the music that you need to think about if you are to arrive at an interpretation, because these are less likely to correspond to simple points of technique or simple instructions in the score.

We can redress the balance by trying some music that forces you to think for yourself because it has no markings for dynamics, tempo, phrasing and articulation. Earlier keyboard music, predating the invention of the piano, is ideal for this, as it was usually written for the harpsichord, an earlier keyboard instrument in which strings are mechanically plucked. (This made it impossible to vary either the volume or the length of notes.) The piece of harpsichord music by Scarlatti that we'll look at next is a perfect example of this.

PHRASING & EXPRESSION (2)

Take a look at the piece by Scarlatti on the next page. As with most music of this period, it has been edited: along with fingerings, some indications of tempo, phrasing and dynamics have been added as a guide to its general character. But a lot has been left to the performer's judgment and imagination. For instance, should the eighth-notes that aren't slurred be played staccato? Should the left-hand chords be arpeggiated? Should we pause on the final note? What should the exact speed be? Your decision about any of these aspects will depend on what you decide about the others, so it must be related to your overall interpretative view of the piece.

EXERCISE 10.1

The title of this sonata by Scarlatti suggests a lyrical, song-like interpretation: an 'aria' is an operatic solo sung by a character to express their personal feelings. Hence the melody should be shaped expressively, carefully matching dynamic shading to the rise and fall of the line. Notice how the last two eighth-notes of most bars involve stepwise resolution of a dissonance – these should be slurred. Other melody notes not slurred can, if you like, be played in a slightly detached way ('non-legato' rather than staccato), for contrast. Aim for rhythmic consistency with the thirty-second-notes, avoiding unintended accents. The leaps of position in the right-hand must be accomplished without taking the hand too far away from the keys. Where does the climax come? What story does the music tell? What feelings does it express? How do shifts between major and minor harmony affect the character of the music?

DOMENICO SCARLATTI

Domenico Scarlatti was an Italian composer employed at the Spanish Court in the early 18th century. After writing many unsuccessful operas he decided to strike out in a quite different direction: he opted to compose only music for one type of instrument, the harpsichord, which was the precursor of the modern piano. He produced more than 550 single-movement sonatas – highly expressive pieces that brilliantly display the technical virtuosity of keyboard players in performance, often with extravagant pianistic acrobatics involving hand-crossing and rapid runs. Modern pianists also love to play his sonatas on the piano, because its modern sustaining mechanism, dynamic range and pedal can be used to achieve musical effects Scarlatti himself could only dream of.

CD TRACK 36

continued over page

EXERCISE 10.1   continued

CD TRACK 37

EXERCISE 10.2

Now here's a different sort of piece – one with a dance-like character. A 'study' is usually a piece illustrating particular technical problems in piano playing. In this case, the challenge is to achieve a good contrast between staccato and legato phrases in the right hand, while combining these with a more consistent pattern of left-hand articulation. Notice how the middle section introduces repeated-note staccato, suggesting that the whole piece should be played at an appropriate speed for hand staccato to be used: ie, not too fast but not too slow. Try to give grace notes a lightly 'clipped' character, keeping this consistent throughout.

EXERCISE 10.2 STUDY

Czerny

LATERAL FREEDOM

One-octave arpeggios and two-octave broken chords have already shown the importance of lateral movements. Now it's time to look at some of the ways these appear in actual music. 'Tracking' the shape of a melody or melodic pattern with the appropriate lateral movements (ie, adjusting the angle of the forearm to the hand, with the help of the wrist, so that a straight line is implied, pointing from the elbow down towards the finger just being played) can sometimes be essential for achieving a natural-sounding legato, or an even rhythmic flow. It can also add a level of subtle and intuitive dynamic shaping to the music, as gradual movements of the arm naturally invite you to also make gradual adjustments of arm weight. (In all of the right-hand exercises below make sure your knuckles are level, with fourth and fifth fingers well-rounded and the weaker side of the hand properly supported from the wrist.)

EXERCISE 10.3

Here's the first of three preliminary exercises that will help prepare your right hand for using lateral motion in the piece we're about to learn. In this case we practice the four-note pattern as a block. This will familiarize you with the fingering and position changes, and make you aware of the way in which the top notes in the pattern also form an embedded melody with a dotted rhythm. When we come to play the piece itself, it's this same line that we'll be trying to highlight through our use of lateral motion. Try just the right hand first, then add left hand as well.

EXERCISE 10.3

EXERCISE 10.4

In this second exercise we'll practice right hand only, aiming to achieve greater rhythmic control by altering the rhythm so that there's a slight pause on the last note of each group. This encourages us to focus on the ascending melodic movement within each four-note figure, which corresponds to the part of the lateral movement in which the forearm swings away from the body. Note, however, that the movement comes from the wrist, not the forearm or elbow: it's the wrist that describes a circular motion around the hand, while the elbow only moves as much as is necessary to relieve the strain of the resulting angle between arm and hand. (In the old-fashioned German style the elbows weren't supposed to move at all, as this was seen as difficult to control perfectly. However, piano teachers now prefer to stress the importance of not straining the wrist.

EXERCISE 10.4

EXERCISE 10.5

In the third and last exercise we change the rhythm round so the pause comes at the start of each group. This time the other aspect of the lateral movement is more to the fore, corresponding to the stepwise movements of the melody line formed by the first and last notes in each group. This requires us to follow each of the gradual movements practiced in the previous exercise with a smaller but faster lateral movement in the opposite direction.

EXERCISE10.5

EXERCISE 10.6

CD TRACK 38

Here we have the piece itself. Notice how the texture changes after the first eight bars as the left hand assumes a more significant melodic role. At this point the right-hand pattern becomes fragmented and should recede into the background: as you approach the last note of each three-note figure, each lateral movement should therefore be combined with a slight lifting of the wrist and release of weight, similar to that employed in couplets. The left hand can sing out more here, but take care to ensure that its dotted rhythms don't upset the rhythmic evenness of the right hand. This will be easier if you maintain a firm sense of the quarter-note pulse. Resist the temptation to rush – you should be able to keep a loose (and low) wrist and relaxed forearm throughout.

EXERCISE 10.6   THE BROOK

Heller

EXERCISE 10.6 continued

CD TRACK 39

EXERCISE 10.7

Finally, try this left-hand lateral movement study, based on similar patterns to the right hand in the last piece. The pattern there has been turned upside down here, so the relationship of movements to fingering is reproduced for the other hand. (This transformation technique is known as melodic inversion, and is often used by composers to generate new musical ideas from existing ones.) Again, you can practice preliminary exercises equivalent to those used for the previous piece, but this time you'll have to work them out yourself. (Devising your own strategies for practicing difficult passages is a vital skill – one that you'll need more and more as you progress towards an advanced level.)

| EXERCISE 10.7 | LATERAL MOTION STUDY |

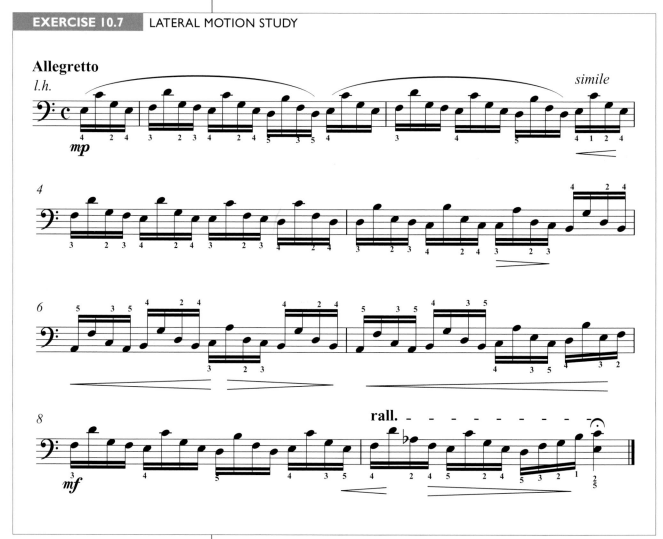

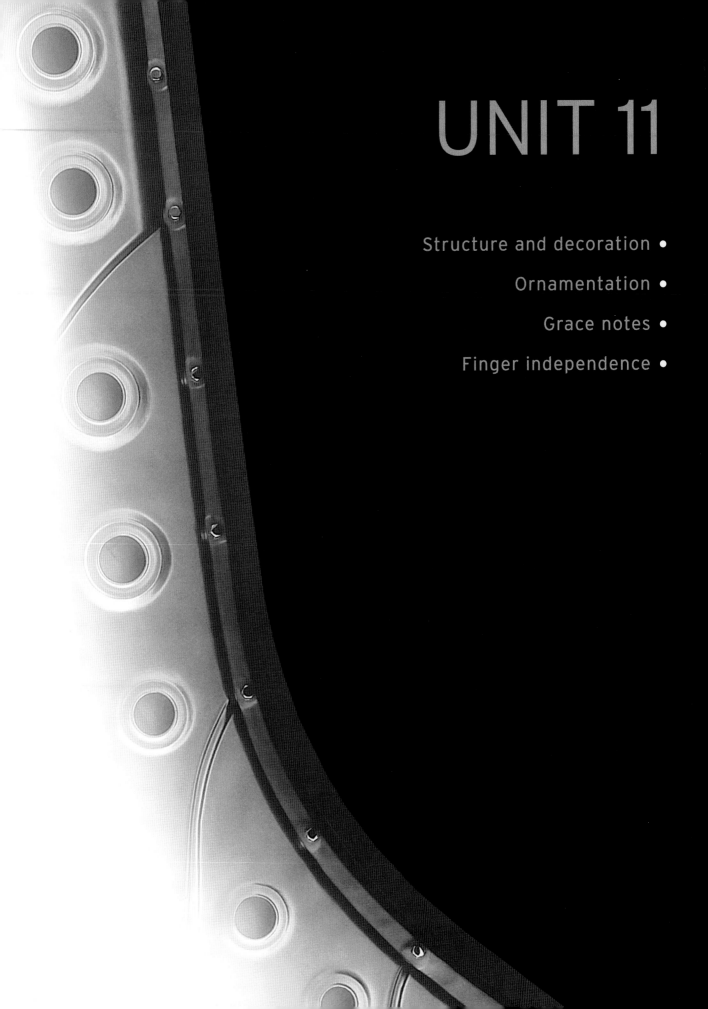

UNIT 11

- Structure and decoration
- Ornamentation
- Grace notes
- Finger independence

STRUCTURE AND DECORATION

Look closely at a piece of music in any style and beneath the surface you'll find a more basic structure or form that could just as easily have been elaborated in other ways. There are reasons for this. It's partly that we naturally perceive and understand music by listening selectively for these simpler structures – in this respect listening to music is no different from any other aspect of how we perceive the world. However, these structures also make it easier to compose or improvise music in a particular style. This is because they correspond to certain formulaic elements that recur across a range of similar pieces.

The basic idea is that if you know these structures, you'll be able to compose and improvise much more spontaneously, without having to write everything down to remember it, and without having to plan out every detail before it makes musical sense. This is especially the case in folk music cultures, where music is created without being written down. As we'll see later, learning a set formulaic structures is also essential for jazz and other modern styles of improvising.

It's easy to forget, though, that classical music also originated from styles that were formulaic in this kind of way, and that involved a great deal more improvising than we ever see in the classical concert hall today. So to properly understand classical music – especially from earlier periods – you need to understand how these basic structures come to be varied and elaborated. The most important way in which this was done was through **melodic decoration**. Understanding how classical music uses decoration will help you see how this music is really organized, and this in turn can guide you towards giving more insightful interpretations as a pianist. At the same time, musical decoration involves special symbols, and calls for special playing techniques. In this unit we'll also be considering some of these.

Looking at different kinds of music in terms of structure and decoration is a good way to see how much different styles of music have in common. Hopefully, by the time you've completed this unit and the next, you'll know that improvising jazz, rock, and blues involve the same kind of underlying musical awareness as interpreting the older classics.

A lot of musicians – not just students, but also teachers – never find this out. Why? Because they haven't learned to look below the surface of the music they play. So they remain trapped in one particular style, and regard other kinds of music as 'out of reach.' That's sad, not just because they're wrong, but also because, as we'll see, these comparisons open up exciting, fresh, new perspectives on all of the different kinds of music involved.

Just take a moment to think back over some of the ground we've covered so far. In Unit 6 we saw that composing a melody involves being sensitive to the harmonic implications of a tune, which means being able to distinguish harmony notes from passing notes. This show that even the simplest melody in a major or minor key already divides into two levels – a more basic structure (corresponding to implied chord changes) and musical surface which includes stepwise melodic elaborations over this.

Now think about how we approached actually harmonizing a melody in Unit 9: once again it was crucial to know which notes in the melody are passing notes, and which are suggestive of the chord; knowing this also enabled us to consider alternative options that made for richer harmonic textures, using inversions and chord substitution. (In a sense these are also forms of decoration in music, as we tend to hear them as referring back to the more basic chord structures implied by the melody itself.)

Finally, consider the issues involved in pedaling: as we saw in Units 7 and 8, whether we use direct and legato pedaling – and when – depends on where the chords change, and on whether melody notes outline the same chord or correspond to stepwise melodic movements that are basically decorative. So you can see, all of these aspects of music making already imply a grasp of structure and decoration in music.

Don't forget: it's not just music that is decorative. Try comparing the music you're listening to or learning with other art forms and artifacts from the same culture or epoch, and you'll start to see that the decorative character of the music is part of something broader: different cultures use decoration in different ways because they are expressing different values, and this finds its way into music too.

For example, European music from the late 16th and early 17th centuries reflects a broader historical movement known as the **Renaissance**. At this time a new view of the world was developing, known as **humanism**, which aspired towards certain specifically human values such as harmoniousness and order, in contrast to the more strictly religious perspective of the Middle Ages. This is reflected in how decoration is used in architecture and music – and in other things, like clothes, furniture, and even everyday human gestures. Everything gets rounded off with a nice decorative flourish to highlight its completeness or resolution. Hence, in Renaissance music, decoration tends to be concentrated around the cadences at the ends of phrases or sections.

In the later 17th century this way of thinking was taken much further, giving rise to what we now call the **Enlightenment**. It became normal to think of the whole world as a harmonious system, which human beings could easily understand through reason and science. This was the period of decorative extravagance, as in rococo architecture and those formal costumes you see in paintings by Rembrandt, with their enormous frilly cuffs and collars.

Decorativeness became a feature of life in general, and likewise became woven into the fabric of the music as a whole. Baroque music is an endless stream of decorative embellishments.

By contrast, the next phase of Classical music, in the 18th century – known rather confusingly as the classical period – emphasizes musical themes and phrase divisions. Decorativeness becomes less central, and was just one of many different ways in which musical ideas could be developed. In the 19th century composers also preferred simpler, less decorative melodies, which could be supported by richer and more complex harmonic textures. This suited the more emotionally oriented outlook of **Romanticism**, in which melodic ideas are more narrative than decorative, and texture is supposed to play a dramatic role.

In the 20th century decoration was eliminated from music altogether – at least by modernist composers – and we can see clear parallels here with the austere, functional approaches to architecture and interior design that are still a major feature of our social landscape.

We'll be learning pieces of music from all of these periods in the remaining parts of this book. Knowing something about their cultural and historical context will make you more sensitive to their decorative style, as well as their use of texture and form.

DECORATION EVERYWHERE
If you think decorativeness is an obscure feature of old music, just pause and look around you. What kind of furniture or architecture can you see? What clothes are you wearing? What gestures can you see people making in the street? When you speak, what expressions do you use? How much of what you see is really essential? The answer, probably, is not much. That's because almost all of these things have a decorative side to them, which we just take for granted, even though it has to be carefully designed by human beings to look that way. Music is just one more example of this.

ORNAMENTATION

In earlier periods of classical music, the performer was expected to add his or her own decorations to what was written by the composer. Eventually, a common set of symbols emerged that allowed composers to indicate how the music should be decorated. Treatises – such as that by the famous C.P.E. Bach – were written that explain how to realize these symbols in performance; this is a specialized and complex area of performance practice. We'll cover the basics of classical ornamentation here, but it's also worth remembering that the few surviving manuscripts in which performers wrote down what they actually played suggest that they often went far beyond what these treatises suggest in terms of decorative extravagance. That's hardly surprising: in the days when keyboard players relied on more primitive instruments such as the harpsichord, or early pianos, the main way to impress an audience was through giving the most virtuosic or imaginative ornamentation so far of a familiar tune.

From the Baroque period onwards there are five basic categories of ornament used in classical music, each represented by a shorthand symbol: acciaccatura, appoggiatura, turn, trill (or shake), and mordent.

(1) An **acciaccatura** is shown by a small note (known as a **grace note**), with a diagonal slash through its stem. It is played very quickly so as not to alter the underlying rhythm, though the exact speed may be adjusted to suit the music. Such notes usually sound just before the beat on which the main note sounds, though in the 18th and early 19th centuries single and multiple grace notes could also sound on the beat, especially if this resulted in a musically expressive dissonance. Two or more grace notes can also be written like this, often with no slash, to indicate a similar effect.

(2) An **appoggiatura** is also shown by a single grace note, this time with no slash, and it sounds on the beat. This means it functions to delay the subsequent main note (ie, the full-size note immediately following it) by a rhythmically significant unit of time. In effect, the written time-value of the main note gets split into two equal subdivisions or, for dotted notes, into two-thirds and a third. Hence whereas acciaccaturas tend to represent purely colouristic additions, appoggiaturas correspond to an element of decoration that is usually part of the more basic expressive unfolding of the melodic line, and should be interpreted as such.

(3) A **turn** is a brief melodic flourish that passes quickly through the note above the written note, then the written note, then the note below, and then comes to rest on the written note itself again: the melody thus 'circles' the main note, much like certain stylised hand gestures that you can still see in ballet. In classical period music (and later), the figure usually starts out with the written note, rather than directly from the note above. If the turn is placed 'after the note' rather than 'on the note' (ie, over it) in the score, then the written note is usually held first, and the turn comes as a rapid flourish that makes up the end of its duration, leading directly into whatever comes afterwards. An inverted turn circles around in the opposite direction, passing first through the note below, and later through the note above.

(4) A **trill** (or 'shake') is a rapid alternation between the main note and the scale-note above. Trills begin on the upper note in Baroque music unless preceded immediately by the same note. However in the classical period the custom changed to starting on the written note (unless preceded in the score by the upper note, marked as a grace note). Because the trill normally ends with a turn, this later style then requires us to use a triplet, to fit all of the notes into time. (The last two notes of the turn are also often indicated in the score as grace notes before the resolution note, to make clear that a turn is expected.) Trills written on short notes in fast music tend to become single alternations, or turns, or a combination of the two.

(5) **Mordents** evolved out of trills on short, fast notes ('Schneller' in German). They later came to consist of a single alternation with the note above or below.

Occasionally you will encounter small accidental signs (sharps, flats, naturals) placed above or below the ornament symbol: these signify a chromatic alteration of the note above or below the written note, respectively. Here is what the symbols for the above ornaments look like:

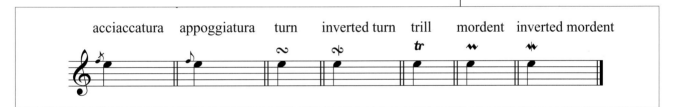

As far as general technique is concerned, ornaments often require you to execute notes at great speed, while remaining relaxed and in control of the movements and weight of your arm, hand, and fingers. They must be fitted into the existing rhythm of the line without sounding forced or awkward. It's helpful to keep the fingers close to the keys, and you should avoid tensing and/or raising the wrist.

Always practice ornaments slowly before bringing them gradually up to speed, and listen out to make sure you've kept a good legato and singing tone. Trills should not be played in any strict rhythmic subdivision: instead, focus on consistency of speed, and learn to judge intuitively when it's right to round off the trill so you land exactly on the beat with the next note. If your other hand is playing at the same time, this requires a high degree of rhythmic independence between the hands, as the other hand must remain strictly in time. This may require careful and patient practice, as you slowly bring the music up to speed.

Now it's time to look at some pieces in which the problems typically associated with realizing and executing ornaments arise.

EXERCISE 11.1

CD TRACK 40

The stylistic ideal for this early classical period piece is a restrained elegance and poise, and this means aiming for a clear sense of how phrase divisions affect the melodic unfolding. Try to feel how each phrase responds to the preceding one. Within each phrase the music carries a strong sense of arrival and departure: in the first the music moves towards the dotted quarter-note E♭ in bar 2, then on to the resolution at the end of bar 4. In the next (and in similar phrases) forward motion is generated by triplet eighth-notes, with a strong sense of arrival at the subsequent dotted quarter-note, even though this is a chromatically unresolved note. Be sensitive to the subtle difference in speed between triplet eighth-notes and sixteenth-notes. Try clapping these rhythms first, until you can move between the two time values with a common pulse. Be alert to changes of hand position in the right hand, and the need to move in and out of the black keys where necessary. The latter will facilitate a good legato, and make ornaments easier to play. The realization of ornaments – as shown in the key – varies depending on whether or not they follow an identical note to that decorated. The trills in bars 13 and 31 are not shown, as they are standard.

EXERCISE 11.1   MINUET

Clementi

EXERCISE 11.1 continued

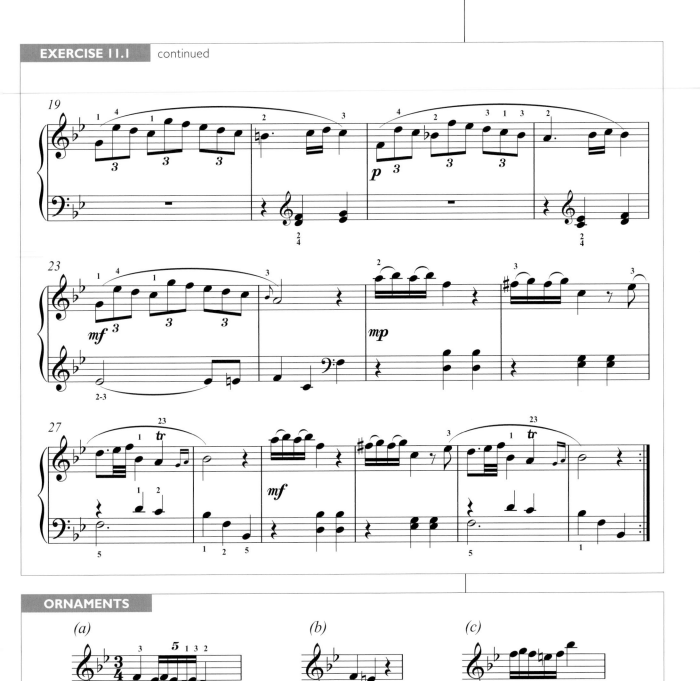

ORNAMENTS

The next piece features written-out turns. Let's start with a couple of preliminary exercises.

EXERCISE 11.2

This exercise focuses on short phrases with a tricky mix of turns and leaps. Turning each one round on itself lets you practice it over and over again, but make sure to give your hand a rest as soon as it starts to tire or tense. Keeping all the fingers about to play in a particular hand position in contact with the keys makes for a smoother, less percussive character, and improves control. Avoid exaggerating the finger movements to speed up the turns: that's a sign you're playing too quickly too soon. It helps to lean over just a little towards the right-hand side of the keyboard when playing in the extreme high register, but your right foot must be on the floor so it still stabilizes you.

EXERCISE 11.2

EXERCISE 11.3

In this exercise, varying the rhythmic relationship between turn figurations and the beat during practicing encourages your fingers to transfer weight and maintain a singing tone through all of the fast notes, and not just on long or accented notes. Once again, a relaxed wrist and fingers close to the surface of the keys is desirable. Can you think of other ways of changing the rhythm that might also help?

EXERCISE 11.3

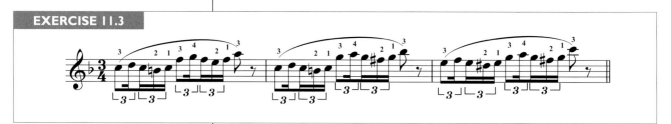

CD TRACK 41

EXERCISE 11.4

Now for the piece itself. Here you'll need to strike a delicate balance. On the one hand, accenting eighth-notes while lightening the fast notes of the turns themselves will facilitate the leap at the end of each turn, as well as increasing rhythmic control. On the other hand, all notes should possess a singing tone and lightness of touch, so that we feel both the continuity of the line and a natural sense of flow. You can tail off at the end of each right hand phrase, as with a couplet, so that the final eighth-note sounds lighter and shorter. Special care will be needed over the move into the extreme high register in bar eight, to maintain rhythmic control and an appropriate gradation of tone. Aim for a strong sense of overall contrast in the second section, with a slightly heavier touch and fuller texture. Here the left-hand written-out turns may benefit from lateral movement of the left forearm and wrist.

EXERCISE 11.4   LA GRACIEUSE

GRACE NOTES

Grace notes that correspond to acciaccaturas (ie, slashed grace notes) don't have a strict rhythmic value, as broadly speaking they are supposed to be played as quickly as possible.

However, in music the phrase 'as quickly as possible' is never interpreted absolutely literally, as this would often mean playing them unmusically. So it can only really mean 'very fast,' but what this means will depend on the musical context: in principle it could actually correspond to a range of speeds. What is important is not so much speed as attaining the musically appropriate character, and maintaining this consistently.

Try the study below, thinking carefully about how you might alter the character of grace notes to reflect the changes in dynamics and the contrast between the right-hand and left-hand material.

CD TRACK 42

EXERCISE 11.5

This study combines grace notes with rapid alternation between the hands, as well as changes of hand position. Note how, with the exception of the last bar, both hands are written on a single staff, as together they form a single line of music. (In such circumstances right-hand notes are shown with stems pointing up, left-hand notes with stems pointing down.) Concentrate on achieving a consistent characterization of the grace-note figure as it passes through different fingerings and between the hands. Be prepared to alter the character of the grace notes to suit the changed feel of bars 9-12.

EXERCISE 11.5   GRACE NOTE STUDY

FINGER INDEPENDENCE

As the music you play becomes more and more demanding, it's vital you start to build up finger independence. When we talk about this, what we mean is the ability to move any one finger without it being constrained by others. However, in fact there are two aspects to this: moving a finger shouldn't produce a reaction in the other fingers, but neither should it produce one in the hand as a whole. The second point is important because students often think it's enough to suppress the reactions of other fingers by force – by tensing up the hand. The problem is that this tensing up is itself an unwanted and uncontrolled reaction to the movement of the finger, and is just as harmful and disruptive to playing. Sure, it may be less visible than fingers jumping around uncontrollably, but its effects are at least as audible.

EXERCISE 11.6

Here are some five-finger exercises for developing finger independence. They are written hands together, but the main thing is to master them hands separately. (Practicing them hands together is more useful later, as a more time-efficient version for general practice.) The same sequence of exercises is given for C major and C minor, to show how the fingering and patterns remain constant. Keep the hand and wrist relaxed throughout, with rounded fingers and level knuckles. Begin legato, keeping tips of fingers close to the keys, then later try a crisp but light finger staccato. Accenting notes on the quarter-note beat may help to achieve rhythmic control in the early stages, but don't force the hand. Start slowly, speed up gradually, and don't feel you have to proceed through the whole sequence in one go. (Repeat each subsection as many times as you want before moving on or having a break.) Monitor posture and keep your shoulders low and relaxed. When you feel confident with it, try transposing the entire sequence into other major and minor keys whose first and fifth steps are white notes: ie, D, E, F, G, and A.

EXERCISE 11.6

C Major

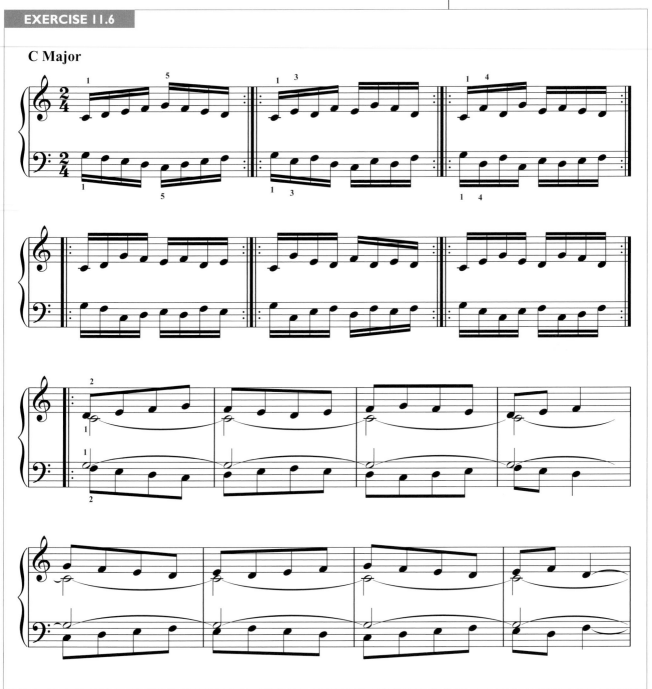

continued over page

EXERCISE 11.6   continued

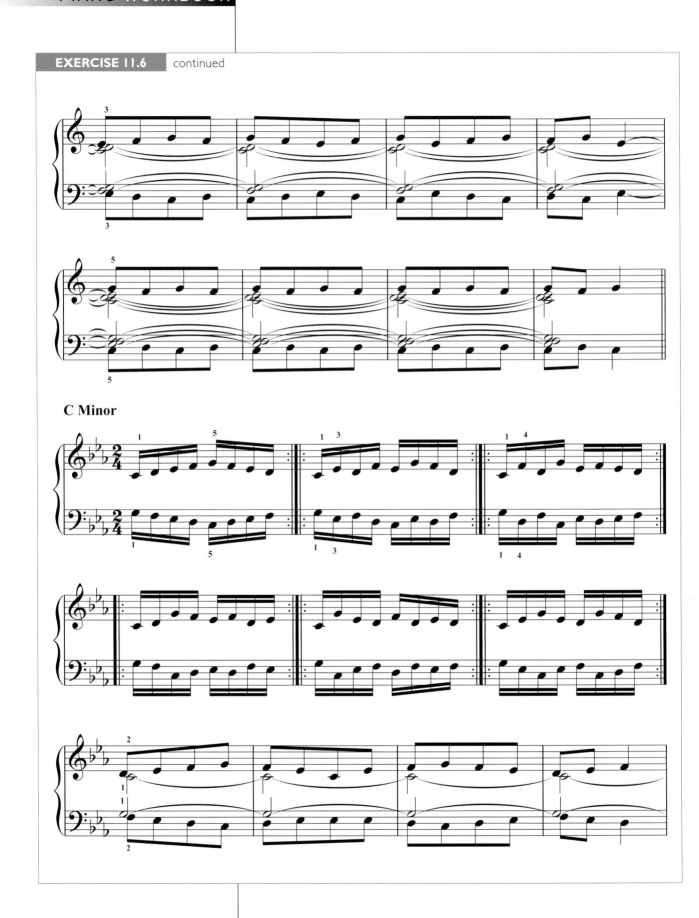

C Minor

EXERCISE 11.6 continued

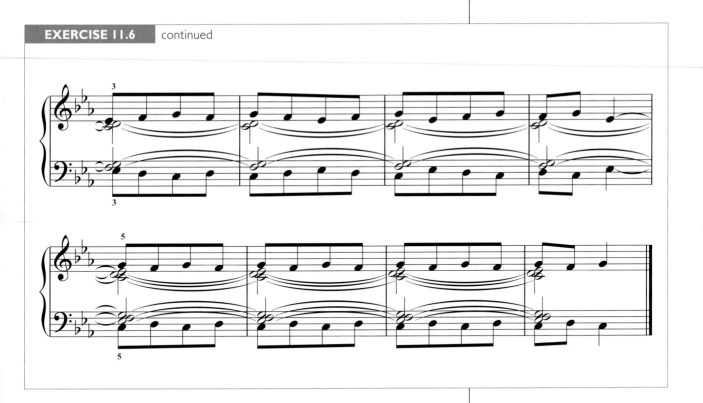

UNIT 12

JAZZ, ROCK, AND BLUES (2)

In this unit we'll be looking more closely at what's involved in mastering rhythms in non-classical styles of piano playing, such as rock, jazz, blues, and Latin, and at how to get started with improvising your own melody lines over chords.

Unlike classical music, non-classical styles have particular kinds of rhythmic feel; these depend on characteristic patterns of rhythmic subdivision and syncopation. You'll need to internalize these so they come naturally to you. Only then will you be able to start using them as a bedrock for exploring melodic and harmonic possibilities with real creative freedom, whether this be through composing or improvising.

SITTING IN THE GROOVE

As we've just said, each style has a characteristic rhythmic feel, and this may correspond to a range of related patterns of subdivision and syncopation. It's known as a **groove**. A good way to master the groove for a particular style is to practice moving to and fro between several of these related patterns. The more comfortable you become with this, the more natural your feeling for the underlying rhythmic unity of the style will be, until your body just naturally wants to keep going in that same way, and spontaneously generates new variations on the same rhythmic patterns – just as your body does in fact, in modern styles of dancing. (That's no coincidence: most of these styles are Afro-American in origin, and so are linked to dance.)

We call this **sitting in the groove**. When you reach the point where your body starts to take over – and don't expect it to happen immediately – you'll feel an exhilarating sense of new-found freedom, as you're now free to shift your attention away from the groove, and focus instead on other aspects of music, such as harmony, melody, and texture. What's exciting about this is that now you have the groove working for you inside your body, so now you can play freely over it or against it, exploring these other aspects of music.

The best way to master grooves is to treat them as two-hand chord patterns – a bit like a basic form of drumming. When you've got the basic feel sorted out, you can then introduce more chord changes, or substitute melodic ideas for chord repetitions. Eventually, you'll want to either convert these rhythms into left-hand accompaniment patterns or team up with a rhythm section (drums and bass). In the latter case you'll still need to feel the groove, but now you'll have both hands available to explore how harmony and melody can work freely over (or against) it.

EXERCISE 12.1

Try playing through each rhythm in a slow and relaxed way, gradually gathering pace. Then try combining two or three, moving between them in sequence. You should expect to play the straight-ahead (rock) and swing (jazz) grooves at a faster pace, with a more upbeat feel, while the blues shuffle should be slower, with a more laid-back, downbeat feel. The halftime groove should be laid-back but brisk, though you'll find the subdivisions here require a steady pulse.

EXERCISE 12.1

'Straight-ahead' rock

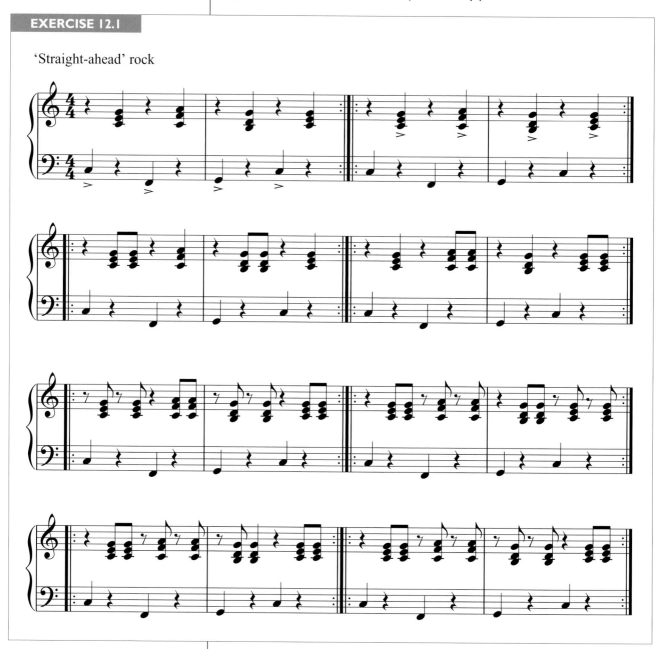

EXERCISE 12.1   continued

Rock and blues 'shuffle'

Jazz 'comping'

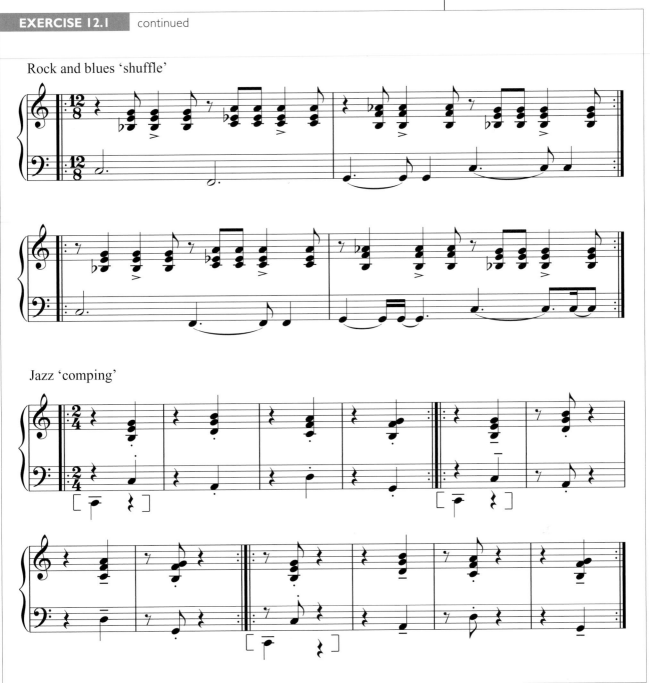

continued over page

EXERCISE 12.1   continued

'Halftime' funk

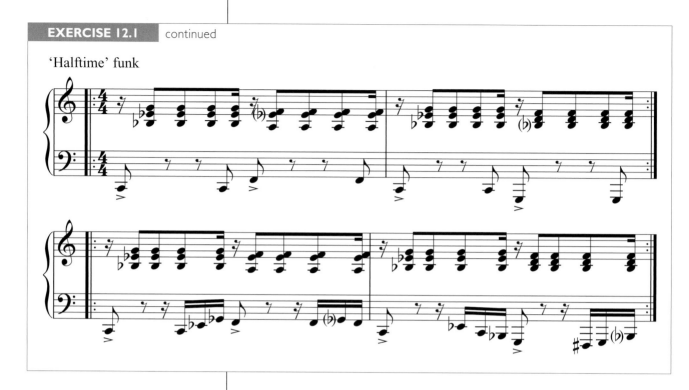

LATIN RHYTHM

Now let's take the same approach to some Latin grooves. 'Latin' here is short for 'Latin-American' – it's a term used to refer to a whole range of music coming from Central and South America and the Caribbean. Strictly speaking, that takes in Cuba, Caribbean countries such as the Dominican Republic and Trinidad, as well as Mexico, Panama, Argentina, Brazil, and other countries on the mainland of the South American continent. Most of these places were colonized by Spanish and Portuguese, who set up coffee, sugar, and cotton plantations that used slave labor brought from Africa. These places became a melting pot for a hot mix of different ethnic cultures, combining Hispanic European (and Arabic) influences with African and native South American Indian elements. The result is a number of distinctive rhythmic and dance-based styles that have become famous the world over. These include **tango**, **mariachi**, **calypso**, **reggae**, and **merengue**, but by far the most famous are **salsa** and **samba**.

From the very beginning there was also a crossover effect: these styles were present in the Creole communities of New Orleans and Cuba, which provided the birthplace for jazz; and as jazz developed into a more harmonically sophisticated medium for improvisation its innovations were readily absorbed into the playing styles of Latin musicians. This bore fruit in fusions such as 'Latin jazz'. Out of this also came **bossa nova** – a commercially successful variant of samba used in many Latin-American hit songs, of which the most famous is probably Antonio Carlos Jobim's 'The Girl From Ipanema.' (If you make it to the last unit of this book, you'll get to study how to do your own solo piano arrangement of that classic number.)

EXERCISE 12.2

Approach these rhythms as in the previous exercise. First practice them by slapping your hands on your thighs, or drumming. The stereotype of Latin rhythms is that they are always fast and furious, full of demonic momentum, but most Latin grooves can be and are played at a variety of speeds. (When used to accompany singers, there are limits on how fast they can be played.) The basic pattern in salsa is known as the 'clave' (pronounced 'clah-veh'): it alternates basic three-note and two-note rhythmic formulas in either 'forward clave' (3+2) or 'reverse clave' (2+3). Bossa nova uses 'forward clave,' but delays the final attack, making the pattern less sharply defined and leaving room for more variation. Samba acquires its primitive, hypnotic character by beginning on the beat, moving through repeated syncopations, and then recapturing the beat again, all within a two-bar cycle, driven on relentlessly by a repeated dotted rhythm known as the 'feet' of the groove, played here by the left hand.

EXERCISE 12.2

Salsa (forward clave)

Salsa (reverse clave)

continued over page

EXERCISE 12.2 continued

Bossa nova

Samba

RIFFS AND LICKS - BUILDING A VOCABULARY

Apart from understanding harmony and learning to feel the groove, the other major skill you need to have to play non-classical styles is an ability to improvise melodically. Basically, there are two different ways to go about learning how to do this, each with its own advantages and disadvantages. Ultimately you should aim to master both, because a good improviser will use elements of both approaches:

The riff and lick-based approach: the basic idea here is that you first learn a range of small melodic units or phrases – what classical musicians call motives and themes – until these become second nature. Then you can weave them together freely into a single seamless line, while adjusting them to fit with the underlying harmony. (**Riffs** are fixed melodic patterns that can be repeated over different chords; **licks** are shorter motives used to fill out or intensify a melodic passage):

PROS: generally easier to learn, and good for improvising freely over an underlying chord structure, as in a jam session (where musicians get together informally to improvise just for fun or to get to know each other's styles of playing), or in an instrumental solo (eg, in a rock song or 12-bar blues).
CONS: melody lines may lack overall shape and direction and precise coordination with harmony.

The 'goal-note' approach: this method treats melodic improvisation as a kind of free embellishment of the voice-leading structures (ie, melodic connections) implied by given chord progressions:

PROS: suited to solo piano playing, where more exposed textures mean that improvised lines must be more tightly integrated with voice leading, as well as to more sophisticated jazz and crossover styles (e.g. mixing classical and non-classical); it also links improvising more closely to composing, allowing you to plan the overall melodic and harmonic structure, and allows for a more subtle awareness of how melodies unfold in relation to harmony.
CONS: generally requires you to think more carefully about how melody and harmony relate to one another.

It's important to note that both approaches can be used to improvise around a given melody. In the riff- and lick-based approach we do this by identifying motives already present in the melody, which we can then explore freely alongside our existing repertoire of riffs and licks, over the underlying chord structure of the melody. In the goal-note approach we strip away some of the decorative elements already present in the melody until we are left with an underlying melodic skeleton that also corresponds to part of the voice-leading structure of the harmony. Then we use this structure to define points of departure and arrival for melodic embellishment.

In this unit our aim is just to get started, building up a repertoire of riffs and licks that you can use whenever you improvise. Later (in Unit 15) we can look more closely at what's involved in improvising around a specific melody and chord structure.

THE LANGUAGE OF IMPROVISATION

Like musical improvising, speaking is also improvised, but we can only do it because we carry around in our heads a vocabulary of words and phrases that can be reused in an unlimited number of ways, plus some basic rules (grammar) for how they can and can't be combined. Think of the rules for scales, chord progressions, and phrase-structure as a musical grammar, with riffs and licks, or themes and motives, as words and phrases (a musical lexicon). Scientists and music theorists such as Ray Jackendoff and Fred Lerdahl have even tried analysing music using models derived from linguistics. (See their book *A Generative Theory Of Tonal Music*.)

So let's consider how we can start building a vocabulary of riffs and licks. A good riff or lick has four ingredients: raw material (scales and chordal patterns), shape or trajectory, a relation to harmony, and a relation to meter. Of course some of this will be determined by the conventions of the particular style of music in which you want to improvise. We've already discussed how different styles of non-classical music take different approaches to chords and use different scale materials (see Unit 9). By now you should also know about swing, and have some feel for other grooves characteristic of straight-ahead rock, shuffle, halftime funk, and Latin styles. So the next step is to be clear about the kind of choices to be made when putting together your own musical ideas, no matter which of these styles you're working in.

MATERIALS: Your basic materials are scales and chord patterns – and intervals. (Actually what really makes a melody expressive is not the notes that it contains, but the choice of intervals – though these still depend on which scale or chord pattern you are using.)

Scales provide the basis for stepwise movement, while chord patterns (as in arpeggios and broken chords) provide the basis for larger steps and leaps. Beginning a chord pattern on any step of the scale, using notes just from that scale, produces a recognizable pattern of larger and smaller leaps. Add the 7th or 6th of the chord to the basic **triad** and you have a four-note pattern instead of a three-note one. Add two notes to the triad (2nd and 6th for major, 4th and flat 7th for minor) and you have a **pentatonic scale** (see Unit 9). This scale is used widely by rock, blues, country and jazz improvisers as it lends itself to being reproduced freely over a range of different harmonies. Add another couple of notes and you get the seven-note major and minor **diatonic scales** of classical music (and rock and pop), and the **modes** used in freer styles of jazz (see Unit 15).

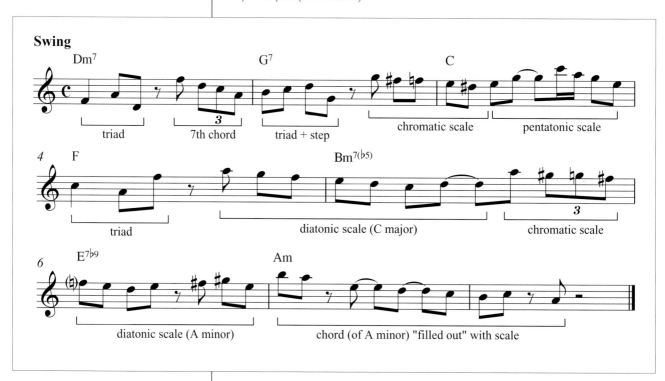

Swing

triad — 7th chord — triad + step — chromatic scale — pentatonic scale

triad — diatonic scale (C major) — chromatic scale

diatonic scale (A minor) — chord (of A minor) "filled out" with scale

At the same time you can stop anywhere in this process of adding more elements, and add alterations based on the **chromatic scale** instead, substituting a note a semitone above or below the normal note and then resolving to the latter by a half-step. A good improvised line, such as the one on the opposite page, will mix up these different kinds of material to avoid becoming too predictable, and will aim to balancing ascending movement with descending movement, and steps with leaps.

SHAPE/TRAJECTORY: A good riff should have a recognizable melodic shape – a rise and fall that catches our interest and stands out, even when repeated. If it's a lick, it should also have a strong sense of movement, with a distinctive trajectory, so we get a clear sense of departure and arrival. In both cases the overall shape should surprise us somehow, but also have a feeling of completeness. Remember: the more distinctive the shape, the more freely you can play around with it, changing different aspects, while taking your listeners with you.

Here's the same line again, with its trajectory marked. Note how it begins with a gradual ascent, followed by more sudden movements, then a couple of phrases beginning high up, and finally a gradual descent from an even higher point. This overall shape provides the context for more local changes of melodic direction, which pull against this.

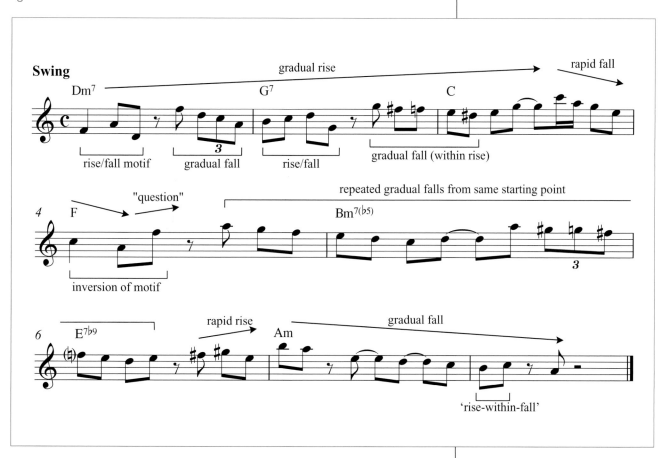

RELATION TO HARMONY: Start by exploring some of the standard licks conventionally used over particular chord changes. Once you've developed an ear for what makes them work harmonically, you'll quickly find yourself branching out in new directions. A good technique is to try transposing them through all keys (along with their chords). You can also try reproducing the same shape one or more steps higher or lower over the same chords, and see which notes have to be changed so that the line still works.

We often feature the 3rd of the chord either on or just after the main beat, as this signals the harmony more clearly, and this is often approached by step (see example b below). Also, each diatonic scale (or mode) contains one or more **avoid notes** – notes that produce an exceptionally strong dissonance when played over particular chords (e.g. the note a perfect 4th above the root of the chord). We tend to be more cautious about using these notes, and if they sound against the chord they are usually resolved by step to a consonance. Both of these points are illustrated in these standard jazz licks. (We'll look again at avoid notes in Unit 15.)

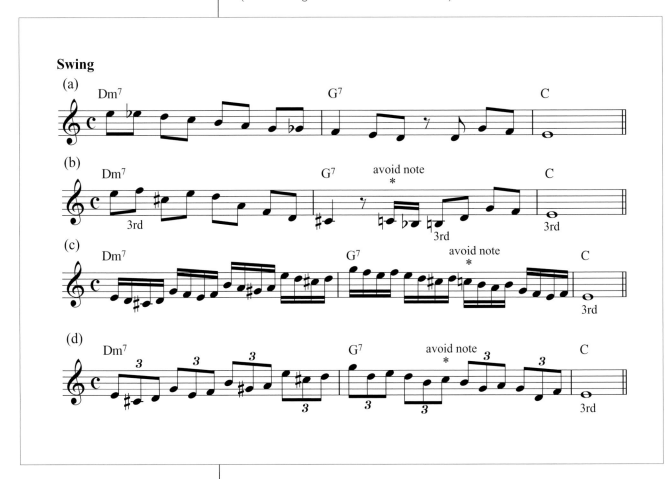

RELATION TO METER: As the example illustrates (opposite page, top), we can alter the relation of a line to the underlying meter in a number of ways: breaking up the line into smaller motifs, displacing harmony notes (eg, the 3rd of the chord) from the beat, or delaying the resolution of syncopated elements within the figure.

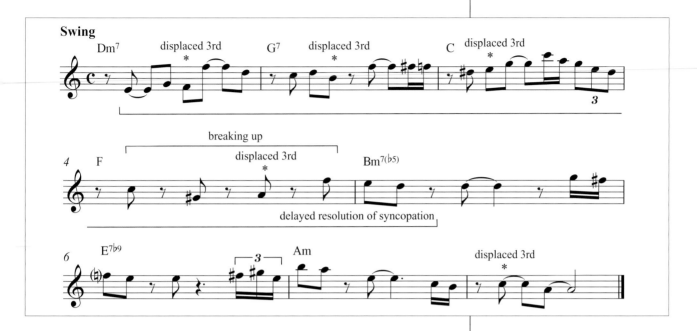

Riffs are often defined by the way they circle round and return after a regular one or two-bar cycle, often using and then resolving syncopations:

Licks, on the other hand, tend to be more fluid, but are usually defined by whether they move towards or away from an important metrical point. (This is usually either the first or third beat of the bar, but may also involve the **backbeat** – the strongly accented second and fourth beat typical of heavier rock and blues, as in the next example.)

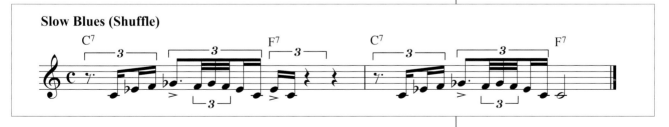

Once you start exploring how riffs and licks work, you'll be surprised how quickly you start to come up with ideas of your own. It really pays to keep a riff diary.

BLUES

Everyone's heard of 'the blues,' but it's easy to forget that practically all of modern pop and rock only came about through the enormous influence of blues on early rock & roll artists, not to mention big-name groups like The Rolling Stones. The blues corresponds to something basic at the heart of modern popular music: a kind of common musical reference point that allows musicians from quite different backgrounds to immediately understand each other's playing. That's why playing blues is an essential skill if you want to work with other non-classical musicians, whether as a professional band or just for informal 'jam' sessions.

The main defining features of the blues are its distinctive **12-bar chord sequence** (sometimes extended to 16 bars), and the distinctive **blues scale**, together with the harmonies and melodies that this gives rise to. Most people recognize the 'bluesy' sound of these, which corresponds to a kind of mixing up of major-key and minor-key elements that is almost never found in traditional classical music, but which is now a common feature of many non-classical styles. We've already had a brief look at 12-bar blues in Unit 9, when discussing the concept of chord substitution. Here's the basic pattern once again:

Standard 12-bar blues (in C):

| C7	| C7	| C7	| C7	|
| F7	| F7	| C7	| C7	|
| G7	| F7	| C7	| C7	:||

Here it is again, this time using classical chord symbol notation, so you can grasp the underlying chord functions. Knowing these will help you to get familiar with the blues in a variety of keys, without having to transpose every time. (You'll find that guitarists like to play blues most of all in 'sharp keys' like A and E major, while clarinet, sax and trumpet players prefer 'flat keys' like F and B♭ major. As the pianist, they'll expect you to adapt.)

| I7	| I7	| I7	| I7	|
| IV7	| IV7	| I7	| I7	|
| V7	| IV7	| I7	| I7	:||

This chord sequence can be embellished in countless different ways. (See the discussion of **chord substitution** and **passing chords** in Unit 9.) What's important, though, is to grasp the logic of the 12-bar blues form, which always stays the same: first we begin on the tonic (I), then in bar five switch to the subdominant (IV), then in bar seven return to the tonic (I), then make a harmonic diversion of some kind (usually involving V and/or modulation through part of the circle of 5ths), and finally in bar 11 return to the tonic (I) again. A common practice consists of replacing the final I7 chord with a V7 chord, as this leads more powerfully back into a repeat of the sequence (which can be repeated as many times as you like.) However, this is optional.

We normally improvise over this sequence using the blues scale, but may also use the pentatonic major scale.

Note how the blues scale itself contains a minor pentatonic scale, with the addition of a flattened 5th. Nevertheless, you should keep in mind that this scale is designed to be played over major key harmony, so we also hear the 3rd and 7th as chromatically flattened – these three notes will all tend to be heard as out-of-tune 'blue notes.' (You should also be aware that while the blues scale tends to stay the same over chords I, IV and V, the pentatonic scale is transposed, depending on the chord. In other words, on chord I we play the pentatonic scale starting on I, on IV we play the pentatonic scale starting on IV, on V we play the scale on V.)

Sometimes the flattened 5th gets written as a sharpened 4th (its enharmonic equivalent) instead. This may reflect the fact that it can also function as a kind of chromatically raised note: a 'leading tone' moving to the 5th of the scale (as if the latter were a tonic), as in classical music. Alternatively, it may be because in certain keys (e.g. with many flats) it is easier to read. It may also be affected by the fact that some classical musicians observe the convention of writing all ascending chromatic motion using raised accidentals (ie, changing naturals to sharps, and flats to naturals) and descending chromatic motion with lowered accidentals (i.e. changing sharps to naturals, and naturals to flats). You can see how this looks in the scale patterns at the end of this unit.

Blues improvisation usually happens over a rhythmically insistent left-hand pattern: this may consist simply of chords repeated on each of the four beats of the bar – known as **stomping** – or of faster patterns, subdividing the beat into two, characteristic of the pounding left-hand of **boogie-woogie**. (Note that the latter can be played in a straight-eight rhythm as eighth-notes, or swung to produce an aggressive kind of shuffle rhythm.)

Left-hand voicings tend to feature the 3rd and 7th of the chord, but players with exceptionally large hands may also voice this in an open position (see below). For those with smaller hands, these open-position voicings are also available in slow blues, as the chord may be arpeggiated, or through splitting the chord and playing the root first. Two-handed blues voicings are also possible, and can feature a striking – and rather dissonant – combination of major and minor 3rds. Note how these chords are notated as dominant 7ths (implying a major 3rd), with a sharpened 9th (corresponding enharmonically to a minor 3rd). You should take careful note of the resolutions and voice leading in the examples of these below.

MEETING THE DEVIL AT THE CROSSROADS

The lyrics of songs by the great blues guitarist Robert Johnson brought about the popular legend that Johnson (and maybe other blues musicians too) had signed away his soul in a contract with the devil, in return for supernatural virtuosity on the guitar. Similar legends surrounded the violinist Paganini in the 19th century. The out-of-tune chromaticism of the blues may have sounded like 'the devil's music' to listeners used to traditional hymns and classical harmonies.

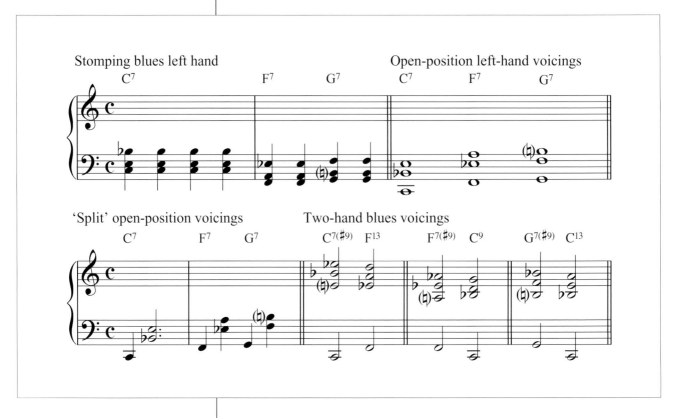

Boogie-woogie patterns tend to be limited to one or two notes sounding simultaneously, and often involve a pattern alternating between the 5th and the 6th or 7th of the chord, or arpeggiated ('walking bass') chord outlines.

Boogie-woogie left-hand patterns

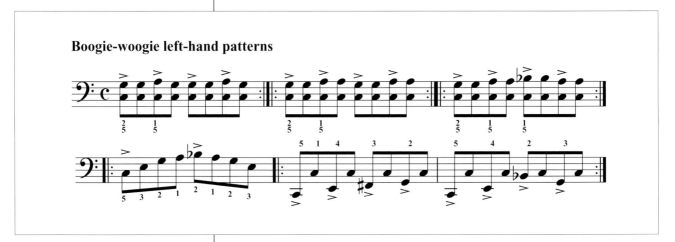

When playing or improvising licks in a blues style it is normal to make extensive use of the pianistic equivalent of 'portamento' – this is the Italian term used by classical musicians for a continuous sliding of the pitch, employed by singers and string players to make certain melodic intervals more expressive. In blues (and country) piano we create a similar effect, with a **slide** of one or more fingers between chromatically adjacent notes – sometimes also referred to in Italian as a 'glissando.' Often this involves a two-part melodic texture, where one note is held while the other moves up or down chromatically. (There may be a literal sliding of the same finger from a black to a white note, or just an impression of this, created with separate fingers playing each note, as when we pass from a white to a black note.)

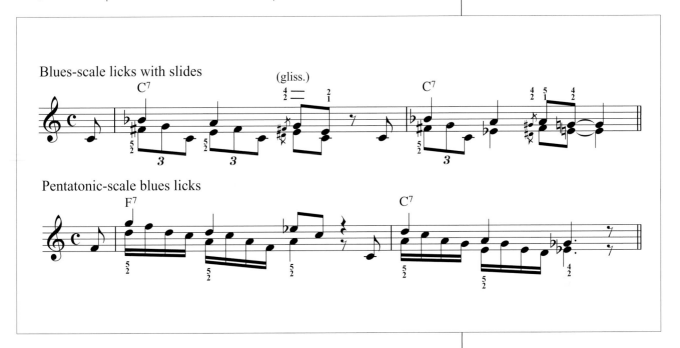

Tremolos – fast alternations of one or two notes – are also common in blues, and should be executed with vigorous rotation.

SCALE PATTERNS FOR ROCK AND BLUES

Fluency in improvising licks and riffs in rock and blues styles requires you to be familiar with the patterns of steps and leaps in different pentatonic and blues scales – especially in your right hand – as well as with the fingerings for these. The patterns below will help you to achieve this, and can be practiced regularly, just like classical scales and arpeggios. (They are fingered for the right hand only. At this stage it's better to focus on learning chord voicings in the left hand. Later you can transpose these scale patterns down a couple of octaves and refinger them for the left hand.)

These examples are all in the key of C. When you feel confident about playing them, try transposing them to related keys. In many cases you'll have to adjust the fingering to accommodate the changed patterns of black and white notes. Don't be afraid of this. In jazz, blues and rock, fingering licks and scales in your own way is part of the process by which you develop your own unique keyboard vocabulary and individual style of playing.

Pentatonic scale: three-note pattern

Pentatonic scale: four-note pattern

Blues scale: five-note pattern (1)

Blues scale: five-note pattern (2)

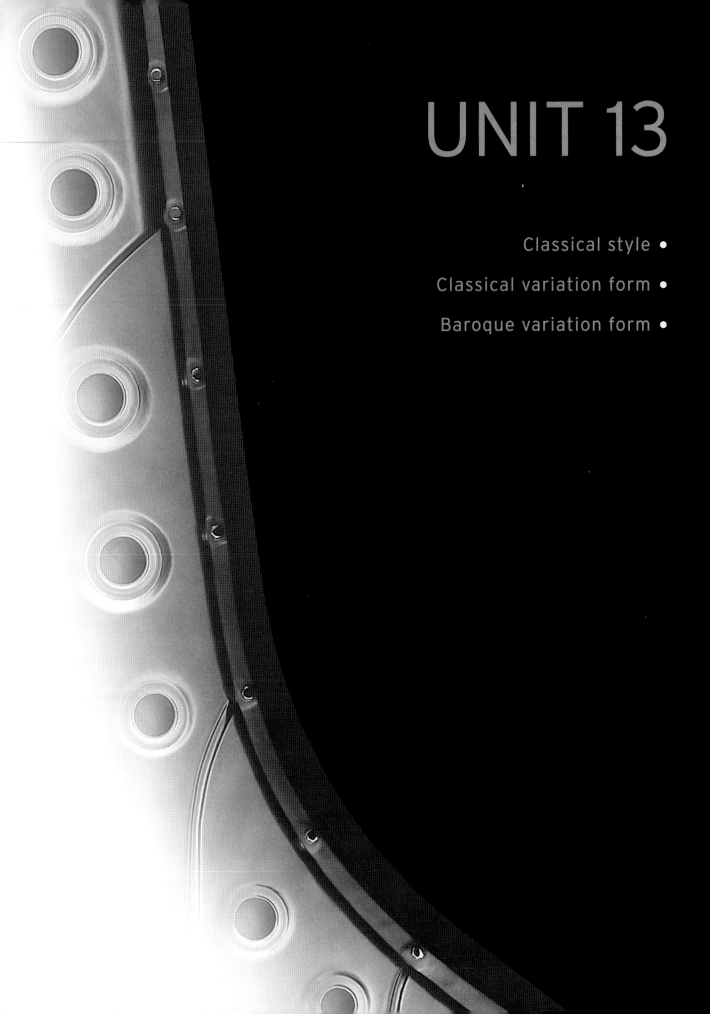

UNIT 13

Classical style •

Classical variation form •

Baroque variation form •

CLASSICAL STYLE

When musicians talk about the 'classical style', they don't mean the style of classical music as a whole, but the style of music written during what we now call the 'classical period'. This period of classical European art music corresponds roughly to the second half of the 18th century and the first quarter of the 19th century, but what really defines it is the music of the great masters of this era: Haydn, Mozart, and Beethoven, and to a certain extent Schubert.

Haydn began composing much earlier, so we can see a gradual transition in his works from the Baroque style of the early 18th century, through the style of the intervening 'Galante' period, to the mature classical style of his late works. By contrast Mozart – the famous child prodigy who died at the age of 36 – developed very quickly into a composer of the classical style, and his early death meant that he did not live past the end of the period in which this style dominated – hence the fact that he is seen as the quintessential 'classical' composer in this more specific sense.

Beethoven, on the other hand, like Haydn, stands in a more complex relationship to this style. His earliest works are classical, in much the same way as Mozart's works and Haydn's later works are, but he increasingly stretched the classical style, reaching out towards the next great phase of development of classical music: Romanticism. (The piece by Beethoven that we will be studying in Unit 16 is an example of this.) Finally, in his late works, Beethoven went even further, combining elements of Baroque and classical styles with others that anticipate both Romanticism and 20th century music. (His last five string quartets are the most celebrated examples of this – you should definitely try to hear them.) Even so, there's something in Beethoven that still clearly defines him as a composer of the classical period.

Schubert, who was born later but died young (he only outlived Beethoven by a couple of years) can also be described, in many respects, as a composer of the classical style. Many critics believe that if Schubert had lived as long as Beethoven, he would have been as great. Even in his short life he produced a large number of masterpieces, and he is especially famous for his songs (known as 'Lieder' in German). These are mostly for voice and piano. One of the best ways to develop lyrical qualities in your piano playing is to accompany singers – only then will you really grasp what it means to make an instrument 'sing'. So it's really worth teaming up with a singer to play through these.

A common misunderstanding is that works of this period are examples of the classical style because they exhibit the kind of qualities we associate with other kinds of art that we might describe as 'classical' or 'classicist' (eg, in painting, architecture, or literature). But actually this is not true, even though it can seem to be the case, especially when we contrast the music of the classical period with what came next – ie, works of the Romantic period.

'Classicism' is a term generally used to refer to the values embodied in ancient Greek and Roman civilizations – we associate it with ideals of harmony, proportion and rationality. But we shouldn't forget that at the time when these composers were working their music was seen as moving away from, rather than towards, these ideals: in fact they were viewed by their contemporaries as 'Romantics', challenging conventions and exploring new and difficult musical forms.

Even so, there is one important feature of the classical style that does justify its name, and this is the central role of **phrase divisions**. Unlike both Baroque and Romantic music, classical period music unfolds as a kind of musical argument or discourse through balancing successive musical phrases. Each phrase (of three, four or five bars) is answered by the next, and together these make a larger phrase, which is also answered by the next, and so on.

This means that classical period music should be played with a strong awareness of phrase structure – something that calls for a more subtle and restrained approach to phrasing and dynamics than later styles of music. The need to present musical structures with a high degree of clarity means that the sustaining pedal should only be employed with great care.

CLASSICAL VARIATION FORM

In this unit our focus will be on a musical form that played an important role in both the Baroque period and the classical period: it's known as **theme and variations**, or sometimes just **variation form** for short. First we'll learn the theme from one of Mozart's finest works for piano in this genre, and then we'll analyze his use of **variation technique**.

Variation form is not the most important form in classical period – that is sonata form. (For a discussion of sonata form, see the equivalent unit to this in the companion volume to this book: *The Piano Handbook*). However, in some ways variation form tells us more about how classical style relates to other kinds of music – both classical (in the broader sense) and non-classical. That's because variation technique is a kind of bridge between Baroque and classical styles, and also between classical music in general and non-classical music.

There's an important reason for this: variation technique is the aspect of composing most closely related to improvising. Nowadays we often forget that Baroque and classical composers – unlike most composers of the Romantic period and the 20th century – improvised as much as they composed, and improvising, whatever the style, generally has to make use of the same basic techniques of melodic variation to be successful. Many people fail to notice that most of the techniques we learn when studying improvised styles like rock and jazz are already in the great classics of the past – especially in variation form – and this is because the great classical composers themselves used those same techniques to improvise, before transferring them to their written compositions!

Learning to improvise in modern styles like jazz, rock and blues, apart from being great fun in itself, should make you more sensitive to these features of classical music, and this will make you a better classical pianist as well.

In classical variation form a theme is usually stated and then followed by a series of variations. These keep closely to the original phrase structure and harmonic structure of the theme, and retain certain important melodic outlines, which are nevertheless varied to produce quite new textures. Exercise 13.3 shows one of Mozart's most beautiful variation themes, but before learning it you'll benefit from practicing a couple of preliminary exercises.

EXERCISE 13.1

Here the theme is reduced to just chords, so that you can focus on precise coordination of notes within each chord, as well as on balancing dynamic levels between all parts of the texture, and on maintaining a steady rhythmic flow.

EXERCISE 13.2

Here the inner parts are removed leaving only the melodic voices. This highlights the parallel movement between the bass line and the melody, which should be brought out slightly. However the top part should remain in the foreground.

EXERCISE 13.3

Now here's the entire theme itself. The melody should sing – especially on notes falling on the beat, as these are usually longer, but the overall texture should be delicate and intimate. Note how each four-bar phrase subdivides into two-bar phrases, which in turn subdivide into one-bar phrases. Feel how the shape and movement of each phrase echoes and answers the previous one, and let this inform your expressive shaping of the music. Lifting and sinking with the wrist will enable you to vary the amount of arm weight, and thus control tone and accent while keeping relaxed. Both the repeated notes in the melody and the chordal passages at the end of each section will benefit from legato pedaling, but this must not compromise the clarity of melodic unfolding.

EXERCISE 13.3   A MAJOR THEME

Mozart

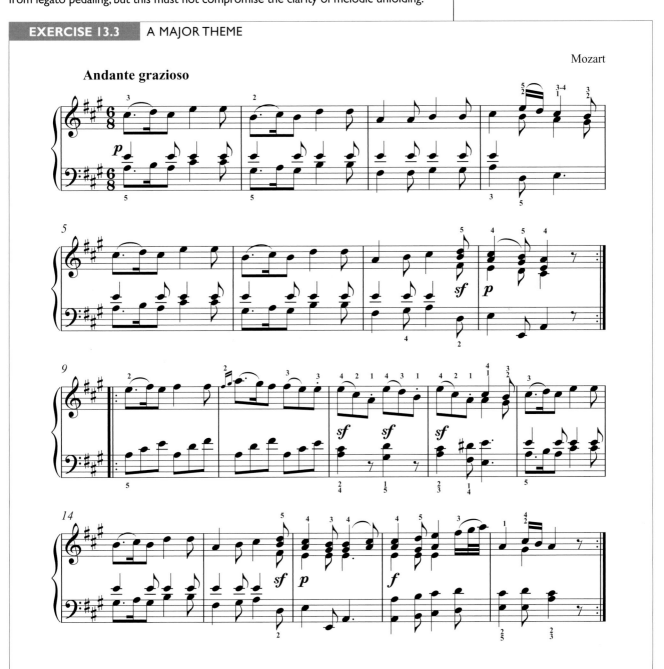

Let's take a look (left) at some of the ways in which Mozart alters this original thematic idea in his variations. We'll concentrate on just the first two bars of the theme.

These examples illustrate this with corresponding material from subsequent variations. The main point to grasp is that variation technique does more than just embellish an existing idea. Immediately below the first two bars of the theme you can see a more basic thematic skeleton. Mozart's variations work by taking this underlying structure of melody and harmony (and voice leading), and building new textures out of this. (This technique of extrapolating a melodic-harmonic skeleton is also used to analyze many aspects of classical music that are not in variation form, and was developed by the theorist Heinrich Schenker. It is significant that it has also been used to analyze how jazz relates to standards and to the harmonic formulae that jazz musicians use when improvising.) Reducing the melody to this core structure gives Mozart more freedom to develop new pianistic textures and melodic ideas that will still be heard as related to the original theme.

In the examples , the notes of the skeleton based on the original melody are circled in the variations. Note how they are carefully placed at prominent points in the line, such as the start or finish or highpoint of a phrase. Notice also Mozart's use of chromatic embellishment in Variations 1 and 3, and how Variation 2 introduces a new take on the bass line, which instead of ascending directly from A, decorated by B, to C♯, passes from A through B to C♯. This means that a decorative feature of the original theme – the B – comes to play a more structural role (connecting the bass notes). This change is taken up again in Variation 6. (See the bass notes marked with asterisks in both examples).

The brilliance of Mozart's use of variation technique lies in the fact that each variation preserves the underlying shape and structure of the two-bar phrase, but gives rise to a completely new and distinctive rhythmic and pianistic texture. (These variations are too advanced for you to learn at this stage, but when you have worked through the rest of this book, why not obtain a copy of the complete movement and learn them? You'll find them in his *Sonata in A major*, K.331.)

Now let's turn to a complete set of variations by Mozart which we can learn straight away. Here is a set based on a French tune which you may recognize, as it is also known as 'Twinkle, Twinkle Little Star'. First let's compare the opening of each variation with the opening of the tune itself. Note how the salient points of the right-hand melody in each variation preserve the outline of the tune, even though the textures vary, while the distinctive melodic leaps and most important pitches (marked with asterisks) of the original left hand are also preserved. Notice also how the variations are arranged in a sequence that highlights well the contrasts of character between them while forming a gradual build-up towards the final variation. The latter combines the faster rhythmic activity of the first variation with chords and a wider dynamic spectrum, producing a denser texture that contributes to a sense of finality.

MOZART'S DEATH

Mozart's death has been the subject of many myths and stories. Legend has it he was visited by a mysterious, nameless duke, who commissioned him to write a *Requiem*, and that from this time onwards he believed himself doomed. Another story, made popular in the play *Amadeus* by Peter Schaffer, has Mozart poisoned by Salieri, a rival composer who may have resented Mozart for his superior musical genius. The truth is that Mozart's life was far less dramatic – he spent most of his time working busily on commissions and chasing deadlines, just like any craftsman. Although he was troubled by debts, he stayed optimistic about his future right up to his death, because his opera *The Magic Flute* had been a great success. The image of him as a tragically persecuted individual says more about those who came after Mozart – the writers and critics of 19th century European Romanticism, who viewed artists as visionaries rather than as craftsmen.

CD TRACK 44

EXERCISE 13.4

Here's the complete set of variations. Notice the across-the-barline right-hand phrasing in the opening theme. This should be supported by a continuous legato in the left hand, so your two hands will need to work independently of each other here. Keep the sixteenth-notes light but singing in the first variation and do not let the sudden leaps or stretches disrupt the even flow of the right hand. The second variation requires close attention to detail, so listen carefully as each hand alternates crisp staccato with held notes; also the transition to sixteenth-notes must be executed here without disrupting the underlying pulse. The final variation will benefit from extensive practicing hands separately, at reduced speeds, paying careful attention to fingering. Accenting the first of each group of four sixteenth-notes will help to ensure rhythmic control, but keep the chords light and firm, using hand staccato. Some rotation may help when practicing alternating sixteenth-notes. Begin the theme at a speed that will allow you to play the sixteenth-notes of the variations comfortably, without any change in tempo.

EXERCISE 13.4   THEME AND VARIATIONS

Theme

Mozart

Var. 1

continued over page

EXERCISE 13.4 continued

Var. 2

GEORGE FRIDERIC HANDEL

George Frideric Handel was the most famous composer and keyboard performer of his time. Although born in Germany, he spent much of his working life in London, where his operas and oratorios were hugely successful. He introduced an unprecedented range of instrumental textures into the style of the day, and his portrayals of operatic characters in music reflect the individualism that was already a feature of English society. You can still see the house in London where he lived and composed. (More recently another famous musician, and another great improviser, the guitarist Jimi Hendrix, spent some time living in the house next door.)

CD TRACK 45

BAROQUE VARIATION FORM

Classical variation form tends to focus on the play of similarity and contrast between an original thematic idea and variations on it. By contrast, in the earlier Baroque period variation form usually consisted of a short chord progression (in the case of a **chaconne**) or melodic bass line progression (in the case of a **passacaglia**), repeated over and over again. A variety of musical textures would then be built on this, only very loosely related to the melodic material associated with its first appearance.

In contrast to the music of the classical period, Baroque music is more focused on achieving a sense of musical inevitability, and it often does this by weaving a seamless web of melody, that is highly decorative throughout. Counterpoint – the interplay of several simultaneous but independently unfolding melodic lines – is also important in music of this period, so there is less emphasis on a division into melody and accompaniment.

You should keep in mind that Baroque music was composed before the invention of the piano, so it would have been played on instruments like the harpsichord, for which no differences of dynamic level or articulation could be made through playing notes in different ways. However, some contrasts and nuances are required when performing this music on the piano, if it is not to sound unmusical. As we saw in Unit 10, unless the music has been edited, you will have to make decisions about this for yourself. You should bear in mind that performers are now expected to capture something of the original character that the music would have had in its own day – this is called 'authentic performance' – so it's worth going out of your way to hear some Baroque music actually being played on the harpsichord, and asking yourself how you might achieve an equivalent musical effect on the piano.

EXERCISE 13.5

In this chaconne only the key melodic points of the original melody reappear in the variations, but the harmony repeats in a strict and exact fashion. The opening melody reminds us that Handel was the greatest operatic composer of his age, and so should be strongly projected; this may be enhanced by arpeggiating some of the left-hand chords. Ornaments should not disrupt the metrical flow of the music, so the four-note decoration in bar two must start on the beat, just as you begin the left-hand chord. In this period dotted rhythms were often exaggerated (making the short notes shorter and the long notes longer – known as the 'French style'), and this might be effective in the first variation. The overall texture of the second and third variations should be legato, but you may still introduce some elements of staccato in the eighth-note lines, as long as these correspond to a regular pattern of articulation (e.g. on the last three eighth-notes of each bar). Variation 4 should be grandiose, with spread chords, but the top notes should still form a clear melody. In the final variation make sure the left-hand texture does not overwhelm the right-hand material. Some dynamics and phrasing have been added.

EXERCISE 13.5   CHACONNE

Handel

continued over page

EXERCISE 13.5   continued

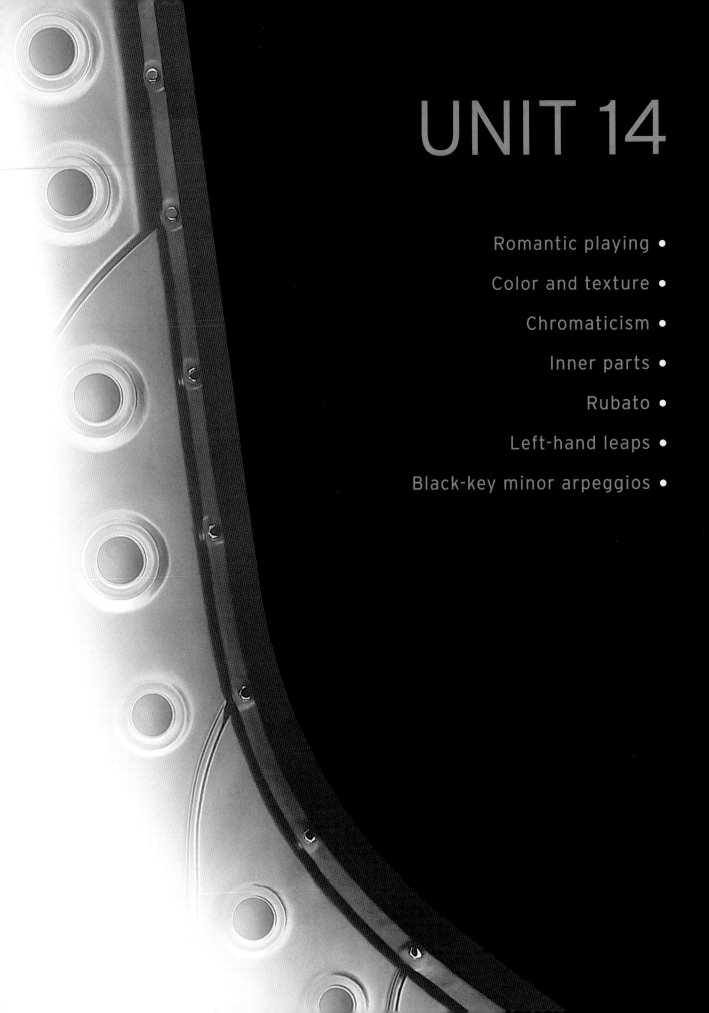

UNIT 14

ROMANTIC PLAYING

The Romantic period in classical music began in the early 19th century, and lasted through to the early 20th century. Romanticism in art, literature and music was not just about a more free exploration of individual human feelings: it was also closely connected to contemporary events, as individual countries in Europe tried to assert their political independence and national cultures. Nevertheless, it is profoundly individualistic, with an emphasis on the inner world of private reflection and personal feeling. Romantic music closely parallels literature in treating life as a narrative or drama of personal development, and music was seen as playing a special role thanks to its ability to directly reveal the unfolding emotional states of human beings. The philosopher Arthur Schopenhauer went so far as to assert that music went beyond human thought and language to directly reveal the spiritual essence of the universe. His ideas were enthusiastically adopted by one of the most important composers of the Romantic era, Richard Wagner.

Compared to earlier periods, Romantic piano music poses a new and exciting set of challenges to the pianist. This was the period in which virtuoso pianists such as Chopin and Liszt dominated the musical scene. The potential of the piano to furnish rich and complex textures was fully explored for the first time: the entire range of the modern piano is exploited, in respect of register, dynamics, and the use of the sustaining pedal. Romantic piano music requires a more forceful emotional, imaginative and physical engagement from the player, which must be balanced against the need to maintain technical control and critical awareness of how the music sounds to others. Classical period music requires the player to focus on phrasing that will articulate the phrase structure of the music, with subtle control of weight and note-length coming mainly from lifting and sinking of the wrist (and occasional use of the forearm). In contrast, the challenge in Romantic music is to combine larger-scale textures, that may sometimes require weight and movement of the player's entire upper body, with a sensitivity to the sort of expressive nuances of phrasing that typically call for great delicacy of touch. Romantic melodies are more freely constructed, and more extended, so it can be harder to perceive their points of overall departure and arrival, but these are often essential to the dramatic and narrative impact of the line. The expressive shaping of accompanying textures – using nuances of timing, dynamics and articulation – normally follows and echoes the expressive unfolding of the melody, and cannot be allowed to overwhelm it.

A great temptation in Romantic playing is over-reliance on the pedal. Because many Romantic piano textures only make sense when pedaled, it's easy to be lulled into a false sense of security, as pedaling can make flaws in technique less obviously noticeable. Remember, the discerning listener hears through the effects of pedaling to the playing itself. You must learn to do the same; it's often worthwhile practicing without pedal, even though this may make the music sound very different from how it is meant to sound.

COLOR AND TEXTURE

Romantic music puts a great deal of emphasis on the capacity of the piano to evoke the colors and textures of everyday experience. Unless you are willing to use your imagination to make sense of the connections that the music suggests, you can't know how textures should be presented. The following pieces illustrate some of the typical contrasts of such music, in which texture and mood are closely interrelated: between light and darkness, floating delicacy and robust heaviness, dreamy intimacy and introverted melancholy.

EXERCISE 14.1

This prelude by Chopin is a beautiful pearly miniature: an upbeat waltz theme is stretched out and transformed into a dreamily intense, lyrical reverie. Melody and chords merge through pedaling into a richly resonant harmonic texture, but the waltz-like simplicity of the line must still come across for the pathos of the music to be realized. The upbeat to each phrase may be slightly lingered over, but the dotted rhythm should be clearly and consistently articulated. Notice how the music falls into pairs of two-bar phrases, each of which initially establishes a sense of forward movement that is then dispersed. This use of classical phrase structure, with a clear question-and-answer character, testifies to Chopin's love of Mozart, but creates a subtle interplay between the impulse to dance and its dissolution into pure reflective lyricism.

EXERCISE 14.1	PRELUDE IN A MAJOR

Chopin

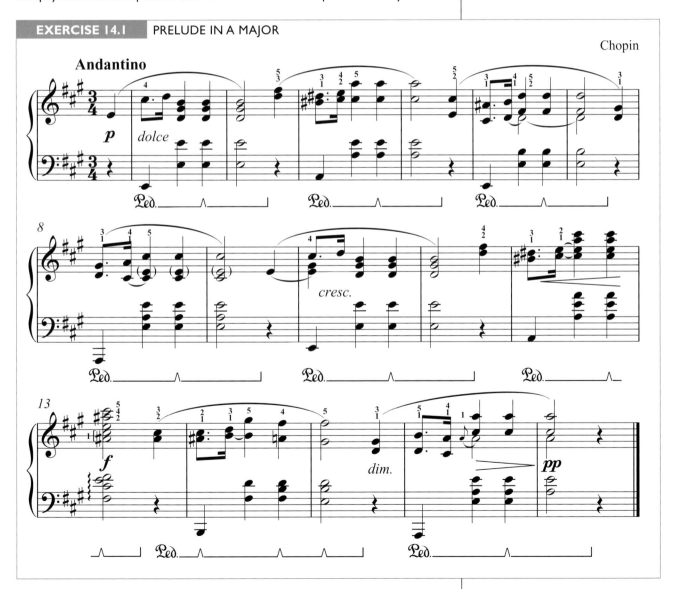

CD TRACK 47

EXERCISE 14.2

Another prelude by Chopin. Notice the extreme contrast of mood and texture created by juxtaposing thick fortissimo chords in the lower register with softer, less densely voiced harmonies in the middle of the piano. The long drawn out melody lines formed by the top notes of chords are a striking feature, and should guide your playing of the chords themselves with respect to expressive dynamics and timing. Your right hand fifth finger must be firm and subtle if it is to highlight and shape melody notes above the chords, and in the first line of music you should also listen for counterpoint between the melodic shapes of the top part and the

EXERCISE 14.2 PRELUDE IN C MINOR

bass line. Pay attention as well to the expressive harmonic effects of the chromatically descending bass line in the later parts of the piece. Dotted rhythms may vary greatly in execution: a more sharply defined rhythm will be more appropriate in the first line, with more relaxed sixteenth-notes in the later, softer passages. Note also the exact repeat of the second line, starting at a softer dynamic level: this throws the entire emphasis on dynamics and their expressive and textural consequences. Contrasts and gradual changes of dynamic level will require a controlled application or withdrawal of weight, using the entire upper body in the loudest passages.

CHROMATICISM

An important development that occurred in the musical language of classical music during the Romantic period concerned the increasing use of chromaticism, both as an expressive melodic device and as a source of unusual and striking harmonic colours. Notice how chromatically altered notes are introduced by Chopin in his 'A major Prelude' as early as the second full bar, in order to add expressive poignancy to the relationship between melody and harmony. Meanwhile in the 'C minor Prelude' the chromatically descending bass lines generate an impression of inexorable descent into gloom and despair in the second half of the piece, while the first line uses chromatic alterations to generate a wider spectrum of chords, which enable the music to move freely in and out of darker and brighter keys with passing modulations.

INNER PARTS

As we've already observed, a big challenge with Romantic music comes from the fact that we have to balance complex textures against single melody lines. Yet this can easily blind us to another important feature of Romantic music, which is that it often blurs the clear-cut distinction between foreground melody and background accompaniment that it inherited from the classical period. This is especially true in the case of a composer like Schumann, whose piano music is less overtly dramatic or virtuosic than Chopin's or Liszt's, but contains many formal and expressive subtleties that, arguably, neither of these other composers were able to achieve. More than any other composer of the Romantic era, Schumann is expert at using voice-leading in the middle parts of the texture – as opposed to the bass or top line – to create a subtle counterpoint with the principal melody line, at the same time as elaborating the harmonic texture that supports the latter.

A perfect example of this is provided by the piece below. It's preceded by two preliminary exercises aimed at helping you achieve greater awareness of the subtle and complex texture that results.

EXERCISE 14.3

This exercise focuses on the first section of the piece. The right-hand theme is given with only those accompanying elements that provide a direct counterpoint to the theme. Note that when the latter also come in the right hand in the piece they are moved into the left hand here for practice purposes. This is a common practice technique for developing awareness of inner parts and contrapuntal relationships. Such exercises should normally be practiced without pedal, and this may require the original lines to be re-fingered.

EXERCISE14.3

EXERCISE 14.4

This exercise takes a similar approach, this time to some contrapuntal elements in the second half of the piece. Once again, practice without pedal. Notice how the inner parts often echo the principal melody line – a loose form of what we call contrapuntal 'imitation.'

EXERCISE 14.4

RUBATO

Before turning to the actual piece by Schumann, let's give a little thought to what's involved in a central concept associated with Romantic interpretation, namely 'rubato'. This corresponds to the Italian for 'robbed time.' It's often interpreted in terms of the idea that when a performer treats timing loosely, by speeding up or stretching out a particular passage, a compensating adjustment immediately afterwards is called for. Thus, if the player speeds up at a certain point, then a certain amount of musical time has been 'lost,' and this must be 'put back' later, or vice versa. Yet this can be misleading. It's certainly true that some 19th century pianists – notably Chopin – employed a particular style of rubato playing in which the right hand melody was played with a certain amount of rhythmic freedom, while the left hand maintained a relatively strict pulse; this would have required compensatory adjustments to bring the hands back into alignment. However, this style of playing has not survived, and it's difficult to make it sound effective. Generally, we don't think of rubato this way, but just as a flexible treatment of the pulse itself, which is expected to return consistently to the same underlying tempo. What's more important is that the rubato in Romantic music must be appropriate to the expressive and structural implications of the music in question – and that's also true of any other kind of music that you play with a degree of expressive nuance.

EXERCISE 14.5

Now here's the piece by Schumann – one of his best-loved classics. The title translates as 'Dreaming,' and gives a good indication of its character. A soft and velvety touch is required, with sensitivity to the relationship between the melody line and supporting texture. Use sustaining pedal to accumulate enough texture to support the line – especially at high points – but do not compromise melodic clarity. Long notes in the melody – especially at the peak of a phrase – should sing, but the immediately succeeding note should generally be played extremely delicately to match the reduced volume of the preceding note after it has subsided. The prevailing

EXERCISE 14.5 | TRAUMEREI

Schumann

eighth-note movement in the melody and texture can be fluid and flexible, adjusting itself to the feeling of the moment. In chords such as that which accompanies the opening, take care that the 3rd of the chord is clearly audible – this will ensure a smoother and richer harmonic texture. Treat chromatically altered notes as expressively significant, and note that in spite of the complex textures there is a well-defined phrase structure to the music whose question-and-answer character should be clearly audible. Unusually, Schumann gives a numerical metronome marking instead of a descriptive tempo indication for the piece, but his suggested speeds are rarely followed these days, as they are considered rather too fast.

EXERCISE 14.5 continued

LEFT-HAND LEAPS

Romantic composers tend to favour right-hand melodies accompanied by richer and more complex supporting textures in the left hand. The latter often require rapid alternation between low bass-line notes and chords in the middle register of the instrument. This can be technically demanding, and often requires special practice. Exercise 14.7 offers an example of this, and is preceded by a preliminary exercise that illustrates how one can prepare the left hand for the difficult leaps and stretches involved.

EXERCISE 14.6

This exercise breaks up the left-hand alternation between bass notes and chords into an easier pattern, allowing you to practice the movements of the hand in a more carefully controlled way. Each four-note pattern corresponds to a lateral movement as the hand swings round towards the thumb, and then back again to the fifth finger.

EDVARD GRIEG

Edvard Grieg was a Norwegian composer and pianist who perfectly illustrates the nationalistic tendency within Romantic music of the second half of the 19th century. He was greatly influenced by Norwegian folk music, and transcribed many folk tunes. His music sought to capture the distinctive national spirit of his country, and to contribute to helping Norway achieve political independence.

EXERCISE 14.6

CD TRACK 49

EXERCISE 14.7

Now the piece itself: 'Albumblatt' by Edvard Grieg. Maintain a steady pace throughout. Note the restrained dynamic levels, which require a lightness of touch especially hard to achieve in the left hand, and certainly impossible if the tempo is too fast. (You don't need actually to join the bass note to the rest of the chord: it's sufficient for chord notes to be slightly softer than preceding bass notes for there to be an impression of a legato join, so keep the left-hand thumb light.) Look out for accents on weak second beats in the right-hand melody. When the melody switches over to the left hand in bar 10, make sure the right-hand chords stay well in the background. Notice how the bass notes in the opening material insistently restate the tonic – this effect is known as a 'drone' and adds to the folk music 'feel.' (With its repeated notes, accents, and intervals of a perfect 4th, it's easy to imagine this melody being played on a Norwegian folk-fiddle.) The expressive effect of the chromatic notes in the melody (eg, bar 6) should be highlighted through expressive delivery, singing tone, and legato phrasing.

THE DEVIL'S VIOLIN

Just like blues musicians, Norwegian folk fiddlers are believed to have acquired their virtuoso playing skills after entering into pacts with supernatural forces – in this case the sinister fairies that live under waterfalls in Norway. Some even say that one of the most famous Norwegian fiddle tunes was composed by the devil himself. Fiddlers were thought to have special contact with the forces of nature, while a piece of really great fiddling could also ward off evil spirits.

EXERCISE 14.7   ALBUMBLATT

Grieg

continued over page

EXERCISE 14.7 continued

BLACK-KEY ARPEGGIOS

Here are some arpeggios starting on black keys, where the minor arpeggio preserves the pattern of black and white notes found in the major, and so has the same fingering.

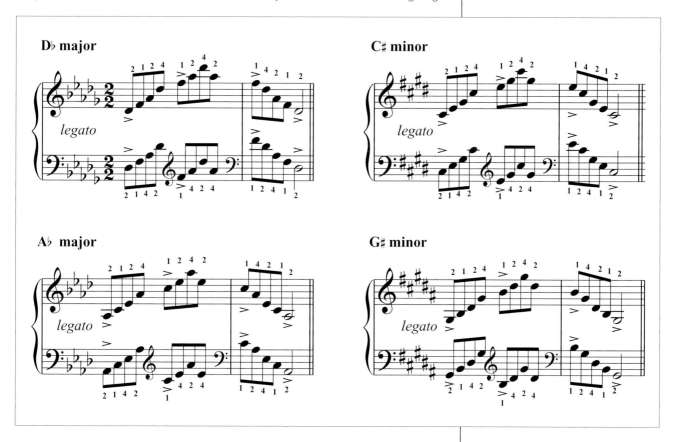

However this is not always the case with arpeggios starting on black notes (see over the page). For example B♭ major and B♭ minor have different patterns, as do G♭ major and F♯ minor, and E♭ major and E♭ minor. (F♯ minor follows the same pattern as C♯ minor, and E♭ major is similar to A♭ major, so you can work these out based on the examples above.)

Note how G♭ major and E♭ minor both only contain black notes. This means they are fingered as if they started on white notes, but the former uses third finger in the left hand, and the latter fourth finger.

Although these arpeggios are shown to only two octaves here, you should also consider practicing them to four octaves at this stage. The fingering will be the same, but you'll need to start lower down on the keyboard, and be prepared to lean over a little more towards where your hands are playing to ensure consistent release of weight as you pass across the keyboard.

As with four-octave scales, the broader sweep of a four-octave arpeggio across the keyboard will be more effective if you let the motion of your arms actively dictate the speed of passage over the keys: individual finger movements then have to keep pace with this overall momentum.

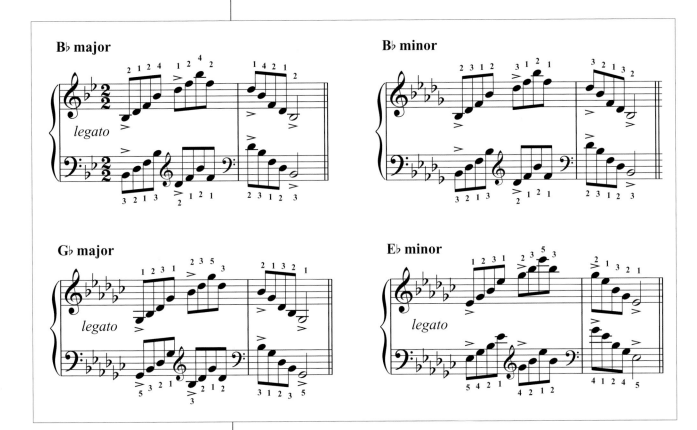

UNIT 15

COMPOSING TECHNIQUES

Composing and improvising are really two sides of the same coin. Learning to compose songs or pieces for piano will make you a more skilled improviser, and vice versa. That's because a lot of the techniques and skills you'll develop first in one of these fields are transferable to the other. So, for example, composing will teach you more about form, voice-leading, and thematic construction (the unfolding of musical ideas) than improvising, while improvising will probably give you a more vivid grasp of the effects of rhythm (eg, syncopation), texture, and register.

Another thing to bear in mind is that there's no clear boundary between composing and improvising. Imagine this. Someone sits in a room trying out ideas on the piano, as and how they come to him or her, and every so often stops to write them down, or to make changes to what's already written. Someone else writes a song lyric, gives it to a friend, who uses his guitar or piano to work out a melody for it, and who then gets together with other musicians to work out some suitable chords and riffs, and instrumental breaks, trying out the different possibilities in live rehearsal. The former corresponds to a typical way for a classical composer to work, while the latter sounds more like the process of creating a rock song. But which is more composed, and which more improvised? At first it may seem obvious, but the more you think about what's really involved the harder it is to say.

The main danger when improvising is that there's a chance you'll 'dry up.' Everything's going great, you've deployed some of your best licks and riffs, you've got into the groove and/or the mood, and your playing has developed its own momentum, so that each idea seems to naturally open the way to the next. Then, all of a sudden, you realize you don't know what you're going to do next. Crisis. A good improviser knows how to deal with this by falling back on a reserve supply of ideas that can be used over a wide range of different musical contexts. They also know it's perfectly okay to make use of these just to 'buy time' until the inspirational juices start flowing again.

With composing, this moment of creative self-consciousness can loom a lot larger. Like writers of novels and poetry, composers can easily find themselves overwhelmed by the range of choices to be made about what to write. Then they end up so confused or self-conscious that they write nothing at all. We all want to find our own unique and personal creative voice, but this only happens through composing – not through planning it out in advance. So don't invest too much significance in the initial creative choices to be made when composing. Whatever makes your music special will be largely independent of these anyway, and remember, when composing any decisions you make are reversible.

Having said this, in our time there are so many different musical possibilities to choose from that it can be useful to have a checklist of questions to run through, just to be clear about the most important choices and options waiting for you when you start a new composition.

MELODY: Do you want to write a melody with a regular ('classical') division into phrases that answer one another, or one that just unfolds continuously (like Baroque lines)? Do you want it to consist of smaller, independently identifiable motives – the sort that leave room for more open-ended development later in the piece – or not?

How will the melody relate to the supporting texture? (A good general rule: the richer or more complex the supporting texture, the simpler the melody must be to cut through it. Romantic melodies from the 19th-century and hard rock tunes are often good examples of this.)

THEMATIC STRUCTURE: A melody or motive usually functions as a thematic idea that can be contrasted with others. Do you want your piece just to explore variations on a single idea (ie, to be '**monothematic**'), or should it play off two or more ideas against each other (ie, be '**polythematic**')? If the latter, then the ideas may be simpler, but there must be a significant contrast between them.

HARMONY: If you've got a musical idea already in mind, you'll probably know its **tonality**: ie, whether it's in a major or a minor key. But do you want the whole piece – or even the whole section that contains that idea, to stay in that tonality? What happens if you switch over and play the same idea using the alternative tonality? If an idea doesn't seem to fit neatly into major or minor key harmony and scale structures, it probably means its **modal**. (We'll look at **modes** in the next section.) Occasionally you'll find that a melody modulates (changes key) in the middle, but this may only become clear when you try to harmonize it.

TREATMENT OF DISSONANCE: This is an important stylistic indicator. Remember, dissonances result when notes clash against the underlying harmony, or against each other. Broadly speaking, the stricter the rules about how you resolve these (to consonances) – usually by stepwise melodic movement – the more you'll be labeled a 'traditional' classical composer. On the other hand, the more loosely you treat them – eg, if you sometimes don't resolve them, but treat them instead as purely harmonic or textural effects – the more you'll be labeled as either 'modern' (in the 'classical' art-music sense) or as non-classical (ie, jazz, rock, etc). But there are practical reasons independent of this sort of cultural positioning for choosing a stricter or looser approach: writing a song-like piece for solo piano, using gentle textures, the harmonic textures will be very exposed, so listeners will be more sensitive to how you treat dissonances, whatever the style. If it's a pounding rhythmic texture that's part of a hardcore rock-band arrangement, they won't be.

(If you opt for a stricter style, take a look at this book's companion volume – *The Piano Handbook*. It gives more information on how to treat dissonances in classical voice-leading style, and recommends useful books on this in its detailed bibliography.)

TEXTURE: This is a very general category, but even when composing for solo piano there are things you should decide early on. Is your style going to be more **homophonic** (ie, a single melodic line in the foreground, supported by a chord-based accompaniment) or **polyphonic** (ie, several independent lines unfolding simultaneously, of roughly equal importance), or something between? (For an excellent example of something between these, see Schumann's 'Traumerei,' in the previous unit.) Also, how much of the range of the piano do you intend to use? Will your accompanying textures be dense and richly elaborated, or simpler and more transparent? Will you use octave doublings to reinforce certain notes or lines, or refrain from doing so?

FORM: It's worth being clear about what kind of overall form you want, even if you don't wish to have a detailed plan worked out in advance. We've already considered Song Form (Unit 9) and Variation Form (Unit 13). Instrumental classical music often uses other forms that are significantly more complex, such as Sonata Form: this is good for more extended compositions, especially if you wish to subject your musical ideas to extensive development. (You can read about this, too, in *The Piano Handbook*). On the other hand, rock and country styles tend to stick to song-based strophic forms (ballads), while jazz and blues are closer to variation form, cycling through a single structure again and again. The latter are good if you plan to compose something that will also serve as basis for subsequent improvisation – like a jazz 'standard' – but otherwise they may sound a bit too primitive and repetitive.

METER AND RHYTHM: In the early stages you'll probably spend a lot of time figuring out how the rhythmic aspect of your musical ideas should be written down. Don't worry, with a little experience it gets easier. It's worth being clear early on about whether you want to use classical notation for things like swing rhythms and syncopations. This may depend on what sort of musicians you're hoping to interest in playing your music. Also, how much and what kind of syncopation you employ can be a powerful stylistic indicator, and will determine whether your music is heard with reference to certain dance styles or not.

SCALES AND CHORD VOICINGS FOR IMPROVISATION

The basis for successful improvisation – especially in jazz, but also many other styles – is a firm grasp of the relationship between scale material and chord structure.

Because of the unusually large role that improvising plays in their music, jazz musicians have developed an especially effective approach, one that allows us to translate a wide range of harmonic structures – including both simple and complex ones – into raw material for melodic improvisation, without the need for the sort of careful working out composers can engage in, which is impossible when making music 'on the fly.' They've also evolved a method for creating chord voicings that allows the player to move through chord changes at speed, and in any key, without expending the time and energy a composer might need in order to work out satisfactory voice-leading.

The practical results of this are that it will give you an enormous freedom and flexibility in how you are able to make use of melody and harmony while improvising. The downside is that to enjoy those benefits you're first going to have to get to grips with some fairly demanding aspects of jazz scale theory.

In jazz, as in classical music, each scale degree defines a distinct chord, but as we've already noted there's more freedom to add chord extensions such as the 7th, 9th, 11th, and 13th. This means that jazz chords often contain all seven notes of the scale corresponding to the key of the music, so we can no longer distinguish them by which notes they contain. But in that case how do we distinguish them? Well, by thinking of the specific relationship they stand in relative to the root of the chord, which is different for each scale degree. This is very similar to taking all the notes in the scale of the key we are in, and arranging them as a scale, but starting on the root of the chord that we happen to be playing, rather than on the tonic of the scale (the 'key note') corresponding to the key we're in. It just so happens that doing this produces another kind of scale, familiar from the very earliest kinds of European classical music. This is called a **mode**.

As was mentioned earlier in this book (in Unit 6), a mode is a scale produced using only the particular notes of an existing scale, but starting and finishing on a different degree from the usual one. So if we take C major, try playing through just the white notes until we reach an octave above where we started. Now start this not just on C but also on each of the other notes in C major. In total we get seven different modes of the same scale – one for each note (including the one on C itself). Because these modes were first explored systematically by the ancient Greeks, we still use their names for them.

So for each **chord function** (ie, each chord based on a particular degree of the scale of the key of the music), the resulting chord notes translate automatically into an equivalent mode. We can practice these modes like scales, but it's more fruitful to familiarize yourself with them from the outset through improvising over the corresponding chords. When you do this, listen carefully to how different notes take on particular qualities and colors as a result of their relation to the harmony. This is also the best way to become aware of which notes count as 'avoid' notes for each mode. (Remember, these are notes that are regarded as a bit too dissonant even for jazz, so they shouldn't be too prominent, and should normally be resolved by step).

More sophisticated jazz musicians then go on to perform a similar operation with the jazz minor scale – building a separate mode on each of its degrees. Although this does provide some scales that could be used for improvising over chords in a minor key, that's not why they do it. (Jazz is rarely actually in a minor key, even though it often uses minor chords and scales that work well over these.) It's because it produces alternative chords (and related scales) that correspond to the more advanced harmonies in major keys that they want to make use of, for variety and contrast.

The examples below show modes derived from both the major and the jazz minor scales, over the corresponding chord extensions. The major-key modes are arranged in a sequence corresponding to the most common kind of jazz progression, in which roots of chords descend by intervals of a perfect 5th, and are all shown in the key of C major. The jazz minor modes are listed as individual chords/scales, however, rather than as part of any progression. This is because they are not all given as modes of the jazz minor scale on C, but are based on whichever jazz minor scale furnishes the notes in that mode that enable it to also function as an advanced chord function in C major. That way you can see how they can be inserted into the major-key sequence as substitutes for chords and scales on corresponding scale degrees there. Note that we identify each mode by the particular scale degrees chromatically altered from the major scale starting on the same note (as in the example below).

(**Avoid notes** – notes that clash with the underlying harmony – are marked with asterisks in the diagram below. Listen out carefully for how they sound over different voicings of the same chord, and experiment with different ways in which they can be resolved melodically.)

Major-key modes and chords

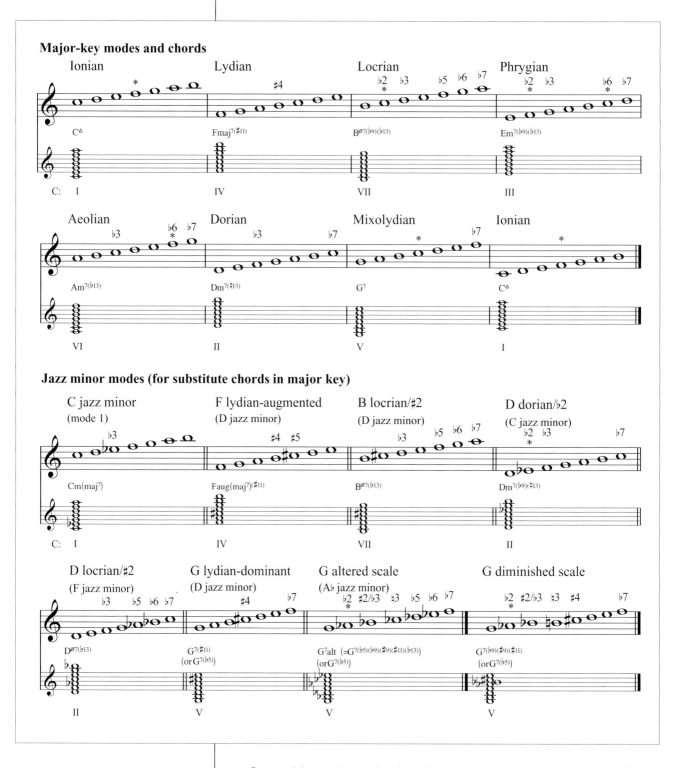

Jazz minor modes (for substitute chords in major key)

Pay special attention to the **altered scale** mode: this is one of the most effective alternative scales over dominant harmony, and is widely used in modern jazz. Because there's no unaltered 4th or 5th step of the scale, the D♭ can function as either a flattened 5th (as in blues, and tritone substitutions) or a sharpened 4th (as in Lydian harmony), and this makes the scale especially adaptable. (Hence it can also be written as C♯, with the C♭ then written as B-natural. Writing these as flats shows the derivation of the scale from a mode of Ab jazz minor, but in jazz highly chromatic scales like this tend to be notated using whatever combination of accidentals are simplest to read.)

Replace both the Ab and Bb in the altered scale with a single A-natural and you're left with a six-note scale, made up entirely of whole-tone steps. It's the **whole tone scale.** You can use it over dominant harmony, in place of the Lydian dominant, treating the chord as V7b5. (It's often associated with 'impressionist' classical composers such as Debussy – see Unit 16).

The last scale shown above, the **diminished scale,** is not a mode of the jazz minor scale at all, but an eight-note ('octatonic') scale, based on alternating semitones and tones. Like the altered scale, it raises the level of tension in dominant harmony. (It has also been used widely by 20th century classical composers, as it can generate a more intensely chromatic feel in which the sense of a tonal centre is suspended.)

Now let's consider the kind of chord voicings jazz pianists use to support their own improvising on these scales. First, we'll consider **two-handed voicings,** which usually consist of three or four notes, normally with one in the left and the rest in the right. Note how a three-note voicing always consists of the 3rd and 7th of the chord over the root, as these are both necessary to identify the functionality of the chord, while with four-note voicings you may opt to add the 5th or 9th (shown here as a filled notehead). When we move through the major-key progression already given above, using these two-handed voicings, all parts except the bass alternate between stepwise descending movements and being restruck in the next chord, so the result is an exceptionally regular and smooth pattern of voice-leading – see the example below. All the improviser has to do is memorize the sequence of downward steps alternating between the upper parts, and learn to apply that sequence freely in different keys. With practice this very quickly becomes automatic.

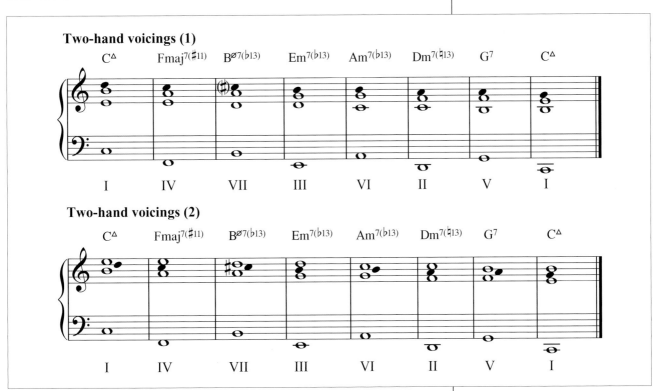

Alternatively, we can use **left-hand voicings**. Here all of the harmony is in the left hand. Smooth progressions can be achieved by alternating between two basic chord shapes (marked in the diagram below as 'a' and 'b'), shifting position down the keyboard (making sure the right black notes are included, of course). We get a different sequence depending on which shape we start with. Note how either the top or the bottom two voices descend by step while the others stay fixed.

Concentrate on the II-V-I progression at the end: this is by far the most important part of the sequence. You can also practice it by itself. When improvising we sometimes base our voicings of other chords on just this progression, treating other chords as variations of II (ie, minor 7th), V (ie, dominant 7th) or I (major), in order to simplify things further, and many jazz standards stick to just these chords. However, it's just here that the underlying voice-leading pattern may be harder to grasp, as we tend to change it slightly to get a more powerful cadence effect. (That's one reason for studying the longer sequence too.) Instead of allowing the 9th of the II chord (E in C major) to drop by step to the 5th of the V chord (D), we tend to hold it over to produce the 13th (or, if you prefer, added 6th) of V. This adds to the tension of V, and so makes for a more effective resolution to I. In both sequences there are alternative options for chord I – we may include or omit the 9th, depending on whether we want some of the tension to be maintained, or prefer a stronger resolution. (To hear how the underlying voice-leading progression carries through to the end, use the voicing for V in the brackets, followed by the first option for I. However in practice you will generally want to use the other, 'altered' shape for V. Notice that this then allows you to simply shift the whole shape of the chord down a step to one of the voicings for I. Nothing could be easier!)

These moves will also become automatic with practice, but you'll need to spend time familiarizing yourself with how they look and feel in different keys. Keep to the same fingering wherever possible, even if this means taking thumb and fifth finger up on to black keys.

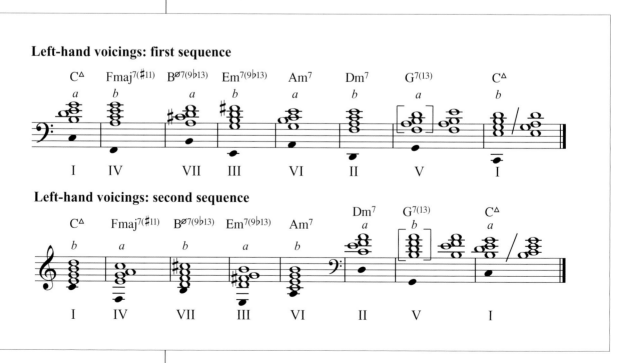

Left-hand voicings: first sequence

Left-hand voicings: second sequence

Notice how in the above example VII and III have the 9th sharpened from the normal mode of C major, giving us C♯ and F♯ respectively. These notes would otherwise corresponding to a flattened 9th over the bass note, and this dissonance is generally considered too strong over anything apart from V. Play the same chords through in the left hand with C-natural and F-natural instead: they don't sound too bad without the root, but try playing them in the right hand with the roots (shown beneath as filled noteheads) in the left, and you'll hear that they really clash. Raising these notes means that VII corresponds to the alternative scale option in the first example above, ie, the Locrian mode with raised 2nd. Meanwhile III will take either Aeolian or Dorian mode on E, thus 'borrowing' the functionality of a VI or a II chord. Likewise we may opt to raise the 4th over chords I and V (also an avoid note), and this will translate into using Lydian (on C) over I, and Lydian Dominant (on G) over V. However, these chords will normally still be recognized as I and V owing to their central role in the all-important II-V-I progression. (There's something similar for VII with the two-handed voicings already shown. Try playing them with C♯, and then C-natural, and feel the difference.)

So how do the two types of voicing compare? **Two-handed voicings** give a clearer statement of the chord, as they include the bass, and are less densely packed. This makes them more suitable for ordinary solo work, but the top voice may have to correspond to a harmonically significant note of the melody line. This can be constraining, especially if you want to improvise fast licks. On other hand, the **left-hand voicings** shown here, associated with pianists such as Bill Evans, free up the right hand to do whatever it wants, but there's a price for this: unless you're playing alongside a jazz bassist you'll lose the bass line. (Experienced listeners still 'hear' the bass as the implied root of each chord, but its absence from the actual voicing weakens the colors that distinguish the chords from one another.)

The denser packing of notes required to fit under a single hand means left-hand voicings have a more 'scrunchy' feel, but as with many jazz voicings, the precise coloristic effect depends on exactly where the particular chord lies in relation to the different registers of the piano. (That's why the choice of key can greatly affect which voicings a pianist uses for a particular set of chord changes.) The lower down you go, the more muddy the resulting texture. Above the middle of the piano they take on a brighter, harder character, but may fail to provide the fullness of sound needed to support expressive melodic lines. An experienced player will shift between these two kinds of voicing to suit the demands of the moment. (For more on advanced jazz harmony and voicings, see Unit 18.)

BEBOP

These techniques let you play around more freely with scale material, because this material stands in a predefined relationship to the underlying chord structure. Think of this as a projection of harmonic color (and functionality) into line. They emerged at a time when jazz was evolving in the direction of a style known as **bebop**.

From the mid 1940s through to the 1950s, bebop (or **bop** for short) moved away from the solid four-beats-in-a-bar pattern that gave a clear outline to rhythm, melody and harmony in previous jazz. It replaced this with a more fragmented, freer approach to melodic improvisation, and made more use of alternative harmonizations, like those shown in the previous section (notably tritone substitutions in II-V-I progressions, and the flattened 5th in dominant harmony). The rhythmic character of the music changed in the direction of a faster, more aggressively 'edgy' feel, with a clear beat often only audible in the cymbal ride pattern of the drums, and in the bass.

Bebop musicians like to introduce an extra note into scales, so that playing two notes to a beat (ie, eighth-notes) results in harmony notes falling consistently on the beat. For example over V they'll often play a scale with both the flattened 7th and the major 7th, while over the I they'll play a major scale with an additional sharpened 5th alongside the normal 5th.

Bebop appeals more to serious jazz aficionados than to ordinary listeners and players. You'd be well advised to hold back from attempting to improvise in this style until you've gained a great deal of confidence with the musical materials and techniques of jazz. But there's nothing to stop you from using the freer approach to playing over chords that goes with this style to get started with improvising. In fact it's an ideal way of getting quickly to the point where you're less dependent on a fixed palette of riffs and licks, and can improvise around existing melodies much more freely, as you no longer need to keep track of the original melody for your harmonic points of reference. Jazz musicians have a special term for the practice of extracting just the chord progressions (or 'changes') from a well-known melody, in order to be able to improvise more freely on these: it's called **contrafaction**. Having said that, you should be aware that the original melody can still serve as an important source of structure for your improvisation, as we'll see in the next section.

ARRANGING (1): EMBELLISHING A MELODY

Take a look at the melody below. It's one of the most famous melodies of the 1930s jazz era: 'Summertime' by George Gershwin. Like many famous songs of that period, it's become a **standard** – a melody that, along with its distinctive chord changes, can serve as a basis for jazz improvisation. Standards were originally published as sheet music: in song arrangements for voice and piano. These were then passed to professional arrangers. However, jazz musicians often work straight from a **lead sheet** – a simplified notation of the song, showing just the melody and chord symbols.

For now, though, we'll concentrate on how a melody in an existing arrangement can provide a basis for improvised embellishment. For this reason the version of 'Summertime' below already has a left-hand part – a simplified version of the original two-hand accompaniment. (Of course you're free to try replacing this with your own harmonization, based just on the chord symbols, perhaps using the examples of left-hand and two-hand voicings given above. You can also get hold of the original sheet music and try incorporating more of the original piano part.)

Gershwin was a sophisticated, classically trained composer. His chord structures reflect classical as well as jazz conventions, and this contributes to the exceptional expressive power of the song. So appreciating the skilful harmonic construction of 'Summertime' will help you take advantage of the possibilities for improvising around its melody and chords.

Take a look at the version of the song below. The chords for the first phrase suggest A jazz minor (with the 6th and 7th from the major), but with the second phrase there's a shift (in bar 7) to chords that suggest A natural minor (in which 6th and 7th are both flattened from the major). The third phrase takes us back to the tonality of the opening, which is reasserted through dominant harmony (in bars 9-10). But the fourth and final phrase of the section shifts again (in bars 15-16), this time implying the Dorian mode on A (with major 6th but minor 7th). In classical terms this implies a cadence in G major, but when it comes the G chord is a dominant 7th, suggesting C major instead. As C major is the relative major of A minor, it prepares us nicely for the return of the latter with the repeat. (Note how the G chord in bar 16 keeps the unsharpened 11th even though this is an 'avoid' note. This is because raising the C to C♯ would give us the major 3rd of a scale on A, which would disrupt the longer-term emphasis on A minor.)

This already tells you something about what scales can be played over the chords, but you need to also take account of the music's stylistic, expressive and dramatic implications. The general mood and content of the song relate closely to the blues, while the opening phrase outlines notes from the minor pentatonic scale on A, a scale which you can find embedded in both the blues scale and the Dorian mode on A. The distinctive blues sound arises when the melody uses flattened versions of the scale degrees present in the chords – typically a minor 3rd over a major triad; but wait a minute, here we don't have major-key harmony! Yet it's enough to use the blues scale or Dorian mode over these chords, as both scales contain the minor 7th, whereas the chords have the major 7th. Adding the flattened 5th of the blues scale will have a similar effect, owing to the presence of the normal 5th in the harmony.

The shift to chords based on A natural minor in bar seven calls for a corresponding adjustment in the line. If you use an A natural minor scale here, it's equivalent to playing Dorian mode over the D minor chord and Lydian mode over the F chords. Once again, embedded in these is a single pentatonic scale (minor pentatonic on D = major pentatonic on F), to which you can also add the flattened 5th for a blues scale on D. (This sets up a parallel to the treatment of the first phrase, one step lower on the circle of fifths. In classical harmony it would count as a modulation to the subdominant.)

In bar eight the chromaticism of the diminished 7th chord can be projected into the melody by using a diminished scale on A, while putting Lydian dominant or altered mode (on E) over the final dominant chord in bar ten adds tension, producing a stronger sense of arrival when the music returns to the opening material.

In the coda, scales are implied by a series of perfect (V-I) cadences in major keys, descending the circle of fifths. However, the final perfect cadence brings us back to A minor through a V chord with a major 13th (or added 6th), and it would make sense to use Lydian dominant over this chord. (All of these scales have been marked above the music in the arrangement given below.)

In a moment we'll consider some of the possibilities for embellishment and improvisation that this melody affords. But note that although it's written out in a way that makes it look like a classical melody, with a strict rhythmic relationship to the underlying meter, this is not how it should be played. As with swing, it's assumed that the performer will treat the rhythm flexibly. In this case, given the downbeat mood of the song, we'd expect some **leaning on the beat** (ie, delaying notes so they come just after the beat, creating a dragging feel). So play the song first without any melodic embellishments. This is the best way to develop a feel for a song's shape and character, and will itself suggest possibilities for improvising.

CD TRACK **50**

EXERCISE 15.1

The aim here is to achieve the right expressive feel through a rhythmically loose delivery of the right-hand melody. First practice the two hands separately, but when playing just the melody make sure that you still feel a steady half-note beat: it can help to tap the pulse with a foot while playing. At the same time follow your

EXERCISE 15.1 | SUMMERTIME

Gershwin

instincts about how the melody can be made to fall around the beat rather than on it. When you're confident about this, introduce the left-hand chords strictly on the beat, and let the right hand play freely against them.

Now we're ready to start embellishing and improvising on Gershwin's tune. There are many different techniques we can use, but the three most basic ones are the following: (1) **filling in** diatonic steps with chromatic notes, and larger leaps with stepwise movement, (2) **leaping past** an expected note by an extra step before moving back to it, and (3) **breaking up** the line into smaller, isolated rhythmic fragments. These are all illustrated in the extract below:

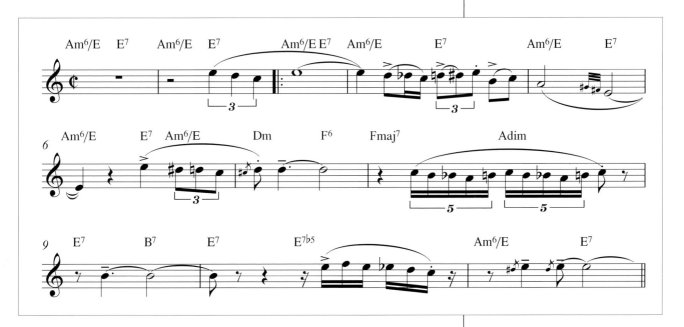

These techniques allow you to embellish the surface details of the original melody, and this still involves sticking quite closely to the original tune. But if you want to improvise more freely – by exploiting the idea of projecting harmony into scale material as described above – then you'll need to find other ways of relating this to the melody. There's a golden rule here: the deeper your understanding of how the original melody works, the more freedom you will have to improvise around it creatively. Let's see a few examples of how this works in practice by taking a closer look at the Gershwin tune.

Firstly, notice how there are four four-bar phrases, and each of the first three phrases begins with a two-note figure leading from an upbeat to a held note, followed by a dotted-note figure that reiterates one or more notes before coming to rest on held notes again. In these phrases the held notes provide points of harmonic arrival for the melody, which proceeds through a combination of variation and repetition of a basic falling shape. By contrast the fourth phrase introduces a new, rising figure, with a brighter harmonic orientation, but at the very end this is reversed as the melody once again falls and the original minor-key tonality reasserts itself.

These points form a **melodic skeleton** that gives us useful landmarks (see below). (In the coda the top notes of the chords form a stepwise chromatic descent that provides a similar framework.) By treating them as **goal-notes** which we aim for when improvising we ensure that there's an audible relationship to the basic outline of the original tune, and a good fit with the harmony, even when we're using scales freely to explore our own riffs and licks.

Secondly, we can pick up on the contrast in the original tune between the varied repetitions that link the first three phrases together and the final phrase. We can use this to give overall dramatic shape to our treatment of the 16-bar structure, say, by treating the first three phrases as opportunities for free embellishment while leaving the fourth phrase relatively unembellished. This makes the latter into a kind of refrain. After cycling through the structure several times we might then reverse the treatment: an effective close to the improvisation would be a final straight rendition of the first 12 bars, climaxing with an opening out of the last four-bar phrase into free improvisation that then runs over into the coda.

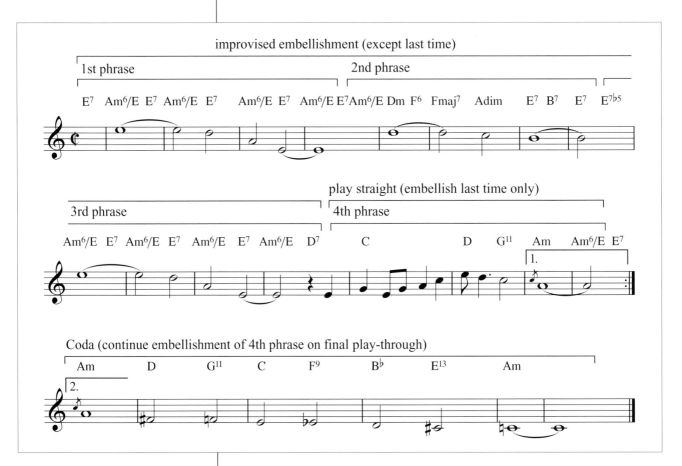

A third aspect involves noticing how the first and second half of each phrase of the original follow a question-and-answer pattern. Much improvisation naturally tends towards this anyway, so it's a feature we'll definitely want to exploit. For example, we might set up an internal pattern, freely embellishing the upbeat figure at the beginning of each four-bar phrase with pretty much anything we want, but always making sure this is echoed or answered by related material in place of the original dotted-rhythm figure.

The key here – as always – is looking beneath the surface of the original song to identify open-ended structuring principles. These will guide your improvising without constraining your creative freedom.

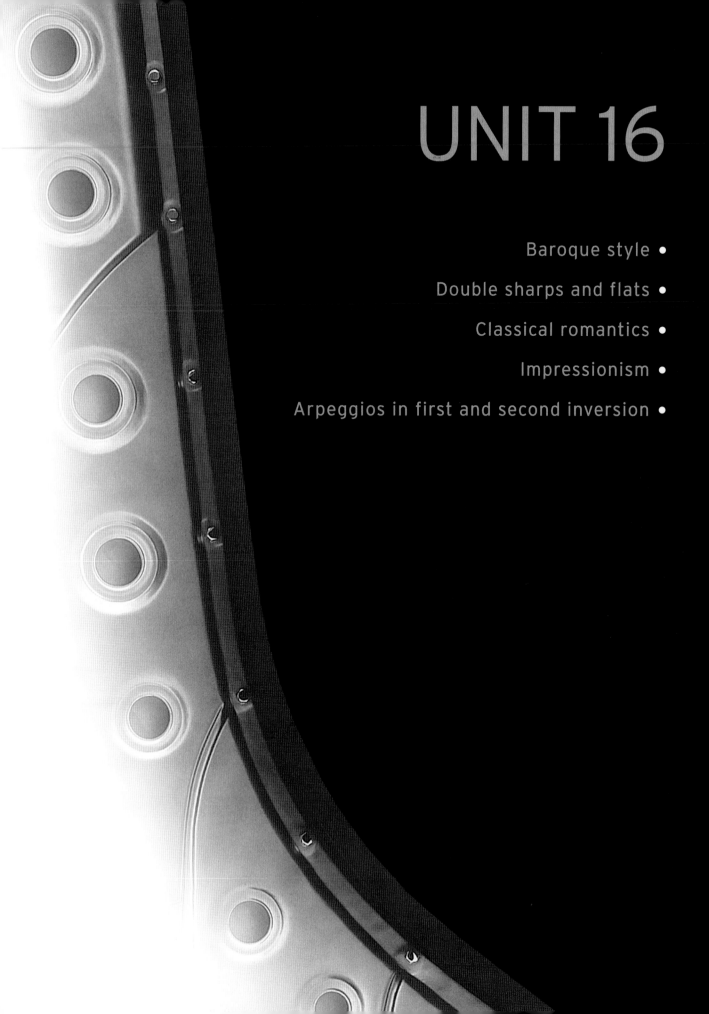

UNIT 16

Baroque style •

Double sharps and flats •

Classical romantics •

Impressionism •

Arpeggios in first and second inversion •

BAROQUE STYLE

The Baroque period in music lasted from the early 17th century through to the first half of the 18th century. It saw the full emergence of the modern system of tonal harmony, as well as an increased interest in virtuoso instrumental writing and dramatic forms of musical expression. Melody lines often unfold continuously without clear phrase divisions, and were extensively embellished through decorative ornamentation by performers. The greatest composers of this period were two Germans, Johann Sebastian Bach and George Frideric Handel, but many important developments originated in Italy. The French composer Rameau laid the foundations for modern chord theory with his treatise on harmony.

Baroque keyboard music was mostly written for the harpsichord, whose dynamics and articulation could not be varied. Hence there are no expressive markings in the score and you must decide what is appropriate. The instrumental music of this period often reflects popular dance forms, so a strong sense of meter and pulse is called for even in highly decorative passages.

THE BAROQUE ARTS

The term **Baroque** refers both to a distinctive style and a historical period of classical art music, but is also used to characterize other art forms, especially painting and architecture. In general it emphasizes dynamic and fluid forms, and dramatic expression. In contrast to the preceding Renaissance period (which is essentially 'classicist' in its pursuit of harmony and proportion), the Baroque seeks to immerse us in the sensual imagery and drama of human experience. With the late Baroque it gave way to a lighter, more playful style, known as **Rococo**, whose equivalent in music is thought by many to be the **Galant** style.

CD TRACK 51

EXERCISE 16.1

Here's one of J.S. Bach's finest slow movements for solo keyboard. It's based on the distinctive rhythm of the sarabande – a stately, dignified dance that stresses the second beat in every bar. This effect is conveyed by the dotted rhythm at the start of bars 1 and 2 (and in later passages), and by the regular appearance of fuller chords on the second beat. Be careful: if you opt for a tempo even slightly too slow, you'll lose the sense of a regular quarter-note pulse, which is essential for feeling the dance rhythm, but if you go too quickly you won't manage the fast runs in bars 13 and 14 while keeping to time. Try working through the piece and thinking about dynamics and articulation for yourself. Afterwards compare your ideas to the suggestions below.

EXERCISE 16.1 SARABANDE

J.S. Bach

continued over page

Let's consider how we might develop a satisfying interpretation of this piece. The main challenge with music of this period is that if we're sensitive both to historical style and to the expressive potential of the modern piano, we find ourselves constantly being pulled simultaneously in two opposing directions. On the one hand, we can be 'purists' and focus on achieving an authentic 'period' style — aiming to reproduce as nearly as possible how the music would have sounded in the composer's day. On the other hand we can concentrate on giving a rendition that makes the most of the expressive potential of the modern piano, which is far greater than that of the harpsichord. Most sensible performers opt for a compromise, but finding the ideal balance is a delicate process. If your performance veers even a little too far in one direction or the other it may arouse critical condemnation from those who profess to be connoisseurs. Even so, the range of successful modern performances of this music proves there's room for a variety of approaches. Personal taste must play its part.

ARTICULATION: Which parts should be played legato, which staccato? With slow movements especially, many pianists opt just to play legato, in order to highlight the lyrical qualities of the melody. Sometimes this is dictated by more specific features: on the piano we expect long notes to be held, so they keep on sounding, while decorative ornaments sound fussy played staccato and very fast runs are only playable legato.

Nevertheless, musicians seeking a strong 'period' feel may introduce some staccato passages to counterbalance the use of expressive legato phrasing. The idea is to bring the overall texture slightly closer to that of a harpsichord, whose notes die away faster but aren't automatically damped, making them something between legato and staccato on the piano.

In bars 1 and 2, however, this would definitely not work: in the right hand the dotted rhythm needs to be firmly enunciated, which requires notes to sound on, and the thirty-second-notes are too ornamental; the sixteenth-notes have expressive leaps whose effect is lost unless played legato.

By contrast the thirty-second-notes in bar 3 provide a good example of where it would be appropriate (but not obligatory) to use a little staccato: they are more integral to the line, rather than purely ornamental, but are limited to stepwise movement. Hence we might play them staccato, but with the surrounding sixteenth-notes still legato. As bars 4 to 6 in the example below demonstrate, we may apply a similar logic in other passages, providing the line is not too close to a dramatic high point:

On the other hand, it may sometimes be preferable to reverse the effect, juxtaposing legato thirty-second-notes with sixteenth-notes that are detached but not too short (what we call 'non legato' – ie, not smooth but not quite staccato either), as in the following extract. This can produce a 'speaking' (parlando) effect, reminiscent of recitative passages in Baroque operas and oratorios:

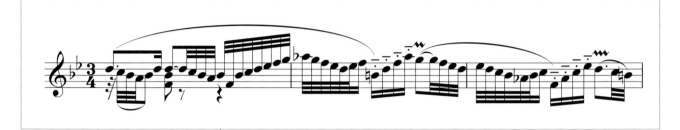

DYNAMIC SHAPING: The overall dramatic shape of Baroque music is often less clearly defined than in later styles, with no single overarching climax. Yet individual passages do usually rise towards or fall away from highpoints, and this can be matched with dynamics.

In the first section the first four bars outline a descending trajectory from the opening D to the D an octave lower in bar 4, and this could be matched with a gradual drop in volume. This is followed by a sequence of rising phrases, each building towards a held chord, each ascending a little further, up to the high G in bar 8. The last four bars begin by dropping back down, before outlining a broader ascending and descending arch, ending on a cadence in the dominant key. (Notice that the modulation to the dominant key is accomplished in bar 9, which makes this is an important point of harmonic arrival.)

The second section reintroduces the opening dotted-note motif, with fuller chords and more exuberant decoration, both of which call for more expansive dynamics. The opening theme is alluded to in bar 16, perhaps suggesting a more restrained moment, while bars 17 and 18 outline a descending sequence, with diminished harmony in bar 17 that calls for dramatic dynamics. The diminished and extended harmonies in bar 19 create a rise in tension, but the C minor chord on the second beat of bar 20 could just as well be dramatized with a sudden drop in volume. The melodic material in both hands in bars 21-24 will require expressive shaping to do justice to its angular leaps, and calls for consistent intensity. The final four bars begin low down with a phased build-up, culminating in diminished harmony on the third beat of bar 26, and the resulting tension is only released with the ascending run and subsequent descent in bar 27.

PEDALING: Musicians who emphasize 'period' authenticity will be cautious about using the sustaining pedal, even in slow movements such as this. However, if you incline towards modern pianistic lyricism and you play the whole piece legato, then the sustaining pedal can be a useful aid. Pedaling repeated-notes figures such as the opening motive is the only way to make these sound really smooth. Quieter chords will have a softer edge to them, and louder ones will be more resonant, with direct pedaling. There are many places in the first section where important melody notes are **anticipated** (ie, first sounded just before the beat and then reiterated on it), and these repetitions can also only be joined smoothly by using pedal.

DECORATION: Bach is exceptional for a Baroque composer, as most of the decorative elements in his music are already written out as part of the melody line. In this case, apart from realizing the ornament symbols in the score in the standard way (see Unit 11), you'll need to add little in the way of additional embellishment, though 'spreading' chords – ie, playing the notes in a rapidly ascending **arpeggiation** (sounding like a harp) – would have been a standard feature in Bach's day.

We may also use this to vary the repeat of each section. There are two possibilities. It's the chords appearing on the second beat of the bar that call for this most, so we can play them straight the first time, and spread them the second time. Or, for a rather florid effect, we might spread these chords the first time, but in addition spread chords on the first beat of the bar in the repeat.

Arpeggiating chords should not disrupt the pulse. If the final, top note of the spread is a melody note, you must decide whether it should come on the beat, with the rest of the chord coming slightly ahead of the beat, or after the beat, in which case the spread may begin on the beat, which will be marked by the sounding of the bass note. The former will be more appropriate to rhythmically strict melodies, while the latter may make for a looser, more extemporized feel.

NUANCES: A striking feature of this piece is the frequent appearance of large descending melodic leaps (usually a 7th), used for expressive effect. The percussive nature of the piano means large melodic intervals often have to be treated with special care, to avoid losing the sense of connection and passage between the notes. It often helps to delay the second note slightly, and you must ensure a careful match of dynamics between the two notes. This is especially the case with descending leaps, as the second note may lie in a louder register than the first, whereas the expressive character of large falling intervals usually requires that we perceive the first note as considerably more intense than the second. Lengthening the first note slightly also helps the listener to experience this.

DOUBLE SHARPS AND FLATS

Some keys require that a note that is already sharpened be raised chromatically by an additional half-step, or that a note that is already flattened be lowered chromatically by an additional half-step. In the first case this is indicated using a **double sharp** sign, in the latter as a **double flat**. Notice that whereas a double sharp looks like a letter x, a double flat is just two flat signs next to each other. A return to a single sharp or flat is indicated by a natural sign followed by a sharp or flat sign, whereas a return to a note not sharpened or flattened at all is shown by just a single natural sign (as there's no 'double natural'). Double sharps and flats only appear as accidentals – they are not used in key signatures. You will encounter some examples of double sharps and double flats in the next two pieces.

CLASSICAL ROMANTICS

If you've worked through Units 13 and 14, then by now you should have a good feel for the differences between classical period music and Romantic period music, and for how we adjust our way of playing to suit these different kinds of classical art music.

As we've already noted, the distinction between 'classical period' and 'Romantic period' can be slightly misleading: the term 'classical' usually refers to classicism in the sense of ancient Greek and Roman artistic ideals, but the period of Western art music most influenced by these is actually that of Renaissance music.

Here, then, it is being used much more loosely, to emphasize the fact that music written in what is sometimes called the 'classical style' achieved a higher level of clarity of structure than in previous or subsequent periods. But this is still a little misleading, as it suggests that the music of this period corresponds to a fixed style. It would be more true to say that this style itself corresponded to a period of transition in European music: a gradual process of evolution from the preceding Galant style to the musical language of 19th century Romanticism.

We can already see elements of Romanticism emerging in Beethoven's early period; perhaps the most striking example is his famous 'Moonlight' Sonata (see below). Here we see a shift of emphasis away from the interplay of musical ideas and towards exploring emotion and atmosphere in music for their own sake, with simpler but more dramatically expressive melodies, and more complex, less clearly defined textures that deliberately exploit the sustaining pedal. (It wasn't Beethoven's idea to call it the 'Moonlight' Sonata, but his publisher's. The latter sensed that Romanticism was in the air and thought it a good idea to give the piece a suitably evocative title.)

CD TRACK 52

EXERCISE 16.2

The tempo marking means 'slowly and broadly,' but this refers to the half-note pulse rather than the triplet eighth-notes, which are quite flowing. Don't be deceived by the fact that the triplets appear at the start in the right hand and with no melody line. (The melody enters in bar 5, with the dotted rhythm and repeated notes of G♯.) They are an accompanying texture, and should stay in the background. From bar 5 there are three levels to the texture: right-hand melody (foreground), right-hand triplets (background), and left-hand bass line. The last of these should be less prominent than the melody, but more clearly audible than the triplets, so your right hand must be simultaneously louder and softer than your left hand. Note the combination of dotted rhythm and triplet, dividing a quarter-note into quarters and thirds. Practice this away from the piano, aiming to achieve an even flow of triplets, letting the eighth-note sound just after the last of these in a way that is natural and expressive rather than mathematically precise. (Keep the sixteenth-note light; feel it falling onto the dotted half-note in the next bar.) Don't let your attention to detail distract you from the overall shape of the music: play through with triplets reduced to single held chords, to get a feel for points of arrival and departure in melody and harmony. The Italian phrase at the top states that 'the whole piece should be played extremely delicately and with sustaining pedal.' There's no suggestion you should use left-hand pedal, which would muffle the tonal colors. It should sound hushed throughout, yet this must be achieved through delicacy of touch alone.

EXERCISE 16.2   SONATA IN C# MINOR – FIRST MOVEMENT

Beethoven

Adagio sostenuto
Si deve suonare tutto questo pezzo delicatessimamente e senza sordino

continued over page

EXERCISE 16.2   continued

continued over page

EXERCISE 16.2 continued

IMPRESSIONISM

In the late 19th century the developments in musical style that led to Romanticism in classical music were taken to an extreme. Composers began to write longer and longer works, for larger and larger orchestras, aiming at ever greater degrees of emotional and dramatic intensity. This was especially true in the Austro-German tradition, which dominated Europe thanks to the overwhelming influence of Wagner. In his operatic works Wagner had replaced the stricter musical forms used in opera with a continuous stream of unfolding textures and motives that could reflect the events on stage more closely. He also took a new approach to harmony – one which allowed for a much freer use of dissonance and chromatic alteration – by exploring ways in which chords could be connected through voice-leading based on the chromatic scale rather than diatonic scales. He sowed the seeds for many of the revolutions of 20th-century classical music, but also provoked strong reactions against his music and what it seemed to represent.

One important reaction was **neoclassicism**: as the 19th century reached its end many composers were looking for ways to escape from the excesses of Romantic music, so they began to adopt classicist values again, often combining elements of traditional pre-Romantic musical styles (e.g. Baroque and Classical) with distinctively modern elements (such as unresolved dissonances). (We'll look at neoclassicism in music in more detail in the next unit.)

Another was **impressionism**, which also emerged in music around this time, especially in the music of the French composers Debussy and Ravel. This was closely related to neoclassicism, though unlike the latter it can also be seen as a continuation of Romanticism. (Debussy and Ravel can also be considered neoclassical in some respects.) These composers opted for shorter forms, and rejected the emotional drama of the Romantics, but they took even further the emphasis on color, texture, and mood that emerged with Wagner. They rejected the use of the term 'impressionism,' even though this refers to a tendency in painting that seems to closely match some aspects of what they wanted to achieve: for example they often produce textures whose atmosphere of vague sensuality recalls the style of Monet and Renoir.

EXERCISE 16.3

Here's one of Debussy's most evocative compositions for piano. Notice the unusual rhythm of the repeated left-hand opening figure, which recurs throughout the piece: the triplet sixteenth-note can be felt as a division of the quarter-note beat into halves (eighth-notes) and then thirds, or into thirds (triplet eighth-notes) and then halves, but must remain consistent. Look ahead and you'll see that the right hand has both ordinary and triplet eighth-notes, so feeling this rhythm both ways will help you maintain a steady pulse. Pay careful attention to pedaling: impressionist music often blurs the distinction between melody and texture, but sometimes clearly defined, 'classical' contours are required. Use pedal for unbroken continuity of sound in the left-hand accompaniment (at the opening and elsewhere), but releasing the pedal briefly with the triplet sixteenth-note will mean that on the third beat of the bar we can hear it as a dissonance resolving. Where right-hand melodic phrases (bars 3, 4, 7, and 19) are deliberately inconclusive, notes can overlap and merge into a texture as a consequence of pedaling, but not where

CLAUDE DEBUSSY

Claude Debussy was perhaps the most important of the composers whose music could be described as 'impressionist.' He introduced the whole-tone scale (see Unit 15), and began to explore the harmonic effects resulting from leaving dissonances unresolved. This corresponds to the use of extended and added-note chords in jazz, and so is something we now tend to take for granted, but in Debussy's day it was considered shocking. He also anticipated jazz with his use of modal harmony and his exploitation of different chord voicings for purely coloristic effects, and a distinctive feature of his music is its fluid approach to rhythm.

CD TRACK 53

continued on p242

EXERCISE 16.3   PRELUDE ('FOOTPRINTS IN THE SNOW')

Debussy

EXERCISE 16.3 continued

KEY TO FRENCH TERMS

French	Explanation
Cédez	slow down
Douloureux	sorrowful
Expressif	expressive
Lent	slowly
Plus	more
Retenu	held back
Tendre	tender
Très	very
Triste	sadly
En animant surtout	getting livelier,
dans l'expression	above all
	through
	expression

there's a clear harmonic resolution (eg, bar 4). Legato pedal the left-hand chords (rather than the right-hand melody) in bars 5 to 6 and 20 to 24, but delay the return of the pedal until just after the triplet sixteenth-note. Legato pedal the bass-line in bars 8 to 10, and individual chords in bars 29 to 31. Aim for an extremely delicate touch throughout.

ARPEGGIOS IN FIRST AND SECOND INVERSION

So far we've only looked at arpeggios in root position, but once you've gained confidence with these in the different major and minor keys it's time to turn your attention to how the same arpeggios can be played in first and second inversion.

Let's look at a few common arpeggio patterns, comparing the fingering for the different inversions. (They are shown here to two octaves, but eventually you should try to extend them to four.) Notice how in C major (and all other arpeggios consisting of just white notes) the fingering shifts from fourth in the left and third in the right for root position, through fourth in both hands for first inversion, to third in the left and fourth in the right for second inversion.

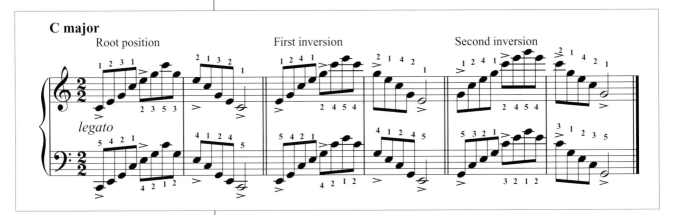

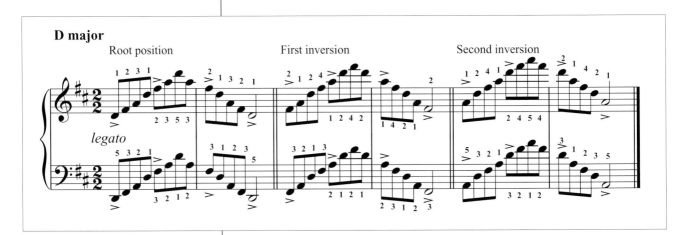

Now let's look at D major, which is typical of arpeggios with a sharpened 3rd (as in A major and E major as well). Here note how we keep the root position fingering in the left hand for first inversion, just starting on the second note of the pattern, while the right hand in first inversion starts on second and immediately goes under to thumb. This right hand pattern is then retained for second inversion, which just starts on the thumb, while the left hand in second inversion begins a new pattern on the fifth.

The next example, D♭ major, shows a typical example of an arpeggio starting on a black note, with a white note as the 3rd and another black note as the 5th (as in E♭ and A♭ majors, as well as minor arpeggios on F♯, C♯ and G♯). Here we begin a new pattern in first inversion in each hand, starting with fifth and thumb on white notes. This pattern is retained for second inversion, which just starts on the second note of the same pattern in each hand.

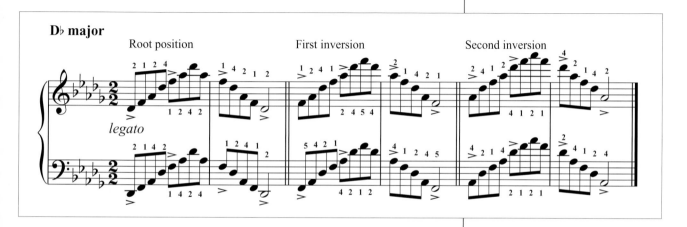

Finally here's C minor, which, like some other minor arpeggios starting on white notes (eg, F and G minor), has its 3rd written as a flat. This follows the same logic as D major in terms of which patterns are retained and which are new, but the use of fourth and third fingers is different, as it must reflect the different spacing between black and white notes.

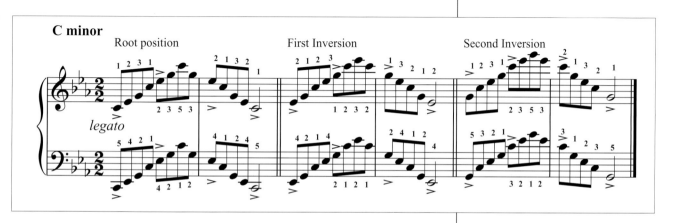

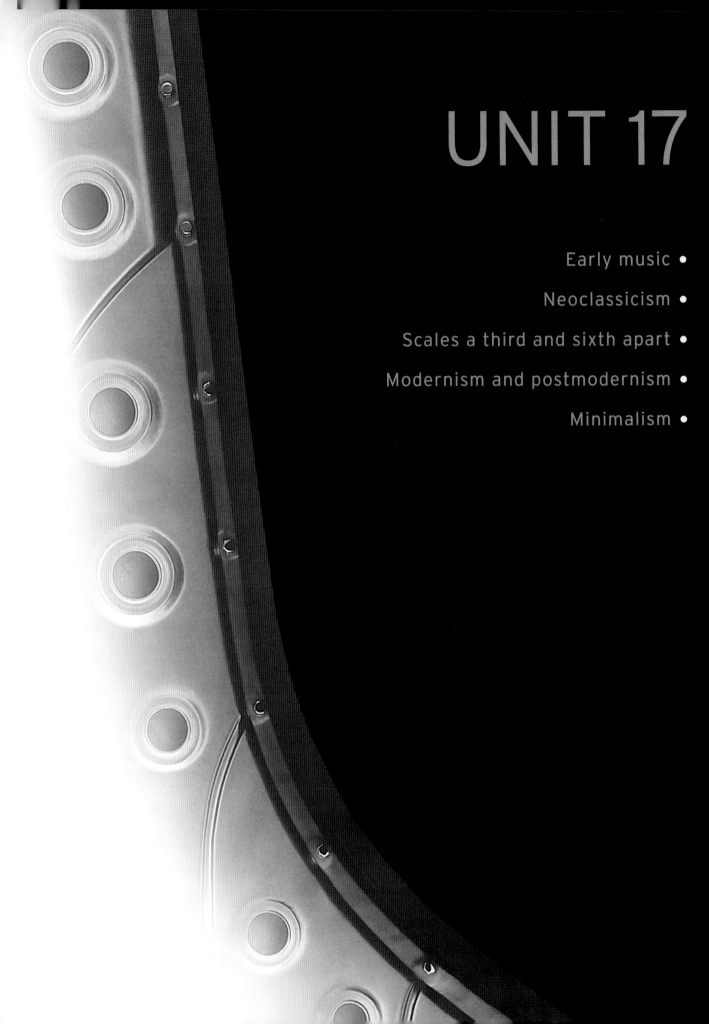

UNIT 17

EARLY MUSIC

The harmonic language of European music, as we know it today in both classical and modern popular music (and jazz), evolved gradually from medieval **plainchant** – ie, religious chanting by monks in which the only harmonic combinations allowed were intervals of a perfect 5th and octave. As medieval music developed, the status of the interval of a 3rd changed from a dissonance to a consonance, and this opened the way for Renaissance composers (of the 15th and 16th centuries) to explore the harmonic implications of combining separate melodic lines into a single texture (ie, **polyphony**). This eventually led to a shift away from harmonic progressions in which the bass or root moved in intervals of a 3rd and towards progressions involving intervals of a perfect 5th (or its inversion, a perfect 4th). The basis for modern harmony was thus established, with its emphasis on tonic and dominant, and the modal harmony of earlier Renaissance music began to disappear. At the same time, the Renaissance saw the beginnings of a more precise and stable system for notating music.

Both of these processes reached a decisive stage in the early 17th century, which marks the end of the Renaissance and the start of the Baroque period. Music from this time onwards starts to display more and more of the standard features that we expect in classical music. By contrast, we are less sure how music from before that time should sound. We use the general term **early music** to refer to the latter, and musicians who aim to reproduce the way in which such music was originally played call this **authentic performance** practice.

EXERCISE 17.1

This piece by the English composer John Blow dates from the mid 17th century. That's already Baroque, but the style developed more slowly in England than in Italy and Germany, so we can still see Renaissance features, such as the simpler phrase structure, marked with strongly defined, decorated cadences, and a straightforward dance rhythm. Like 'early music,' it's been notated in a more open-ended way, with performers understanding what's required even when the instructions are vague (see below). A 'jigg' is a sailor's dance, so you should keep a strong, regular pulse, with a clear stress on the first beat of each bar. The version here shows the original notes (though the ornamentation signs have been modernized), so you can first try playing it through as written, with no ornamentation or changes to rhythm.

ENGLAND'S RENAISSANCE

English culture of the Renaissance reached its peak later than on the continent, and so was more influenced by the Reformation. The reign of Queen Elizabeth I (1558-1603) saw the emergence of Shakespeare, the development of the English madrigal, and the appearance of great composers such as William Byrd, who enlarged and advanced the keyboard repertoire of the day. You can see this from the works gathered in an important collection of the time: *The Fitzwilliam Virginal Book.* The Reformation and a desire for a more English style both favored simplicity and naturalness, in contrast to the more decorative and artificial style of the Italians. The English organ music of this time subsequently influenced great masters such as J.S. Bach.

CD TRACK 54

EXERCISE 17.1   JIGG: ORIGINAL

Blow

Now here's a realization of the right hand, printed above the original for comparison. Note how dotted rhythms are played 'in the French style' – as double-dotted rhythms. Groups of four stepwise descending eighth-notes get treated as 'notes inégales' (ie, 'unequal notes') – this means playing them in a dotted rhythm, often with the first of each pair as the quick note or sixteenth-note. Chords tend to be spread, and sections repeated with different ornamentation. When it was written, a change in dynamic level could only be achieved by switching between manuals (ie, keyboards) on the harpsichord – something only possible on larger instruments. We can achieve an equivalent effect on the piano by restraining dynamic variation within sections, reserving more significant changes to the overall level for each section repeat. Work through the right hand, then combine it with the original left hand. Finally play from the original, but keeping the embellishments.

EXERCISE 17.1A   JIGG: RIGHT HAND REALISATION

IGOR STRAVINSKY

The Russian émigré Igor Stravinsky was the most important exponent of neoclassicism, as well as one of the most original composers of the 20th century. His output covers almost every major style of the 20th century. The best-known works are his earlier ballet scores, written for Diaghilev, such as *The Firebird* and *The Rite of Spring*. These introduce a strong element of primitivism and already feature polytonality; but in the 1920s he turned in the direction of neoclassicism, writing smaller works such as his wind Octet and *The Soldier's Tale*. Eventually he also produced a neoclassical opera, *The Rake's Progress*. Finally, he adopted the serial technique of atonal composition developed by his contemporary Schoenberg. All of his works are distinguished by his harmonic and rhythmic ingenuity and wit, and his unusually subtle ear for orchestration. His influence on the direction of 20th-century music has been enormous.

CD TRACK 55

SERGEI PROKOFIEV

The Russian composer Sergei Prokofiev was one of the most original personalities of early 20th century classical music. At the beginning of his career, when piano music was still dominated by the influence of Chopin, he rejected all elements of Romanticism. His *First Symphony* is an example of neoclassicism, and many of his works deliberately avoid any traces of lyricism and traditional Romantic textures, preferring brutal percussive rhythms and ironic musical parody instead. Even so, many of his finest works (notably the ballet *Romeo And Juliet* and the *Fifth Symphony*) have beautifully lyrical passages. He left Russia after the communist revolution in 1917, but eventually returned. His funeral was also strikingly unsentimental. The composer and Stalin died on the same day – within an hour of each other. As a result there were no flowers for Prokofiev's funeral: they had all been reserved for that of the dictator.

NEOCLASSICISM

In the period between the World War I and World War II, **neoclassicism** emerged as an important new tendency in 20th-century classical music. For composers such as Busoni, Poulenc, and Prokofiev it continued the reaction against late Romanticism present in Impressionism. For others, such as Stravinsky and Milhaud, it also represented a fresh alternative to **modernism** – the harsher rejection of traditional approaches to harmony, melody and rhythm that had been a feature of the more experimental works produced in the first two decades of the 20th century, including Stravinsky's own earlier compositions.

There were two aspects to neoclassicism: a revival of classical ideals of clarity and detachment (which in practice meant a preference for small-scale forms and instrumentation) and the deliberate imitation of Baroque and Classical period musical styles, usually with a strong element of irony and **pastiche** or **parody**. (Pastiche is a light-hearted imitation or juxtaposition of elements of existing musical styles, while parody mocks the latter through exaggeration or caricature.) Neoclassical composers favored traditional phrase-structure and tonal harmony, but complicated by irregular phrase-lengths and meter, by **polyrhythm** (ie, several independent rhythmic patterns superimposed), and by **polytonality** (music simultaneously in more than one key). Dissonances were often deliberately left unresolved. Some composers, such as Stravinsky, were also influenced by jazz, but this was a two-way relationship: for example, Milhaud taught and influenced the great jazz pianist Bill Evans.

EXERCISE 17.2

This movement, from his collection *The Five Fingers*, is fairly typical of Stravinsky's neoclassical style. Note the scarcity of expressive markings for dynamics and articulation, which makes the score resemble Baroque music. It suggests that what matters is precision and clarity rather than nuances of feeling. In the first section you could contrast sharply defined staccato right-hand eighth-notes with legato sixteenth-notes, with a slightly detached touch in the left-hand. The second section (from bar 16) calls for a legato left hand: this is implied by the quarter-notes, which must be held while the eighth-note thirds sound above them, while the right-hand repeated notes can only be performed staccato. Although no dynamic change is marked, there is a softening of harmonic texture here, suggesting a drop in volume. Notice the sudden contrasts of loud and soft in the third section (bars 24-37). Aim for a strict and precise rhythmic feel, with a clear accent on the first beat of each bar. Note how the opening sixteenth-note figuration implies polyrhythmic groupings of three sixteenth-notes over a quarter-note pulse.

EXERCISE 17.2   ALLEGRO

Stravinsky

continued over page

EXERCISE 17.2 continued

EXERCISE 17.3

This piece by Prokofiev also features neoclassical elements, but with a more lyrical aspect: note the regular four-bar phrase lengths and tonal harmony with unprepared dissonances. There are also features of 20th-century piano music, such as abrupt switches between high and low registers, unusual leaps and stretches, and unfamiliar harmonic outlines. These often call for unorthodox fingering patterns, as in the left hand (bars 9-13) and right hand (bars 17-18 and 21-22). Aim for clarity, but with sufficient expressive nuancing to ensure the music does not sound flat and uninteresting. Pedal repeated notes and chords for continuity of texture. Legato pedal each harmonic change or stepwise movement. The tempo should not be too slow.

EXERCISE 17.3   REGRETS

Prokofiev

continued over page

SCALES A THIRD AND SIXTH APART

So far we've only practiced scales hands together an octave apart. However, we can also play them with the hands separated by an interval of a 3rd or a 6th. This is harder, but it's an effective way of further reinforcing the fingering pattern in each hand, as the latter must operate more independently of each other than when playing the same note in each hand.

Starting a scale on the 3rd step sometimes allows us to simplify the fingering at the beginning and end. Note how in C major (hands a 3rd apart), below, the right hand can start with second finger instead of third, making it easier for the thumb to pass under, while in D-flat major (hands a 6th apart) the left hand begins with the little finger, as there's no point in using thumb on a white note if it's the first note of the scale and is going to be followed straightaway by the fourth finger.

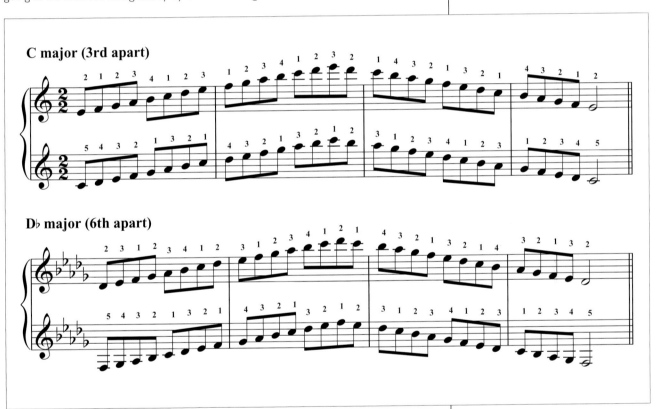

MODERNISM AND POSTMODERNISM

The 20th century saw two periods of revolutionary development in the language of classical music. The first took place in the opening decades of the century: a small number of composers began to reject some of the longstanding conventions of classical music. Composers such as Schoenberg, Stravinsky and Bartok explored new approaches to rhythm, meter, and harmony, using dissonance and large melodic leaps more freely. Like Debussy (and Busoni), they also began to explore the textural possibilities of the modern orchestra for their own sake. Schoenberg began writing music that was **athematic** (ie, with no distinguishable musical themes) and **atonal** (ie, with no stable key centers). As we've just seen, Stravinsky experimented with polyrhythms and polytonality.

These developments were connected with historical events of the time, and mirrored wider trends in European culture. In the run-up to World War I, people had a strong sense that the existing social order was disintegrating: it seemed that long-cherished certainties were being overthrown by the claims or discoveries of intellectuals and scientists like Nietzsche, Freud, and Einstein. In the wake of the brutality of the war, a strong sense of disillusionment with the existing social and political hierarchies was added to this, fostering political movements such as socialism and fascism. These developments were reflected in broad artistic movements such as primitivism, expressionism, and surrealism, and in more specific trends, such as the emergence of abstract art and formalist architecture, all of which had social and political implications.

By the 1930s much of the impetus behind these radical developments had been dispersed, but with the ending of the Second World War a new generation of artists and composers emerged, who demanded a fresh start. The 1950s and 1960s thus saw a rapid succession of developments as composers such as Boulez, Stockhausen, and Cage sought to define themselves as part of an experimental avant-garde – often in ways that were more and more extreme and individualistic. To begin with many of these figures were reacting against the growing influence of commercialized popular music, and so opted for a severe and austere style of atonal composition influenced by the pre-war composer Webern (a pupil of Schoenberg). However, as time went on they relaxed: the 1960s saw a degree of interaction and convergence between avant-garde and popular music. By the 1970s many composers were starting to reject the more extreme innovations of post-war modern music in favor of neo-Romantic styles, or alternative approaches such as **minimalism** (see below) that reflected the influence of popular and ethnic music.

The term **modernism** is used to describe the more serious and individualistic aspirations of artists and composers working during these periods of radical innovation, but critics have coined the term **postmodernism** to describe the trends that have followed in their wake, in which a more playful, ironic, and multicultural perspective on contemporary culture is articulated. More recently it has been argued that postmodernism is really just another kind of modernism, as it also involves stepping outside of one's own traditions. Others claim that the neoclassicism of the inter-war period was already postmodernist. Postmodernism as an artistic approach can be interpreted in the context of the idea, put forward by some social theorists and philosophers, that we live in a postmodern society (ie, **postmodernity**) – a society in which it's no longer possible to hold up any particular beliefs or values as more central than others, or as absolute or universal. This kind of **relativism** can seem natural in the age of globalization and the Internet: how far it appeals probably depends on how you yourself are affected by these sorts of changes in society.

MINIMALISM

Minimalism is a general term for the tendency to reject all extravagant forms of expression and ornament in favor of a 'stripped-down' feel. You'll find examples in many kinds of modern art, architecture, literature, and music. However in classical art music of the last 50 years or so – what's known as 'contemporary music' – it refers to something more specific. It's a style that emerged in the US in the 1960s, in which textures, rhythms, and motifs are repeated over long periods, evolving through very gradual processes of subtle change. These involve gradual alterations to the harmony and slight shifts in the rhythmic or metrical relationship between different layers. (The latter, known as **phase-shifting**, gives rise to interesting cross-rhythms and shifting melodic figurations.)

The result is a peculiarly static feel, given the amount of rhythmic activity and melodic movement going on: this reflects the influence of African drumming and South-East Asian music. Minimalism has proved especially popular as film music, thanks to composers like Philip Glass and Michael Nyman, but its reception in the concert hall has been mixed. Nevertheless, it has entered the vocabulary of many contemporary composers, if only in subtle ways, and is, perhaps, the quintessentially 'postmodern' musical idiom.

EXERCISE 17.4

CD TRACK 57

This short study piece will give you a feel for the shifting patterns of minimalism. Notice the juxtaposition of block-like textures, each with its particular register, color, articulation, and dynamic level, as well as internally static harmony and cyclically repeating rhythmic figures. Aim for extreme precision in terms of rhythmic accuracy, without letting changes in register disrupt the flow. Note how accents are often indicated on the beat to ensure the underlying meter remains audible as a foil for syncopated melodic figures. Legato pedaling bars 29-32 will add a brief contrast of mood, and in the rest of the piece you should keep a firm touch – with fingers well rounded – even when playing quietly.

EXERCISE 17.4 MINIMUM LOAD

Rhythmic and flowing

EXERCISE 17.4 continued

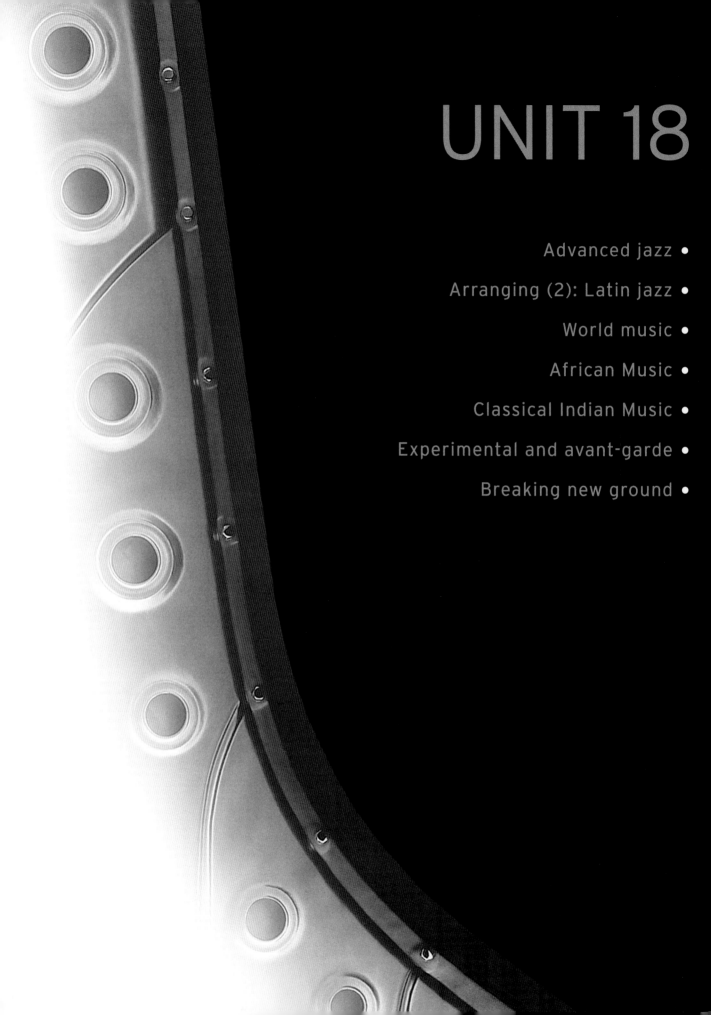

UNIT 18

ADVANCED JAZZ

Now that you've had some experience of how scales and chords work in jazz as a basis for improvising, it's time consider some of the more advanced techniques that can be used to enhance the overall effect of jazz arrangements.

Remember, the basic idea behind all of these methods is that they can be applied to the kind of simple melody and chord symbols you'll find in the lead sheet for a jazz standard. Lead sheets are published in large collections known as *Fake Books* or *Real Books*. (These are just different names for the same thing. *Fake Books* are no less real and no more fake than *Real Books*.) That means that the general context for these techniques is harmonizing and reharmonizing a well-known tune. But this not just a question of producing more interesting harmony: it's also a question of finding harmonizations that bring the tune itself to life in new and unfamiliar ways. So you should always ask yourself how a harmonization impacts on the expressive color of notes in the melody line or in related improvised material.

Let's run through some of the more commonly used advanced techniques for treating chords.

VOICINGS: In Unit 15 we considered the kinds of left-hand and two-hand voicings that can be built using chord extensions (7th, 9th, 11th, 13th) based on the major scale and its modal derivatives. We also examined how alternative, altered-note harmonizations could be derived from modes based on the jazz-minor scale. However, jazz musicians mostly use shortcuts to generate more complex voicings, as these enable them to identify chords by how they look on the keyboard, which is quicker than working out each voicing from scratch. Here are some examples:

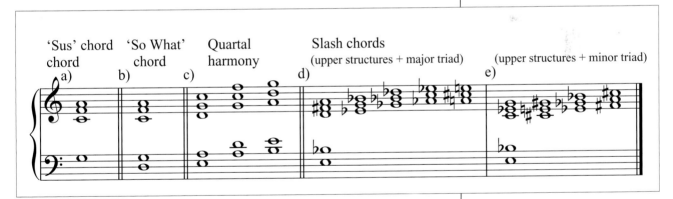

'Sus chords' (above, a) introduce the 11th (or added 4th) in a V (dominant 7th) chord. 'So What' chords (above, b) do the same in a II (minor 7th) chord. In both cases this results in intervals of a perfect 4th between the lower parts. Taking this idea further we can build chords entirely out of perfect 4ths, resulting in what's known as **quartal harmony** (above, c). Note how in the first two cases the top three notes of the chord form a triad whose root is different from that of the chord as a whole. Hence it can be easier to remember these voicings by remembering what triad to play over what root: a major triad whose root is a whole tone below the overall root for a 'sus chord' voicing on V, or a minor third above the overall root for a 'So What' chord voicing on II.

This is the basic idea behind **slash-chord voicings**: there are all sorts of more complex harmonizations that can be broken down into combinations of a right-hand triad and one or two left-hand notes. The examples above shows how we can arrive at some of these by playing the 3rd and 7th of the V chord in the left hand, while shifting a major triad (above, d) or minor triad (above, e) up and down over it. (Note that all of these voicings also function with the corresponding tritone substitutions: try thinking of them as dominant chords on F♯ instead of C: just think of the left-hand B♭ as an A♯. Try moving each of the right-hand triads through its inversions to see which sounds best within the voicing. This may also vary depending on the key, so try transposing all of these voicings through different keys as well.) These particular voicings are all known as **upper structures**: you can learn more about them in Unit 18 of the companion volume to this one: *The Piano Handbook*. Of course there are also lots of more specific voicings associated with particular jazz pianists, such as Bill Evans, Herbie Hancock, McCoy Tyner, Mulgrew Miller, and Kenny Barron. That's why you should get to know as many recordings as possible by these musicians.

If you're playing with others and are not sure what voicing to put down over a V chord, because you don't know what they're going to do, try playing a **neutral voicing** first time around, while you get acquainted with their approach. You can just play the root, 3rd and 7th in any arrangement. Any V-based scale will work over this.

SEQUENCES: Jazz musicians often like to use set sequences of chords. That way everyone in a group knows where they stand, at least at the outset. The classic, of course, is the **12-bar blues** (see Unit 12). Another famous sequence is '**rhythm changes**,' based on chords adapted from Gershwin's song 'I Got Rhythm.' (That's the piece you may have learned in Unit 8 of this book). Here is the basic chord sequence for the verse.

C	Am7	Dm7	G7	C	Am7	Dm7	G7	

| C | C7 | F | Fm | C | G7 | C | | ‖ |
| | | | | (C | Am7 | Dm7 | G7 | :‖) |

Jazz musicians like to cycle round these eight bars before moving to the middle-eight, so they often replace the last two bars with the opening four-chord sequence (as shown in brackets above), keeping the closing three chords shown above for the final time, just before the move to the middle-eight, which looks like this, and will of course lead back to a repeat of the verse:

E7	E7	A7	A7	

D7	D7	G7	G7	‖

A lot of jazz chord sequences consist of a succession of II-V-I (or V-I) progressions, each in a key a perfect 5th, whole-step, or half-step (semitone) below the previous one. But in 1960, in his famous number 'Giant Steps,' John Coltrane went a step further and introduced progressions in keys a major 3rd apart. Compare the following examples.

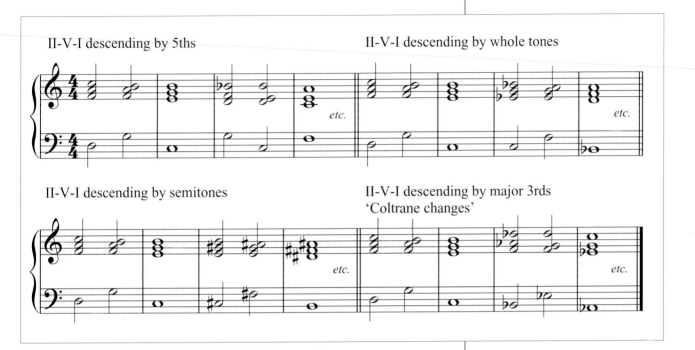

The last group are known as '**Coltrane changes.**' He went on to develop ways of integrating these into reharmonizations of more conventional chord sequences.

FUNCTIONALITY: As you become more expert with jazz chord structures, you'll notice that not all chords fit the II-V-I pattern. Good musicians look at context to see whether a chord marked in a lead sheet as a minor 7th chord really functions as part of a II-V-I or not. If not, then it's probably a minor-key I chord, that could sound better voiced as a minor triad with the added major 6th or major 7th (both taken from the jazz minor scale) rather than a minor 7th chord. If it's a major chord, it may be functioning as IV rather than I, in which case a voicing with sharpened 11th will become obligatory, rather than just being an option for removing avoid notes. (Having said this, if the normal 4th isn't sounding above them in the melody, most I chords lend themselves in jazz to Lydian treatment with a sharpened 11th.) So the lesson is that you do, after all, have to be aware of the broader harmonic structure of the chords you use.

APPROACH CHORDS: The effect of a chord is always partly a function of how it is approached. In jazz the impact of almost any chord can be changed by inserting a chord beforehand that functions as V relative to that chord (just like the idea of **secondary dominants** discussed earlier in this book). Another similar technique (**chromatic approach**) involves arriving at a chord via a similar one, a half-step (semitone) lower or higher – usually the latter. Here the chord may also be voiced as dominant harmony (e.g. V7♭9 or Valt), in which case approaching from a half-step above may be heard as a tritone substitution for a dominant.

CONNECTIONS: Unlike in classical music (except for composers such as Debussy and Ravel), jazz musicians go in for **parallel block chords** as an easy way of connecting up chords. This involves all parts of the harmony moving together, and is sometimes known as **locked hands**. You can apply it to any kind of voicing, but it's most commonly used with the kind of block chord layout in which the right hand plays three notes and the left hand one note, all of them grouped together in close position. It's a natural option when approaching a chord chromatically from an identical voicing a semitone above or below.

BASS-LINES: Playing solo you'll soon be aware of the need to incorporate some interesting bass-line movement into your style: just playing rootless left-hand voicings all the time, leaving it to the listener to imagine a bass line, quickly begins to sound one-dimensional. As in classical music, elaborating the steps or leaps between successive roots through stepwise bass-line motion is a natural option, but in jazz this tends to be used as a pretext for also inserting transitional chords over each bass note. (This is easiest when the whole voicing shifts in parallel motion, as described above, but letting the right-hand move as a separate block in contrary motion to the bass is often more striking and effective.) **Pedal points**, in which a bass note is held suspended or repeated while the chords change above it, are another device familiar from classical music, which jazz also uses to build up a sense of unresolved expectancy.

FREE VARIATION: The essence of jazz harmony lies in exploiting the ambiguities and loopholes of the Western tonal system of chords and scales. The aim is to open up as many options as possible for freely varying the chord structures you're playing without losing all sense of underlying structure. Try the following experiments:

1) Take any chord that you use in a jazz progression and see what happens if you substitute any of the other eleven notes of the chromatic scale in the bass, while leaving the rest of the progression intact. It's surprising how many of the new possibilities will work.

2) Take any melody note from the lead sheet for a standard that you're interested in playing on the piano. Note the key of the music at that point. Then work out all the other keys that also contain that same note. Now transpose the chord that you play underneath that note into all of those other keys. How do they make the note sound? Which of them could substitute for the original chord, or function as an approach chord?

The most radical variation technique that jazz musicians use is to let their improvised embellishments of an existing melody and chord structure go **out-of-key**. Here the chords stay the same, or are reharmonized within the key, but there is a shift of emphasis in the melody line. Instead of mainly using notes that belong to the scale that corresponds to the actual harmony, the player emphasizes the remaining notes of the chromatic scale. These notes are foreign to the scale and chord, and are known as **off-notes**. More often than not they will imply a different key from the chords sounding at the same time, producing the effect of **bitonality,** which, as we noted in the previous unit, is also a feature of some 20th-century classical music.

ARRANGING (2): LATIN JAZZ

In Unit 15 we considered some of the ways in which we might embellish an existing tune, such as a jazz standard, as part of arranging it for piano. In such cases the supporting texture created through chords and/or bass line is likely to be kept as simple as possible – at least in the earlier stages. But we may we want to transfer a song to piano while leaving the melody line largely untouched, either because it's too beautiful to mess around with or because the creative emphasis of the arrangement lies elsewhere.

A good example is **Latin jazz** – a rich fusion of Latin-American rhythms (see Unit 12 for these) with jazz-inspired harmony and licks. This music quite often keeps to a fairly straightforward rendition of the melody, so that the spotlight falls instead on how rhythmic and harmonic features of the texture are elaborated. Let's take a look at the most famous Latin bossa nova song of all, 'The Girl From Ipanema,' composed by

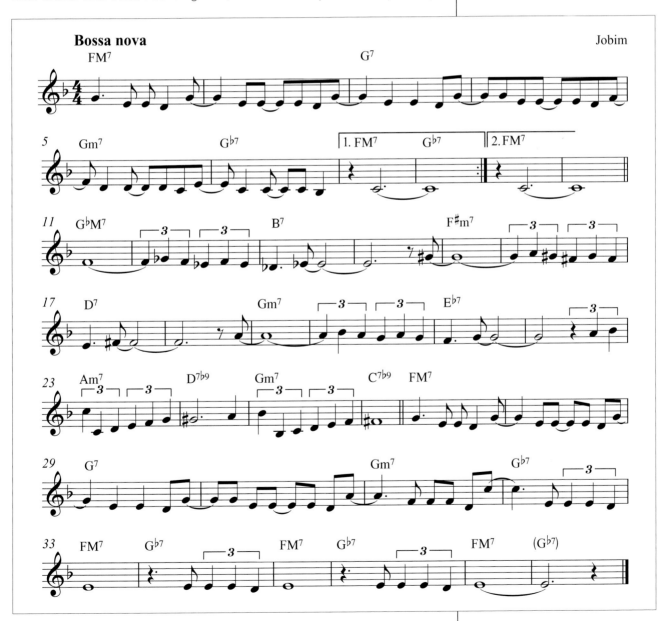

Antônio Carlos Jobim, and consider some of the choices we might make in arranging it as a solo piano version. First here's the lead sheet.

Note that the melody line is more rhythmical in the first section, with repeated notes and continuous syncopations, but opens out into more sustained gestures in the middle section. Hence the first section calls for a texture that puts across the Latin feel of the rhythm. Let's focus on achieving this first. The example below shows a basic harmonization of the first section: note how placing chords exactly on the first beat of the bar – which is where the changes are actually indicated in the lead sheet – produces a fairly pedestrian effect, leaving the rhythm of the melody without any support at all.

We can generate a stronger effect just by shifting the chords forward half a beat in those places where they're not already aligned with the melody, at the same time as restating them at or around the start of each new bar and half-bar. This sets up a two-

chords-per-bar pattern that reinforces the rhythmic outline of the melody. Note how in the final two bars the left hand must supply rhythmic material to fill the gap created by the lack of rhythm in the melody.

This is better, but styles like bossa nova are normally heard against the background of a rhythm section with the feel of Brazilian salsa and samba, even if this is toned down by focusing on the drum kit and bass, without the more sensual and exotic sounds of Latin percussion. It provides a rhythmic bedrock separate from the melody, which can fall more freely around the beat. Let's try turning our left-hand bass line into a samba pattern.

This sounds more Latin, but there are places where the left-hand pattern definitely doesn't sit right with the melody and chords, leading to a mechanical feel. We need a more flexible approach, as in the next version. Note how it keeps the samba effect on the half-bar but lets the bass shift from playing on the first beat of the bar at the start to moving with the right-hand syncopations, making for a more fluid and integrated texture.

Finally, lets turn to harmony. Actually we've introduced a few subtle enhancements as we've been going along. Take another look at the above versions. In the first, the Gm7 chord in bar five is already extended to include the 9th – always an expressive addition to a minor II chord in jazz. (Notice how the chord sequence Gm7-G♭7-FM7 is really a II-V-I in F major, with tritone substitution applied to the V chord so that C7 becomes G♭7). In the second example the more coordinated relationship between the chord changes and the melody allows us to take this further: the G7 chord is extended to include the 13th, and the 9th is added to the G♭7 as well, producing a more consistent overall level of harmonic tension. The third version adds a 9th to the last G♭7 chord before the repeat, making for a stronger sense of arrival back on the more resolved opening FM7 chord. However, it's only in the fourth version that we can really get to appreciate these improvements, as the more flexible approach to the left-hand pattern ensures that the first appe arance of each chord is supported with the root in the bass.

This might work for the theme the first time round, but as it returns several times over the course of the song we'd definitely want to vary the harmonization, adding a few surprises each time around. Here's a version based on the last example, but with several alterations. Note how the general effect is to further increase the level of harmonic tension. It's better to do this gradually over several appearances of the music rather than straight away, and you should be careful not to do this all the time, as the harmony can lose its underlying character, becoming undifferentiated.

EXERCISE 18.1

Taking the previous examples as a starting point, try to develop further variations on the harmony and texture for the opening measures of 'The Girl From Ipanema.' When you've done that, take the melody and chords for the middle section of the song through the same process, starting with simple chords and following the lead sheet. An important hint: you can keep the samba rhythm going right through, but as in the first section you'll need to use it in a flexible way. It's best not to use it in bars with triplet quarter-notes, as combining the two rhythms will produce an overcomplicated texture.

WORLD MUSIC

In the 1980s an increasing number of recordings of non-European folk music began to appear in Western record shops. This music didn't fit into any existing categories used by record companies. Sometimes it was simply recordings of local 'native' music from exotic parts of the world: what's rather misleadingly called 'ethnic music.' (It's misleading because 'ethnic' here implies 'non-Western,' whereas it should mean any music connected with a particular cultural heritage – and that's pretty much all music.) More often than not, the music had been adapted by Western popular musicians, using studio techniques, or introducing Western song lyrics and titles. After much discussion record company executives settled on the term **world music** as a general label for this. In effect it refers to any music that doesn't fit neatly into the categories of Western popular or classical music, so it can refer to non-Western folk music (eg, African tribal music) and Western folk music (eg, traditional Celtic music or Eastern European folksong), but also to the more formal styles of non-Western music making that have undergone extended periods of development comparable to Western classical music – the so-called 'classical' traditions of countries like Persia (now Iran), Japan, China (and Tibet), and the Indian subcontinent.

The development of the world music scene, which now extends to large international festivals such as WOMAD, is closely intertwined with several other tendencies in music and culture. For example, a lot of **new age** culture centers around the idea that music with an 'ethnic feel' is believed to be helpful in opening doors to lost forms of spiritual insight, coming from traditions that offer an alternative to stressful modern Western lifestyles. At the same time, the gradual emergence over the last century or so of **crossover** styles, involving fusions of different musical traditions and languages, has also raised the profile of world music. Think of tango and ragtime, then samba and bossa nova, then the folk-rock of Bob Dylan or Fairport Convention, and then fusion-based styles such as funk and reggae: all of these involve a more or less deliberate merging of Western classical or popular idioms with non-Western or folk idioms to create fresh new styles. Even so, many of these would be considered more mainstream than world music, as they are not so strongly distinguished by the use of alternative scales, inflections, and instruments. Yet they are definitely part of the same wider phenomenon, which is the cultural appropriation of indigenous musical traditions by Western artists, for Western commercial markets – something we can now see as part of the more general trend towards 'cultural tourism' that is part of globalization.

MUSIC AND LIFE

Ethnomusicologists study how the music of particular cultures relates to the ways of life of their traditional inhabitants. When we talk about the ethnic character or identity of music, this is what we are really referring to. Often in such cultures the form and style of the music makes sense as part of wider activities: for example it may reflect its role in rituals or as an accompaniment to manual work, or express collective forms of experience specific to a region or community. By contrast the musical styles we tend to call 'classical' are usually performed in a more formal setting (like a classical concert), by specially trained musicians, and it's harder to say how their musical language and form relate to the patterns of life and experience of those taking part in the performance.

(Actually the cult of the exotic – 'orientalism' – has a long history in European culture. In music it stretches back at least to Mozart, who incorporated Turkish elements in some of his compositions. Debussy was also strongly influenced by Japanese and Indonesian music.)

These days, though, people are more aware of the downside to this. The dangers of unlimited cultural fusion have become obvious: the price of global branding and recognition is that indigenous local styles get watered down and homogenized, losing any connection to the wider fabric of the centuries-old communal ways of life that produced them, and which often provide the only context in which they are genuinely meaningful. Perhaps as artists we need to learn to respect local traditions more, resisting the temptation to treat non-Western musical styles as a global resource from which we can just take what we want, when we want it.

Yet this needn't mean closing our ears to the alternative sounds and possibilities that these traditions offer. A better model – at least in some ways – for how we might make use of these new horizons to enrich our artistic potential is offered by some contemporary classical music, which sees the music of other cultures as opening up alternative ways of thinking about musical sounds, instruments, and practices at a more abstract, conceptual level.

These traditions, then, can offer us something more than just exotic sounds and an increasingly familiar 'ethnic feel': they can teach us alternative ways of understanding what music can be and what it can mean to take part in creating it. Let's have a look at a couple of these possibilities as they relate to piano playing.

AFRICAN MUSIC

THUMB PIANOS
Mbira and **kalimba** are amongst the African names for the various instruments grouped together into a single common category by ethnomusicologists, known as lamellaphones. These include any instruments with protruding metal tongue-like keys that can be plucked directly with the thumbs and/or fingers, and which are attached to a soundboard, in turn often connected to a resonator. Because the metal tongues resemble the keys of a piano and are also played with fingers and thumbs, they are known as 'thumb pianos.'

Ask someone about African music and they're sure to mention drums. Most people these days are familiar with the sound of African drumming, whether from films, holiday trips to Africa, or recordings of native musicians. (By 'Africa' I mean sub-Saharan Africa, as distinct from North Africa, where the musical traditions are really part of Middle-Eastern culture.) Even if you haven't heard it, you're sure to have been exposed in some way or other to many of its most striking rhythmic features, thanks to Afro-American music. Why? Because it's where all those syncopated and swung rhythms and offbeat accents typical of jazz and other modern popular styles like rock and pop originally came from. Nevertheless, this familiarity can be deceptive, as it can suggest that this all African music has to offer, whereas actually there's another, deeper sense in which it opens up fresh perspectives on our relationship to musical sounds.

This concerns the way instruments define different physical possibilities for playing, depending on how they are built. Take the modern Western piano, with its keyboard in which the pitches of the scale are laid out in a simple ascending order from the lowest on the left-hand to the highest on the right. The result is they form a linear sequence (each one step higher or lower than the next), encouraging us to think of the range of pitches available on the piano as something like a continuous dimension in space.

The idea of a scale, in classical music or jazz, is a perfect expression of just this sort of conception of musical pitch, so it's natural to think that it must be universal feature of all music.

But is it? Let's contrast this layout of pitches with the one we typically find on the most common keyboard-like instrument in Africa: what's known in the west as the African 'thumb-piano' or 'finger-piano.' (These names are misleading, as from the point of view of the mechanics of sound-production the thumb-piano is quite different from the piano. Even so, they provide fixed non-technical names for all such instruments, whereas African names (such as mbira, kalimba, etc) vary considerably depending on the type of instrument and geographical region.

Scales in African music also vary from one region to another, but what's striking is that often the pitches are arranged starting with the lowest in the centre of the 'keyboard,' ascending outwards in both directions, alternating between the two sides. Keeping in mind that African tunings are different from Western ones, so the pitch-names here are only an approximation anyway, let's consider what a thumb-piano' might look like:

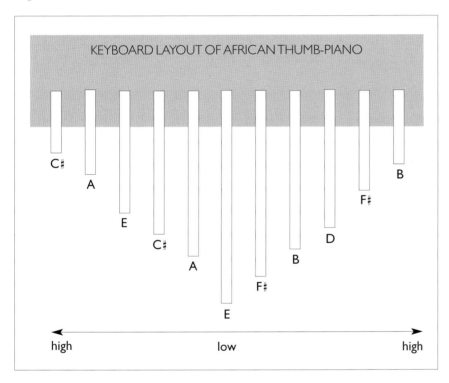

KEYBOARD LAYOUT OF AFRICAN THUMB-PIANO

C♯ A E C♯ A E F♯ B D F♯ B

high   low   high

Straightaway we can see our attitude to pitch would be quite different playing an instrument like this. The alternation between left and right sides involved in ascending or descending would make it impossible to feel any direct correlation between one's playing movements in space and the overall direction of the melody, forcing one to focus more on the sheer rhythm and color of the texture, leaving the exact rise and fall of the melodic material almost to chance. A natural response to this situation is to limit one's harmonic and melodic material to a minimum, while letting the patterns unfold and vary quite loosely and freely. Translated onto the piano (using the scale material shown in the diagram, but switching the relationship between left and right hands for ease of playing), a typical example of the kind of texture that would result might be the following (which you can also use as an exercise in crossed-hands playing, with the left-hand positioned over the right):

Gently flowing

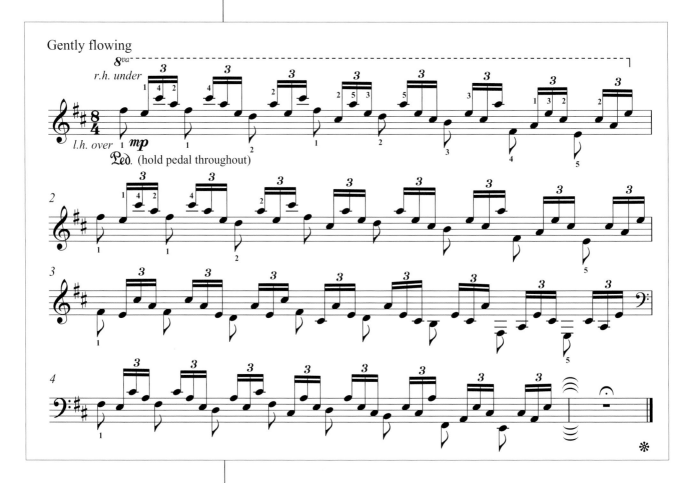

CD TRACK 58

In classical and popular music of the West the central role of pitch is to produce a sustained line, while rhythmically patterned melodic figurations form a secondary feature, usually in the background and derived only indirectly from the scale, via harmony. In the mbira-inspired piano texture shown above, on the other hand, these figurations become part of the foreground. This is a reflection of the fact that on the mbira this mix of left-hand and right-hand material moving in different directions is our most basic way of experiencing the scale itself, given how this is made physically accessible on this instrument. But as pianists we don't need such instruments ourselves: all we need do is imagine what it would be like to play them to grasp the underlying concept, which can then be applied directly to the modern piano in whatever way we want.

This also points to a more general contrast between African and Western music that can open some new doors for us. The most basic form of Western music is a sung melody line – something that contrasts with both human speech and human dance. By contrast the melodic patterns of African music relate closely to the pitched patterns of speech in their languages, which are often tone-based. That's why melodic patterns and pitched drum patterns can actually count as verbal language as well as music.

At the same time in many African cultures there are no distinct concepts for music and dance, so the physical movement involved in *playing* the music and in *dancing* to it form a single activity. We don't need to think of the movements of the performer just as a means to an end, which is how they are basically viewed in the West: they are part of your performance, part of your involvement in something richer than sound. Realizing and experiencing this can often be psychologically liberating for musicians trained in the West, and may also help them to overcome inhibitions about performing in public.

If you want to hear an early example of Western non-classical music influenced by some aspects of the African thumb-piano, listen to Miles Davis's *Kind Of Blue* (1959). Davis said that it was the music of the African mbira that inspired him to keep the scales and chords to a minimum throughout the material on this recording.

For a recent example of a Western classical composer absorbing some related possibilities connected with African music, see the three cycles of *Études* for piano (1985-2001) written by the composer György Ligeti.

CLASSICAL INDIAN MUSIC

Ever since George Harrison, the Beatles' guitarist, picked up a sitar and recorded the result, classical music from the Indian subcontinent has been a powerful influence on the imagination of Western musicians. It's common knowledge that it's based on a different scale system from Western music – the **raga** system – and uses complex metrical cycles – **talas** – as well as belonging to a sophisticated tradition of improvised music making that reaches back as far into the past as Western classical music.

From the late 1950s onwards, jazz musicians have also engaged with this music: John Coltrane, an important figure in the development of modal jazz in the 1960s, is thought to have been inspired by his encounters with the music of Ravi Shankar. For some, the appeal of Indian music lies in its scale-based improvising, for others it's the more fluid approach to rhythm and metre, and for others it's the sheer sound of instruments like the sitar, together with the effect of single-line melodies unfolding slowly over a **drone bass** (that's an unchanging bass tone).

Of course there's also the whole ethos of traditional Indian culture, philosophy and spirituality, with its connections to practices such as meditation and yoga, whose appeal in the West is as an antidote to the speed and stress of modern urban lifestyles.

There are countless examples of crossover styles emerging from interactions between Western and Indian music. These range from the classical-Indian fusions of the composer and violinist John Meyer, through 1960s 'raga-rock' to 'indo-jazz', and of course there's also the huge phenomenon of the Indian popular film industry, whose products are full of Indian sounding, rock-inspired tracks. Yet beneath this lies the fact that Indian classical music represents a tradition in which improvisation has survived as an essential feature, in a way largely absent from Western classical music (from which improvisation largely disappeared during the 19th century).

As such it also offers a contrast with jazz. Jazz, though improvisation-based, relies on Western musical structures (of harmony, melody and form) that were largely defined by their role in classical compositions of the preceding centuries. (Hence the general tendency for mainstream jazz to become less and less improvised in recent decades as it becomes more and more of a technically precise concert art-form, mirroring the process of change that Western classical music went through earlier and more gradually.)

That's why, when jazz musicians want to inhabit a radically improvised zone – as in 'free jazz' – they are generally forced to reject most of the familiar forms of musical structure of jazz itself (as well as Western classical music). The musical results are then

GYÖRGY LIGETI

György Ligeti (1923-2006) was a Jewish Hungarian classical composer born in Romania. He is best known for having written the music subsequently used (without permission) for Stanley Kubrick's film *2001: A Space Odyssey*. The matter was eventually settled out of court. Kubrick went on to use Ligeti's music (with permission, and on payment of a fee) in *The Shining* and *Eyes Wide Shut*. In his later music, Ligeti was especially influenced by African rhythmic textures and fractal geometry.

closer to improvised contemporary classical music, which usually explicitly aims to distance itself from all recognizable conventions and structures. By contrast Indian music is 'improvised all the way down,' meaning that the improvised approach is reflected at all levels of music making, no matter how conventional, even when elements of composition are introduced as well. What can we pianists learn from this?

What's really striking is that when Western musicians actually work closely with classical Indian musicians, they discover the latter have a very different fundamental concept of making music. All cultures use metaphors to capture their sense of what is happening when human beings make and experience musical sounds. Often they use the same words and images to describe this, but this can be misleading, as often these are really understood in a completely different way.

For example we naturally tend to think of Western music as beginning from a musical idea, already complete in itself, which is then varied, repeated, and developed, and contrasted with other ideas to produce a larger musical structure. It's tempting to think of improvisation as a variation on how this process is accomplished. In this framework, we may talk about how particular musical ideas undergo 'organic' transformation and development over the course of a stretch of music — rather like living plants and animals that often seem to us to be evolving towards some kind of fulfillment of their potential, rather than just changing at random.

Indian musicians also conceive of music using such terms, but there are big differences in how they are applied. It's not individual musical themes or ideas that are evolving towards their fulfillment over the course of a musical happening, but an overall idea which always takes in the entire character of the music so far. That's the real meaning of raga, which is much more than just a scale.

It's probably impossible to really understand this without getting serious about Indian philosophical thought about time and human consciousness — something we won't get into here — but we can still spell out the fundamental difference between Western and Indian attitudes towards music that this implies. In essence, for Western musicians a musical performance is an event that frames various processes happening within the music. (If you like, it describes a sort of 'temporal landscape' within which musical phenomena are heard to come and go.) For Indian musicians, though, the performance is itself the fundamental process, which at any moment represents in its entirety the unfolding potential (the 'bearing fruit' of a 'musical seed') that is a raga.

That's certainly a very holistic conception of music and music making. It explains why Indian musicians like to improvise using a set of open-ended conventions that allow and forbid particular ways of connecting up notes and intervals in the context of a raga, rather than working from a fixed structure or a given musical idea, taken as a starting point for variation and embellishment, as in the Western approach to improvisation. In practice a raga corresponds to a family of interdependent features:

- five or more notes that function as a scale/mode
- a specific tuning
- distinct rules for melodic ascent and descent, specific to the raga (aroha/avaroha)
- a few specific phrases (chalan/sanchara)
- specific notes for starting and finishing phrases (nyasa, apanyasa, graha)
- melodic resolution notes (modal pitch centres) (vadi)
- specific forms of microtonal inflection (sruti).

This conception can be liberating if you're the sort of musician who is drawn to freer styles of melodic improvisation, as in bebop and modal jazz. Maybe you find the tendency of jazz musicians to use and reuse the same harmonic and melodic skeletons, as provided in jazz standards and other established progressions, constraining. The Indian approach shows that it's possible to identify unifying principles other than these, sensitizing you to something you might otherwise be unaware of: that when you are improvising the character and quality of your personal style is defined largely by things you are not so conscious of, such as your particular habits for connecting certain intervals with others when ascending or descending melodically or when approaching certain melodic resolution notes, and is less a matter of what particular riffs and licks you've worked out and incorporated into your playing.

When it comes to relating this more directly to the piano, there are some other important features of Indian music we should take account of, even though these seem to make it more problematic for pianists: they include the extensive use of **melisma** (expressive changes of pitch within a single sustained sound) and **microtonality** (pitch intervals smaller than a semitone), as well as the rich effects of harmonic **resonance** on instruments like the sitar. Together these allow performers to create subtle coloristic inflections of harmonic tension within individual notes, whose vividness is enhanced by the fact that we typically hear them over a drone-bass.

Melismatic inflection offers a striking contrast to Western piano music that can help us bring the real nature of the latter into much sharper focus, precisely because it's impossible to literally achieve it on the piano. (It's actually a widespread phenomenon in Asian music: try listening to the Japanese shakuhachi flute music as well.)

In Indian music, the unbroken continuity of a melismatic melodic line is connected with the singing voice: in that context it manifests the breath (central to yoga and meditation) and is thought to directly mirror the continuity of human consciousness through its continuous sounding, which nevertheless must be actively sustained by the performer.

The piano, on the other hand, is actually a percussive (stringed) instrument: its central limitation is that we cannot physically make adjustments to a note while it is sounding. This brings to light a fact that is so obvious that we normally forget to notice it, which is that we don't really sustain notes actively on the piano at all. In literal terms, the piano is the least melismatic of Western instruments, and perhaps the farthest removed from the human voice. Its tuning is also fixed. Yet when we learn to produce expressive legato phrasing in our performances of the Western classics — as you'll know if you've worked your way through this book — we are, above all, attempting to imbue melody lines with precisely this kind of melismatic feeling of unbroken continuity of sound.

So contrasting the piano with music such as this, that is literally melismatic, alerts us to the fact that much of what we are doing when shaping melodies expressively on the piano is creating an illusion that the steps and leaps of a line or phrase are in fact changes to the pitch of a continuously held sound. And when we succeed in this we are suggesting that there really is a continuously sustained underlying tone similar to that of a singing human voice there.

In the recent past music therapists and music psychologists have found that imaginatively identifying with this sustained tone can help players achieve a fuller sense of involvement in their own music making — bringing psychological as well as artistic benefits, enabling them to overcome performance-related stress or other emotional difficulties.

EXPERIMENTAL & AVANT-GARDE

We've just seen how knowing something about the classical Indian approach to melodic line and inflection can change how we experience tonal continuity on the piano, as this relates to legato playing. You should now be aware that the percussive nature of the piano means that each note in a melody played on the piano really is a separate sound – a separate sounding event with its own beginning, middle and end – in contrast to the voice, and wind and stringed instruments, where this need not be the case. But it's the piano that has functioned as the central reference point for classical composers, who often wrote their music in a simplified form for piano before orchestrating or arranging it for other instruments. Why? Partly, of course, because keyboard instruments like the piano allow a single person access to melody, harmony, and counterpoint all at once.

However, there's another reason why this seemed natural. It's because Western music from the Middle Ages onwards has been notated using variations of a single underlying system that treats individual notes as the most basic and indivisible elements of a melody line, corresponding to points or dots on a staff. So Western musicians have grown used to thinking of musical lines and harmonies as arrangements of notes, while what goes on within a note has tended to be sidelined and seen as an optional extra which is the province of the performer but not intrinsic to the music itself. Because Western music, like all music, uses sustained sounds, this creates a division between the structure of the music and its actual physical realization, which is often identified with the distinction Western musicians make between a work and its performance.

A consequence of this is that there is a tendency to think of a musical work as something abstract that has its essential form independently of how it might be realized in different arrangements or performances. This is a feature of Western music that is almost entirely absent from non-Western traditions, and while it's responsible for a great deal of the richness of both classical and non-classical Western musical traditions, it isn't a universal feature of all music making. In particular, contemporary improvisation specialists often find it especially useful to question this basic conceptual framework underlying Western music, which may be less helpful for them than for other musicians.

In fact Western music has witnessed its own evolution away from this more abstract model of musical structure, in the field of contemporary classical music. This is part of a larger musical tendency that has impacted on our understanding of the potential of the piano and its relationship to the materials of music in a variety of ways. In the first 60 years or so of the 20th century, Western classical music underwent a period of radical and revolutionary change, connected with modernism and other trends. During this period, modernist composers tended to reject tonality, preferring methods designed to creating **atonal** music (ie, music with no key centre at all). These methods were often very abstract: they involved ways of organizing pitch relationships that were hard to relate directly to what listeners could hear in the music itself.

In the 1960s this ceased to be the dominant tendency within contemporary classical music, and many composers turned their attention towards non-Western music as a source for a new set of alternatives to traditional musical idioms. (Others became interested in past styles, often ironically. See the discussion of postmodernism in Unit 17 of this book.) What struck these composers above all was the fact that non-

Western music often seemed to be as much focused on the internal characteristics of sounds as on the possibilities for combining them into larger sequences and structures.

One of the first composers to explore harmonic textures in these terms was the French composer Olivier Messiaen. (It's no coincidence that he was also a leading organist and improviser: organ music is the only area of classical music where the tradition of improvisation survived after the 19th century.) Inspired by Balinese Gamelan and classical Indian music, Messiaen assembled chord structures that were entirely static, as they were based on special kinds of scale in which it was impossible to a hear a single unambiguous tonal centre. As a result, the listener is forced to hear these chords purely with reference to their internal coloristic character, rather than as part of a progression. Here are some examples of the scales he used, which share the common characteristic of being only transposable to a limited number of other degrees before they repeat the same combination of pitches. Because of this they are known as **modes of limited transposition**. They form an important harmonic resource for pianists wishing to improvise or compose chords and structures outside of the Western system of 'functional' tonal harmony. (Others not shown here include the whole-tone scale and the diminished scale, already considered in Unit 15.)

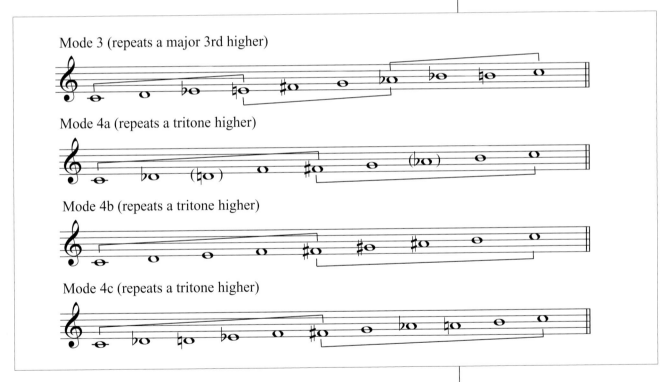

After Messiaen, other composers pursued this direction even further. The American composer John Cage began making use of what he called the **prepared piano**, placing various objects in between the strings of a piano to alter their sounds. This had the effect of breaking the illusion of the piano as a neutral medium, as different notes in the same phrase now sounded as if they were coming from different instruments. (In effect, Cage showed listeners that every pitch on the piano was, in a sense, a separate instrument, in contrast to the human voice.) This disruption of the linear character of musical lines and harmonic progressions also forced listeners to refocus their

OLIVIER MESSIAEN

Olivier Messiaen (1908-1992) was a French composer and organist. His music was inspired by religious ideas and was influenced by his own detailed studies of birdsong. He probably had more influence on contemporary classical music in the second half of the 20th century than any other composer of his generation, with famous pupils including Pierre Boulez, Karlheinz Stockhausen, and Iannis Xenakis. The rhythmic complexities of his music reflected his interest in Ancient Greek and classical Indian music, while his attempt to develop alternatives to the linear sense of musical time emphasized in Western music led him to explore scales and compositional approaches that at the time were considered highly unorthodox.

awareness onto the individual character of sounds and the internal character or texture of chords. (Another composer whose music leads the listener into an intensified contemplation of individual sounds and their internal characteristics was the Italian Giacinto Scelsi.)

Perhaps the most radical step in this direction came with the emergence of a new tendency in contemporary classical music in the late 1960s, known as **spectral music**. Of the creative figures associated with this tendency, the most radically original is the Rumanian-born, Paris-based composer Horatiu Radulescu.

To understand spectral music we need to know something about the acoustic basis for harmony, which lies in the relationships between **overtones** of a pitch. Overtones – also known as partials or harmonics – are additional, higher pitches which we do not normally experience, because they are too faint, but whose presence and strength nevertheless noticeably affect the tone color or timbre of the sound that we do hear. The overtones of a definite pitch follow a particular series of intervals, known as the **harmonic series** (first discovered by the Greek mathematician and mystic Pythagoras). Here is the beginning of the series for a low G. Note that some pitches can only be notated approximately, as they do not correspond to the pitches of the Western scale system, either in its natural form as used sometimes by singers and string players, or in its equal-tempered form, which serves as the basis for the tuning of modern pianos. Some harmonics are therefore indicated using quarter-tone approximations.

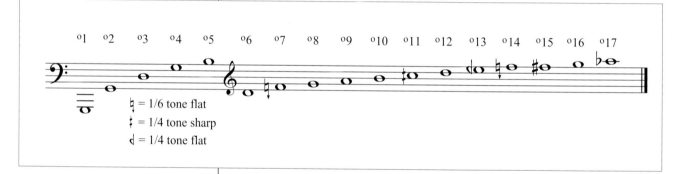

Radulescu's music represents the purest form of spectral music, owing to its concentration on large-scale, slowly evolving textures that consist of projections, into an audible register, of the pitch relations internal to a single fundamental pitch, which is not itself sounded but is mathematically implied. Hence this music can be said to consist entirely of an exploration of the overtone structures within a single sound. Radulescu made dramatic use of the grand piano by turning the instrument on its side so that it could be played in ways that bypass the keyboard mechanism completely, stroking the strings with bows and metal objects. His sonatas for piano require the instrument to be tuned to **alternative tunings** in order to reproduce elements of the harmonic series in their pure form, giving rise to quite new and subtle harmonic effects.

The subsequent development of spectral music from the 1970s onwards has also tended to mainly involve Parisian composers, though these have often adopted a different approach to Radulescu, in which particular kinds of internal unfolding of sounds are first computer analyzed and then recreated on a different scale as orchestral textures. This trend was connected to the development of a research centre in Paris (IRCAM), devoted to exploring the creative possibilities for musicians that have been opened up by the development of computers (and the study of psychoacoustics).

Spectral music has had a significant influence on the approach to harmonic texture of contemporary composers writing for the piano, alerting them especially to its potential for rich and complex forms of resonance and sympathetic vibration (where strings that are not struck directly nevertheless vibrate in sympathy with others), made possible by the sustaining pedal. (The third or middle 'sostenuto' pedal has also proved useful, as it allows just those notes held down by the pianist at the moment when the pedal is depressed to function as if the sustaining pedal were depressed, letting the strings vibrate freely, while others are unaffected.)

Try out the examples below of spectral voicings (all derived from the harmonic series in the previous example) with the sustaining pedal, noting their unusual qualities of resonance, which are audible in spite of the inexact relationship between the tempered tuning of the modern piano and the natural intervals formed by the overtones. (Note how overtones tend to remain fixed in the octave in which they first appear as part of the harmonic series of the fundamental tone.)

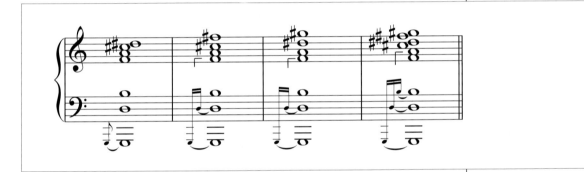

BREAKING NEW GROUND

In the previous section of this final unit I've tried to show how our understanding of the piano and its potential has changed as a result of the exposure of jazz, rock and classical musicians to non-Western cultures. The piano remains the quintessential instrument of the Western tradition, embodying as it does many of the distinctive features of the latter in its physical construction, as well as in its role as a sketchpad for musicians and composers.

But this is a two-way process as well. If we are able to hear the great classical masterpieces, and the finest recordings of jazz pianists, in a different light as a result of this change in our cultural horizons, then we should also realize that the piano has brought something quite special into the world of music – something that, in turn, has been taken up enthusiastically by many musicians working outside of Western musical culture. Only with the piano did it become truly possible for the individual creative musician to explore melody, harmony, and counterpoint all at once, along with a wide range of textures and shades of colour, of difference of articulation, and nuances of dynamic level. The result was a personalization of the experience of playing a musical instrument that has empowered individual musicians everywhere to seek to realize their artistic personality in their own playing, whether it be performing a classic of the repertoire, their own improvisation, their arrangement of a well-known tune, or an original composition.

Only a fool would try to predict the next exciting developments in the world of the piano, but its important role in jazz, rock, classical, and contemporary music suggests that there are sure to be some. Artists who break new ground often don't realize that that's what they're doing at the time – they're usually just following their instincts, doing what excites them right there and then. I hope that working through this book will have enabled you to do just that – and to take a step closer to fulfilling your potential – each time you sit down and play the piano.

ON THE CD

You will find the accompanying CD for this book in the pocket attached to the inside of the back of the jacket. The performances by Carl Humphries on a Steinway piano were recorded on December 22-23rd 2006 by John Taylor at Potton Hall, Dunwich, Suffolk, England.

The following list indicates track number, exercise number ("Ex") where relevant, and the page number(s) where the music for the exercise or piece appears in the book.

ABOUT THE AUTHOR

Carl Humphries was born in London in 1966. He studied piano and composition in London, Berlin, and Turin, and pursued theoretical studies at the University of Cambridge. He works as a pianist, teacher, and composer, specializing in the relationship between theory and performance. His lectures and workshops are in demand at universities and music conservatoires in Europe and in the United States, and he has performed at a number of major classical and jazz venues, as well as for television. He has written extensively on music education, contemporary music, and the philosophy of music.

MUSIC PERMISSIONS

Copyright material reproduced with thanks to the following:

'The Jolly Miller' by Leslie Fly, from *Canterbury Tales: Nine Miniatures For Pianoforte*. © 1927 Forsyth Brothers Ltd.

'Allegro' by Igor Stravinsky, from *Les Cinq Doigts*. © 1921 Chester Music Ltd.

'Repentirs' by Sergei Prokofiev, from *Musique D'Enfants, Op.65*. © 1935 Boosey & Hawkes, G. Schirmer, and Alfred Music Publishing.

'I Got Rhythm' by George Gershwin, from *Girl Crazy*. © 1930 WB Music Corp.

'Summertime' by George Gershwin, from *Porgy And Bess*. © 1935 (Renewed 1962) George Gershwin Music, Ira Gershwin Music, and Du Bose and Dorothy Heyward Memorial Fund. All rights administered by WB Music Corp.

'The Girl From Ipanema' ('Garôta De Ipanema'). Music by Antonio Carlos Jobim, English words by Norman Gimbel, original words by Vinicius de Moraes. © 1963 Antonio Carlos Jobim and Vinicius De Moraes, Brazil. Copyright renewed 1991 and assigned to Songs Of Universal, Inc. and New Thunder Music, Inc. English words renewed 1991 by Norman Gimbel for the world and assigned to New Thunder Music, Inc. Administered by Gimbel Music Group, Inc. (P.O. Box 15221, Beverly Hills, CA 90209-1221 USA). This arrangement © 2007 Songs Of Universal, Inc., New Thunder Music, Inc. and Gimbel Music Group, Inc. All rights reserved. Used by permission.